Winged Odyssey

by

Lettice Curtis

Air Research Publications

First published 1993 by
Air Research Publications
PO Box 223, Walton-on-Thames,
Surrey, KT12 3YQ,
England.

Printed in Great Britain by
MBA Group Ltd
London N17 0HW

ISBN 1-871187-19-2

Permission for use of the painting of The Duchess's Gypsy
Moth 'Curlew' (G-ACUR) kindly granted by the artist, E A
Mills of Aviation Art International, Bridlington. Copyright,
Audrey Taylor (née Todd) daughter of J W Todd, Ground
Engineer to Mary, Duchess of Bedford.

Winged Odyssey

The Flying Career of Mary du Caurroy,
Duchess of Bedford

By

Lettice Curtis

CONTENTS

Foreword by The Marquess of Tavistock
Introduction by Sir Peter Masefield

Appendices

Foreword

My great-grandmother, Mary, Duchess of Bedford, is without a doubt the relative I would most liked to have met. She was, I believe, a most amazing woman. She took up flying with characteristic courage and enthusiasm at a little over the age of sixty and subsequently the press laballed her 'The Flying Duchess'.

Although greater prominence has always been given to her work as a pioneer in flying, it was only part of her life's achievements. She was also a highly trained surgical nurse, a skilled radiologist, a naturalist and zoologist of some repute and a competent watercolourist. As if these major interests were not enough, she succeeded in becoming a crack shot, a fine angler and an experienced yachtswoman.

It is to my great regret that I was never to know Mary, as she disappeared in 1937 whilst on a routine flight over the flooded Fens. However, two personal achievements have, I feel, brought me closer to this lady I so admire. In 1985 my own long-standing dream was fulfilled when twenty Pére David deer were reintroduced to China from the Woburn herd. It is from the original eighteen deer saved from extinction by the 11th Duke and carefully monitored at Woburn by Mary in the late ninteenth century that the entire world herd is descended today. Then, in the autumn of 1986 a scientist in Tennessee telephoned Woburn to ask if the same family lived there who had done so in the 1930s! It transpired that for eleven years he had been the owner of a Rolls-Royce Phantom II built in 1934 for the 11th Duchess of Bedford and now hoped it could return home. Needless to say I bought my great-grandmother's car, brought it back to Woburn by container and subsequently totally restored it.

I was thrilled when Lettice Curtis chose to tell Mary's story and hope you are as fascinated by it as I have been over the years

Marquess of Tavistock

Introduction

by

Sir Peter Masefield

No more devoted advocate and parcipitant in the delights of light aeroplane flying can be imagined than Mary du Caurroy, Duchess of Bedford (1865 - 1937), wife of the 11th Duke and a fabulous character in her own right. Miss Lettice Curtis, herself a renowned aviator, has brought Her Grace engagingly back to life in this, most readable and splendidly researched, biography. It is written with a deep and sympathetic understanding of the complex, but endearing, personality of the Duchess. It is written, too, with a wide knowledge and experience of flying. That has enabled Lettice Curtis to present a sound, and highly probable, explanation for the hitherto unexplained dis-appearance of the Duchess of Bedford on a short, solo, flight from Woburn on a cold winter's afternoon in 1937.

How remarkable, as Lettice Curtis so well relates, was her life. Daughter if an English country parson (who became Archdeacon of Lahore in India) she married at the age of 23 a British Army officer, equerry of the Viceroy. In 1888, five years after her marriage to Herbrand Russell, the second son of the Duke of Bedford, Herbrand succeeded his brother to the Dukedom. Twenty-eight years after her marriage and thirteen years after the Wright Brothers first flew she made a record flight to India and back and was rightly proclaimed as a leading protagonist of British aviation and of Imperial Communications an example to Imperial Airways.

Always energetic, the new Duchess trained in hospital work, specialised in radiography, opened her own hospital, gave sterling service throughout the First World War, became an authority on birds and then, in 1926 at the age of 61 - though seriously afflicted by deafness - decided to take up flying. For the next 11 years that became an increasing joy to her, a means of travel and in learning to fly herself, an absorbing pleasure. In all of this she had the good fortune to be able to taste the delights of carefree aviation in its golden years between the wars - a time when the aeroplane had emerged as a reasonably reliable, and tolerably comfortable, means of journeys of some length - albeit subject to frequent landings. By then, aircraft were still able to fly with freedom, without the imposition of pre-flight plans and the trammels of air traffic control, which increasing congestion began to make necessary.

Against such a background, the flight by the Duchess of Bedford - and her crew of Charles Barnard, pilot, and R.F.Little engineer/navigator - from England to India and back in seven-and-a-half days during August 1929, was properly hailed as a remarkable achievement. Charles G Grey - the not easily impressed editor of *The Aeroplane* - called it, 'the finest possible demonstration of the uses of air communications. Thanks to the energy and the initiative of the Duchess of Bedford who, as a sportswoman, has shown what can be done with Imperial Communications.' Charles Barnard remarked that 'throughout the flight she had been an active, useful and efficient member of the crew.' Her Grace was fortunate in all but the last of her personal pilots. She enjoyed a warm and cordial relationship with those who shared her relish of the air - and they with her. Thus, the loss of her most devoted pilot Bernard Allen in December 1933, was a heavy blow. Subsequent flights with the autocratic Ralph Chevallier Preston were never the same.

Lettice Curtis handles all this with insight, clarity and an engaging regard for her subject. Her account of the tragic final solo flight of the Duchess culminates in a well considered suggestion for the cause of her loss which is, I believe, almost certainly correct - a solution to the mystery which has lain unresolved for more than half a century. I will not give away the solution to be found in the final chapter. I commend with enthusiasm this warm-hearted book. It will, I am sure, be relished by everyone who reads it.

Acknowledgements.

First and foremost, I have to thank the Marquess of Tavistock and the Trustees of the Bedford Estates, for giving me access to their documents, photographs and above all, the personal diaries of Mary, Duchess of Bedford without which it would not have been possible to put together the story of her flying.

There are also a number of individuals to whom I am specially indebted. Firstly, my grateful thanks go to Lavinia Wellicome who on behalf of the Marquess of Tavistock, never failed to find time to help me sort through essential documents and photographs. Thanks also to Roger Jackson and Richard Riding for providing additional photographs; to Betty Ewens of the D.H Museum and Darryl Cott, for extracts from the *DH.Gazette* of 1927 and to Chris Hobson, Librarian at the RAF Staff College, Bracknell, where I spent many hours researching aeronautical events of the era.

I am also indebted to Mrs Ralph Preston for the loan of her husband's diaries; to Mrs Audrey Taylor, daughter of J W Todd the Duchess's mechanic, for childhood memories of Woburn as it was then and for the photograph of her painting of Moth G-ACUR. Last but by no means least my grateful thanks go to Sir Peter Masefield, for his support of this project and for writing the Introduction.

Chapter One
Prologue

This is a story about flying as it once was, when lightweight radios had yet to be invented and the 'Mark I Eyeball' was the only aid to navigation. It was a time when owners of light aircraft could land without fear of prosecution on field or golf course and when private aircraft were welcomed at military aerodromes. Days when there were no landing fees and, when travelling abroad, an Aviator's Certificate issued by the Royal Aero Club was as good as a passport. Times that the modern owner of a light aircraft can only dream about.

The story revolves for the most part around the flying carried out by Mary du Caurroy, Duchess of Bedford DBE, RRA, FLS, Honorary Liveryman of the Guild of Air Pilots and Air Navigators and wife of the 11th Duke. It was not until the arrival on the scene of the de Havilland Moth in 1925 that private flying in the United Kingdom became a practical proposition. The Duchess took her first flight in 1926 at the age of 61, and bought her first aircraft, a Cirrus Moth, in 1927. Her foreign holiday in May 1927 with Charles Barnard, the first of her pilots, covered 4,500 miles and was seen by the flying fraternity as proof of the reliability of the Moth. It was seen also as an important pointer as to how private aircraft could and would in future be used.

Between then and her death in 1937 in an air accident, flying became the Duchess's hobby and main means of transport both within the United Kingdom and, at a time when there were few if any bars to international travel, abroad. Her Moths took her and her pilots to Jerusalem and Petra, Egypt, The Gambia and the Canaries and finally across the Sahara. Between 1928 and 1930 she sponsored and, as a crew member, took a full part in record flights to India and back in eight days, the Cape and back in twenty. These records, which at the time were given much publicity, were not made simply for records sake, but were attempts to show the sort of schedules that could - and should - be achieved by Imperial Airways. An avid diarist, these flights were documented in rare and absorbing detail.

Between 1926 and 1937 the Duchess employed three pilots, each of a very different character. The first, Charles Barnard, an extrovert with a good sense of fun, was an ideal pilot during her introduction to flying. Bernard Allen who came next, was another capable pilot but without Barnard's wide experience; he flew simply because he loved it. Moving to Woburn, which was much more convenient for the Duchess, he took full charge of her aeroplanes which from now on were based there. Allen shared with the Duchess her love of birds and animals and her love of travelling. He was an ideal flying companion for her and, when he was killed in a flying accident in 1933, she lost, in her own words, not only a pilot but a loyal and trusted friend. After his death, although she continued to use her aeroplanes as before, much of the enjoyment went out of flying. Ralph Preston, an Irishman, the pilot she now engaged perhaps a shade too hastily, was a man of entirely different character. Forty-one years of age and with some sixteen years of flying experience behind him, he had already travelled widely. He took on the job one feels not so much for the love of it but because flying had become his trade and way of life. Temperamentally, Preston and the Duchess had little in common. A public schoolboy and ex-RAF flying instructor, Preston was used to organising - a little too much so for the Duchess. He had no real interest in country pursuits, and when travelling with her preferred to sit and sketch while the Duchess preferred walking and sightseeing. During his years in the Services and in civil aviation, he had inevitably crossed paths with many individuals who turned up at various places during their travels, involving her with people with whom she had little in common and who often bored her.

During her eleven years of flying the Duchess spent no less that 2,600 hours in the air. As her pilot invariably went with her to look after her aircraft and generally deal with administration, although she often took the controls, only two hundred of these hours were logged as 'solo'. But more of this later. First a brief look at her background and how she came to take up flying.

Mary du Caurroy Tribe was born on 26th September 1865, in the Rectory at Stockbridge, Hampshire, where her father, the Reverend Walter Tribe was the incumbent. Her mother Sophie was the daughter of Charles Lander, British Consul in the Dardanelles during the Crimean War and later, Vice-Consul in the Netherlands and Germany. Mary had an elder sister and three brothers the eldest of whom served on the Northwest Frontier of India and in China at the time of the Boxer Rebellion. One cannot but wonder therefore whether this led to the rescue by the Duke of the last of the Pére David deer.

When Mary was two years old, her father accepted a chaplaincy in the North West Province of India, leaving her and her elder sister Zoe with relatives in Pulborough. When Mary was twelve the girls were sent to Cheltenham Ladies College only to be removed a year later and sent to Switzerland, to study languages and painting and to learn to ride. From there in 1879 Zoe, older by two years, joined her parents in India while Mary returned to Cheltenham. Two years later she too joined her parents in India. Soon after arriving in Lahore however, Mary caught typhoid fever, which led to the deafness that, increasing with age, greatly affected her whole life and even contributed to her decision to take up flying.

When she was well again her parents moved to Dharmsala in the Himalayan foothills. Here Mary accompanied her father on his tours of the district, which were often undertaken with a single shared pony, which, when there were no Europeans around, Mary would ride 'astride'. She was to look back on these years in India, of which she wrote later, 'we each had our ponies, there were no horrid motors and where our very faithful servants loved us.' as gloriously happy times. During this period with her father's encouragement, she built up her interests in nature and in painting.

In 1886 Mr Tribe was appointed Archdeacon of Lahore and transferred to Simla, where the family were in frequent contact with the Staff and Household of the Viceroy, the Marquis of Dufferin and Ava. It was here that she came to know and love Herbrand Russell, second son of the 9th Duke of Bedford, a

11

subaltern in the Grenadier Guards and one of the Viceroy's Aides de Camp. They were married in 1988 somewhat to the consternation of Herbrand's family who considered him worthy of something more than an Archdeacon's daughter. After their marriage they returned to England where, as both preferred country life to London Society, they took the lease of *Cairnsmore*, a house near Newton Stewart in Galloway. Here, a year after their marriage, their son and only child Hastings was born. Two years later Herbrand's father died. This was followed shortly afterwards by the death of his elder brother at the early age of 41. So it was that in 1893, Herbrand succeeded to the family title, becoming the 11th Duke of Bedford and, reluctantly one must assume, moved to Woburn.

Woburn at the time was still run following years of family tradition, by a hierachy of heads of departments without thought to expense or manpower. Thus, even if the new Duke and his wife had wished to make changes, they would have found them virtually impossible to carry out. As it was, the Duke settled into the routine of his ancestors and the new Duchess, when free from social obligations, looked outside the household for fulfilment and freedom.

By the turn of the century the Duchess had opened a small cottage hospital in Woburn, which after taking a course at the London Hospital, she personally directed and managed. This, at the outbreak of World War I, became an arm of the larger military Base Hospital at the Abbey, which she also supervised. She took training in theatre work, in radiography and radiology and, when the Abbey hospital closed in 1920, her smaller hospital again became a civil one in which she herself worked as Chief Theatre Sister and radiologist. In all this work, she had the unstinted moral and financial support of the Duke even when in later years, the cost of running the hospital became prohibitive.

The Duchess's main recreation and lifetime interest was bird-watching. Before World War I she at first hired and later bought a yacht, SY *Sapphire*. In this she made regular excursions to the Scottish Isles to study birds, using her yacht to get from place to place in much way she later used her Moths. Through the prolific records kept of her observations,

In July 1901 the Duchess travelled to Spitzbergen in 'Sapphire' to extend her birdwatching. The Duchess is seated middle row right, with the 11th Duke, Hebrand back row left and their son Hastings, Marquess of Tavistock in front with a friend of the family Flora Green. (Woburn Archives)

she became a recognised authority on birds and in due course, a Fellow of the Linnean Society. On the outbreak of World War I she put both yacht and crew at the disposal of the Admiralty - an offer that was rejected because she insisted on being included in the crew. The yacht was later impressed anyway and was not returned till after the war by which time the Duchess was otherwise involved.

In the New Year Honours published 2nd January 1928, Mary de Caurroy, Duchess of Bedford R.R.C (Royal Red Cross), F.L.S (Fellow of the Linnean Society) was awarded the Order of Dame Commander of the British Empire (D.B.E) for Public Services. 'At the end of the war when honours were freely distributed,' the Duke wrote after her death,

"She received the Order of the Red Cross Second Class and nothing more. True eight years later when War Hospitals had

13

long since been forgotten, she received the Order of the D.B.E. She used to say that for five years she had worked really hard without any recognition and then received the D.B.E. for flying as a passenger to India."

In fact in January 1928 this particular flight had not yet been made but having received considerable publicity for her continental tour in 1927, people tended to associate the award with her flying. The excuse made for the award of Order of the Red Cross Second Class was that 'the Order, First Class was reserved for professional nurses'.

Chapter Two

1926 - First Flight

The years had now passed, the Duchess was 61 and deaf. She also suffered from tinnitus, a distressing middle-ear disease that produces continual head noise for which to this day there is no cure. Some years later Ralph Preston, the last of her three pilots, wrote that she used to liken the continual head noise, which was far worse than deafness, to railway trains rushing through a station. She could, he said, hear better against a background noise and would frequently leave her car running when speaking to him at his house. In an aeroplane he said, she heard better through the speaking tubes - in those days the only means of communication between front and rear cockpits of a Moth - than some of normal hearing. Lawrence Wingfield one-time pilot in the Royal Flying Corps and first Clerk to the Guild of Air Pilots and Air Navigators also relates how, when lunching with her one day, she turned to him and said, 'Can you hear your passenger talking to you in an open cockpit?' and on receiving the answer 'No.' continued, 'I have the sort of deafness which can hear better in a lot of noise.'

During the war and for a time afterwards the Duchess had been fully occupied with her hospitals. Now, as the hospital work declined, she found herself again, with time for travel and for bird-watching. Use of the Woburn cars was strictly controlled and, impatient by nature, time spent in trains irked her. Moreover the time she could spend away from the hospital was still limited. Aeroplanes flying over the Abbey in wartime had already stimulated her imagination and this compounded with her interest in birds, turned her thoughts to recent developments in light aeroplanes. When someone suggested that flying might bring some relief from her head noises, the time for action had arrived.

The first step of the Duchess was to approach the Private Hire Department of Imperial Airways with a request to fly her from Croydon to Woburn - in those days a particularly slow and tiresome journey. In reply they offered her a flight in a DH.50, a cabin machine that carried four passengers. But this, the Duchess told them, was not at all her idea of 'emulating the birds.' Imperial Airways next got in touch with de Havilland's at Stag Lane, who lent them aircraft from time to time. So it was that on 11th June 1926, the Duchess at the age of 61, made her first flight with Sydney St. Barbe, the London Aeroplane Club's chief flying instructor, in the front seat of what she termed 'a two-seater Moth (open) travelling at 70 mph.' Her comments on the flight, unusually perceptive for a first-time flier, were recorded in her diary thus:

'There was a little wind but not enough to make things unpleasant and I enjoyed the experience enormously. I did not experience the slightest feeling of apprehension, nausea or cold in fact all was pleasant *except the noise.* The Aeronaut must be grateful to the Romans for their straight roads for they and open sheets of water, must make things easy for the pilot in clear weather. It is curious that although I have not a good head for looking down precipices as when climbing Mont Blanc and the Otler, I could look over the edge of the machine from the first. I suppose it is confidence in my pilot. My only apprehension (as I could only communicate in signs with the pilot) was that we should land in the Bison enclosure which from the air looked particularly attractive, instead of in safer but less open parts of the Park.'

This inevitably was where, in spite of much gesticulation from the from the front cockpit, St. Barbe chose to land - fortunately without unduly frightening the animals. She flew again from Croydon to Woburn on 15th July, her pilot this time Hubert Broad, de Havilland's 'test' pilot - later to become the chief production pilot for Hawkers. This time she recorded that there was a strong wind and 'a good deal of bumping' but that she enjoyed the flight very much all the same. She was particularly impressed by the fact that only the week before, Broad had won the Kings Cup in a similar DH.60 Moth. The flight from Croydon to Woburn took 40 minutes. Although a distance as the crow flies of only some fifty miles, it could have taken between two and three hours by car and train.

Mary du Caurroy, Duchess of Bedford,
wife of Herbrand, 11th Duke.
1865-1937

On 30th July, the Duchess and Mr Ogilvie the Surgeon at her hospital, went by train to Leeds to spend an afternoon watching operations carried out by Sir Berkeley Moynihan. They spent the night in Harrogate, moving on the following day to Manchester where they watched more operations, this time by a Mr Burgess at the Royal Infirmary. Leaving Mr Ogilvie to return by train, the Duchess had arranged for a Moth to pick her up at Woodford and this dropped her off at Woburn an hour and forty minutes later. The Duchess who intensely disliked trains, had discovered an alternative means of transport, much to her liking. From then on she hardly set foot in a train again.

The Duchess now started hiring Moths from de Havilland's for her social visits thus at the end of August, Broad collected her from Woburn to lunch with friends at Lyndhurst. After diverting to view the *Mauritania* in Southampton Water - the largest passenger ship then afloat - they landed on Lyndhurst golf course. They left again at 3.45 pm and flew home via Netley, Hayling Island and Bosham where they circled Mr Ogilvie who in his boat, was taking part in the local regatta. They then made their way home via Chichester, Hindhead and Windsor arriving home at 5.20 pm. 'It was a lovely day,' the Duchess wrote, 'and altogether a delightful and most interesting expedition.'

Each autumn the Duke and Duchess returned to *Cairnsmore*, their first home near Newton Stewart on the borders of what was then Kirkcudbright and Wigtown, which they continued to rent for the shooting. The Duke's method of travel was by train, in a private carriage that dropped them at Palnure station within a mile or so of the house. This year however while the Duke and members of the household went as usual by train, the Duchess hired a Moth for the journey. Her pilot on this her longest flight so far was again Hubert Broad and, much to her pleasure, he collected her in G-EMBO, the Moth in which that year he had won the Kings Cup. For a description of the flight one can do no better than quote again from the Duchess's diary:

'September 20th - I went to *Cairnsmore* by air for the first time in the same machine I went to Lyndhurst in viz. the Moth which won the Kings Cup, with its pilot Captain Broad. We left the Park at about 11.35 am in rather dull weather and inclined to be foggy. With a fairly strong headwind the whole way we had to fly low ie. about 700 ft but we kept up a steady rate of 75-80 mph. We stopped at Birmingham aerodrome to get enough petrol to carry us to Manchester as Captain Broad had come from Lympne that morning. At Manchester we again landed and Captain Broad and I had lunch of boiled eggs and bread and butter at a delightful old farmhouse adjoining the aerodrome. We had to wait some time for petrol to come from Manchester and set off again about 2.30 pm.

'After Manchester as we approached the hilly country the sky cleared and the rest of the flight was in bright sunshine. The vast panorama of our own distant hills in front, the Isle of Man to westward, the hills of the Lake District to the east and the sea below us was wonderfully beautiful. Truly it could be said of such towns as Blackpool, Barrow and Workington 'Distance lends enchantment to the view' for all look so attractive from above. We crossed Morcombe Bay and the Solway and landed in a field at the foot of our drive and I felt a little sad that it was all over and sadder still when the little white Moth sailed away without me in the bright sunshine next morning.'

They remained in Scotland until mid November when the Duchess wrote:

'November 15th - My pilot and aeroplane having arrived last night I left at 10.30 am from Linnie Meadow (Barholm), Captain C.D.Barnard being my pilot this time. It was fine at starting but the Cumberland hills were covered in cloud so that there was not the same view as when going to Scotland. Still as we skirted the hills by the shore and rose above the clouds, there was a beauty of another kind. Soon we ran into thick weather and owing to the mines and manufactories having re-started work after the long coal strike, we could not see Manchester aerodrome so pursued our way south till we had to land in a field at Knowsley for petrol. Whilst my pilot went for petrol some very dilapidated rustics came up to look at the aeroplane, the first they had seen on the ground they told me. An old fellow sheltering himself from the rain under the last rags of an overcoat informed me that, 'it was generally the young people who took to flying' and added 'I suppose you are over 60'. We resumed our flight in about half an hour and the weather was so thick that there were thoughts of returning to our Knowsley field to seek Lord Derby's protection for the night. However we got through to the clearer atmosphere but as visibility improved the wind freshened and the last part of the journey was exceedingly lively. It seemed very wonderful that the little machine could be kept on anything like a straight course. My pilot tells me that I may consider myself a proved Air Sailor as many pilots would have been ill. *We landed in the Park at 4.05 pm beating Herbrand and Jemima who started in the train at the same time that I did by three and a half hours.'*

The Duchess's last flight in 1926 took place on the day after Christmas when with Barnard, she took a brief flight from the Park to test a speaking tube, which would enable her to communicate with her pilot. 'It was a glorious day,' she wrote, 'and I longed to go further.'

Chapter Three
1927: A Moth Abroad

1927 opened for the Duchess with an invitation from de Havilland's to fly in their new DH.66 Hercules. This was a three-engined wooden biplane that they were building for Imperial Airways and a project that, like all too many others, was killed by 'improvements' and modifications imposed by the Air Ministry. There were nine other passengers and the flight had to be curtailed because one of propellers began to 'skin'. In March the Duchess flew up to Cley-on-Sea on the north Norfolk coast, where she had rented the Mill as a base for birdwatching - her lifetime hobby. The flight took one hour 20 minutes, as opposed to the eight hours that it took her when she went by train to Ely and motored from there. 'I had control of the joystick for half an hour on the way there,' the Duchess wrote, 'my first flying lesson!' On the return journey she was allowed to take control for a short time of both stick and rudder.

The first flight of the de Havilland Cirrus Moth had taken place in February 1925 and sales were now taking off. With its tail-wheel configuration and stalling speed of some 40 mph it could be landed in parks, fields or indeed, any reasonably flat or open space; Geoffrey de Havilland, its designer, recommended a minimum field length of 300 yards from the hedge. It was the machine that every club and private owner had waited for. Its popularity can be judged by the numbers produced, fifty in 1926, 117 in 1927 and by 1928 there were no less than 136 on the UK register. Remarkably too during this period, the price had dropped from £830 to £650 and it was even being advertised in shops as shown by the following extract from the *DH Gazette* for April 1927:

"It is of singular interest that the first sale of an aeroplane from a London shop occurred early this month. Much interest was aroused when William Whiteley Ltd the well-known London emporium decided to include a Moth amongst the 'lines' handled by their motor department. Under their enterprising policy their customers are offered Moths either for cash or by a convenient system of deferred terms. Their first exhibition machine which was attractively displayed in a central position on the ground floor was sold within ten days".

The purchaser of this machine was a Mr L G Richardson of the Fleet Air Arm who it was said, intended using it purely for pleasure and travel. The shop asking price was £730 cash, or £230 with either twelve monthly payments of £47, eighteen monthly payments of £32.5s.0d or twenty-four payments of £24.15s.0d. A couple of years later the Honourable Mrs Victor Bruce was to set course on her noteworthy career in aviation after seeing - and subsequently buying - a Blackburn Bluebird in a shop window in Burlington Gardens.

By now one feels, de Havilland's would have been pressing the Duchess to join the fast-growing band of private owners and in this they clearly succeeded as on 18th May, Cirrus II Moth G-EBRI was registered in her name. It was not however until July that it obtained its Certificate of Airworthiness and was delivered. Meanwhile she continued to hire and in April that year, set out on the first of her many foreign tours in Moth G-EBPM, rented from the Hon. Geoffrey Cunliffe. She had by now engaged Charles Barnard as her private pilot. He had been a Flight Commander in the Royal Flying Corps and, for a short time after the war, had acted as test pilot to Sopwith Aviation. After obtaining his commercial 'B' Licence (No.81), he had joined the de Havilland Hire Service of which Alan Cobham was then manager. When this closed in 1925 he became chief instructor for the de Havilland Reserve School at Stag Lane from where in 1927, he joined the Duchess. A highly professional pilot, intelligent and with a delightful sense of humour, they got on well and it was at Barnard's instigation that the Duchess undertook her first unforgettable and, for her, totally absorbing experience of foreign air travel. For a description of the early part of this trip one cannot do better than quote directly from her diary.

'April 21st - Left Woburn at one pm for my first long flight abroad. Departed amidst much photography. We had to land at

*The DH.60 Cirrus Moth G-EBPM, which the Duchess hired from the
Hon. Geoffrey Cunliffe for her first continental tour in 1927.*
(A J Jackson Collection)

Croydon for a few minutes and at Lympne where one of the big
airliners was taking off. My luggage consisted of two small
suitcases, a small attache case carried on my knees, a hat in a
bag and a little leather hand bag. For the rest Capt. Barnard
had a suit case and we carried as much extra petrol and oil as
space permitted. The suitcases (three) on either side of my legs
and a couple of oil tins at my feet left just comfortable room and
on occasions later, kept me warmer I think than I would have
been without them. It seemed to take an amazingly short time
crossing the channel and I have never done it more supremely
comfortably. Capt. Barnard swooped low to show me places of
interest such as the Cathedrals of Abbeville and Beauvais and
after two hours flying, we arrived to my great regret at Le
Bourget in bright sunshine, and were immediately pounced on
by photographers. Capt. Barnard having expatiated upon the
marvellous restaurant arrangements for travellers at Le Bourget took me hither and thither only to find everything in the
hands of painters and builders, so I waited outside whilst he
put the Moth to bed, watching aeroplanes constantly coming
and going. We stayed at the Ritz Hotel and our road from Le
Bourget (Via Dolorosa) might have led to Hades itself for there
were funeral processions by the score.'

Next day, owing to sundry delays at Le Bourget, it was nearly lunchtime before they got away. They flew over Versailles - the first time the Duchess had seen it - dipped down over Chartres Cathedral and, after two hours flying, landed at Tours to refuel. They then left for Biarritz where they had planned to spend their second night, often following roads that dwarfed in length Roman roads in England. Nearly two and a half hours after leaving Tours with fuel running low and still well short of Biarritz, Barnard climbed to 5,000 feet in preparation for a possible forced landing. The Duchess meanwhile blissfully unaware of the reason, continued to enjoy the view. 'After flying at this height for some time,' she wrote later, *'the engine stopped and I wondered why.* I was to be enlightened shortly by Captain Barnard who said, 'I don't know why the engine stopped like that, I think it must have been an airlock'. He then told her that because of headwinds they would only just make the airfield and asked if she would mind a quick descent. 'As the petrol gave out at that moment,' the Duchess continues 'my reply was not of much importance and we did come down quickly by some amazing corkscrew turns, landing neatly at the bottom. All experiences being new to me and having implicit faith in my pilot even when short of petrol, I had done nothing but enjoy myself.'

When the petrol ran out they had been flying for two hours and fifty minutes, rather longer in fact than the Moth's fuel could be expected to last. It so happened that at the time they were over the aerodrome at Bordeaux. Later as we shall hear, Sir Sefton Branker was to refer to Barnard as one who, besides skill possessed 'that divine thing called luck.'

After refuelling, although it was now well into evening, Barnard took off again for Biarritz, a good hours flying away. Approaching the coast however he was again forced to climb, this time into sunshine over a layer of fog rolling in from the sea. When this showed no sign of breaking, he had no option but to return to Bordeaux, where they landed at five minutes to eight on an April evening. Here after a very full day and a long wait for a cab, they dined and went to bed.

Next day in bright sunshine, they retraced their route of the previous evening, this time scudding along some twenty to

The Duchess with Bernard at Woburn before the start of the 1927 tour in G-EBPM. (DH Gazette)

thirty feet above the sands with the sea on their right and the vast forests of Les Landes on their left; for the Duchess this was another new and wholly captivating experience. The aerodrome at Biarritz was small and they were told, few planes landed there.

Seated at lunch in the gay well-filled dining room of their hotel, Barnard, whose thoughts were evidently elsewhere, suddenly remarked, 'Tomorrow we go over the Pyrenees and if the engine fails, we will either crash or come down somewhere inaccessable.' 'Yes,' the Duchess replied, 'it is strange how calmly one can look forward to it.' She then asked Barnard if he thought about such things when he was flying or whether he tried to put them out of his mind. *'I am always thinking of it.'* he replied. *'A pilot who is not always thinking of it is no use.'* - and the Duchess, although not yet a pilot, thought that he was probably right.

Next morning rain and low cloud made the chance of further progress look pretty hopeless and at the agreed time of departure the Duchess, noting Barnard's shoes and suit still lying outside his door, assumed that he thought it unnecessary to rise. She was to find however that Barnard's late rising could not always be attributed to weather! When the rain stopped, Barnard suggested taking a short local flight along the lower

Pyrenees. 'It was my first view of the mountains from the air,' the Duchess wrote, 'and a very beautiful one. We flew over the very picturesque town of San Sebastian and along the coast and back over the Pyrenees. Just as we were approaching the aerodrome and about 3,000 feet up a voice from the rear asked if I would 'like to try a little spin and nose dive'; he said it made some people giddy but as I felt my education would not be complete without it I said 'Yes' and away we went. I saw the earth once in the middle of it but how anybody ever guides an aeroplane out of a spin I am at present at a loss to understand. I suppose most people are more or less giddy the first time whilst it is going on but as the aeroplane straightened, so did I. As Capt. Barnard described it as 'rather jolly', later I hope I too may get to think so!' Meanwhile at the aerodrome, onlookers unused to such displays had concluded that they were about to crash.

In the evening, they met up and dined with one Leslie Hamilton who a few months later, was to be lost in an attempt on the first east-west crossing of the Atlantic. As second pilot to Colonel Freddie Minchin in Fokker G-EBTQ, owned by and carrying Princess Lowenstein as passenger, they took off from Upavon and although reportedly seen by a tanker in mid-Atlantic, were thereafter never seen or heard of again. As at the time the Newfoundland coast was enveloped in thick fog, it was generally assumed that they had gone off course and crashed, either in the sea or in deserted inland wastes.

The next day a further depression had arrived bringing rain, wind and low cloud over the mountains. They nevertheless prepared the Moth for departure, although with little hope of getting away. To pass the morning the Duchess went out and bought herself an umbrella and a warm garment to wear while over the mountains. She then helped a woman who lived at the aerodrome to pluck five Dottrels. By afternoon as the clouds had risen a little, they decided to take off if only for another local flight. As they approached the mountains however, the clouds broke sufficiently to allow them to cross into Spain. 'When nearly at our highest point,' the Duchess wrote, 'the sun came out and the scenery was wonderful beyond description *and I am indeed thankful that I have had the courage to fly before my course is run.. Not that any great courage is needed to fly for I had always longed to do it but one has to run the gauntlet of ones friends and relations who think it is silly and foolhardy and done from a desire to show off.'* She had, she continued, wanted to fly ever since aviation became generally available and since her first flight, had never had any qualms about her personal safety, *'but only for Herbrand's sake.'* On all her trips throughout the coming years, she was to keep in touch with her husband from wherever her 'planes took her.

South of the Pyrennees all was blue sky and sunshine. As they descended, Barnard swooped down first on an Egyptian Vulture which owing to its colour stood out below them, then on a flock of common Vultures, which fortunately alighted - as they had been known to attack aeroplanes. Their first night in Spain was spent at Burgos where as darkness fell shortly after they arrived, there was little time for sightseeing. In the morning therefore they made a hasty visit to the Cathedral before they set off for Madrid. At first the scenery on this leg was less interesting but of the Sierra Guadarrama which rise to some 8,000 feet, the Duchess wrote, 'It seems futile even to try to record the marvellous beauty of that flight. It was pretty cold at the highest point which at 9,000 feet was about the snow line. Heavily laden as we were it seemed a wonderful performance for the little Moth that on the ground looks so small and frail.'

After crossing many miles of orange orchards they arrived at the large military aerodrome at Madrid where they had been given special permission to land. Here they were welcomed by the officers who even provided with them with an interpreter. As there was little time left for sightseeing, they took a quick drive round the town which, the Duchess commented, was one of the finest she had seen. They stayed at the Ritz Hotel and indefatigable as ever, dined, went to the theatre and then went on to a Cabaret that did not start until 1.30 am!

Next morning Barnard went up to the Aerodrome, the Duchess arranging to join him later. When she got there she found her pilot 'somewhat ruffled' because he had to hang around for more than an hour while a search was made for the keys to the hangar. The flight to Seville involved two stops for petrol, the first at Daimiel, a military emergency landing ground where they were refused fuel until the Duchess in her best Spanish, explained that they had permission from the military authorities to land there. At Cordoba, Barnard not liking the look of the usual landing ground, selected his own field and refuelled with petrol from their spare can, something he was always happy to do to show how much faster he could do it than aerodrome ground staff.

At Seville the hangar was already full and, as the aerodrome was populated by goats, and bees were said to block any pipe left open, they were not a little relieved when Mr Hatchett, a friend of Barnard from his de Havilland days, appeared on the scene and arranged for the Moth to go inside. Hachett had for the past four years been flying on the Seville-Larache mail run and was to prove a valuable friend to them. While they continued their tour, he undertook to supervise the construction of an extra fuel tank. Without this, they would have to return the way they had come instead of, as they had hoped, by the east coast; there were as yet no landing grounds between Alicante and Barcelona.

They spent two nights in Seville. On the day they left, Barnard took the opportunity to display the Moth at an aviation meeting laid on by King Alfonso for his guest the Prince of Wales. After watching displays at Hendon however the Duchess reckoned that the Prince was unlikely to have been greatly impressed! They left shortly afterwards, the Duchess remarking that she was glad to be back in the Moth as Seville had been the least enjoyable part of the trip so far.

Their next port of call was at Jerez where the long grass and the short landing ground raised doubts about whether they could take off again. They were met by Mr Williams the British Consul and a Spanish Marquis who claimed to have sent Herbrand a donkey from his piebald herd some two years earlier. 'During the day,' the Duchess wrote, 'I continued to be introduced at frequent intervals to other friends, all of whom claimed to have sent us a Spanish donkey. As I knew we had received only one I began to be rather puzzled until I was told that the Marquis had seven sons, a fresh one turning up at every place we visited.'

Captain Barnard poses with Moorish helpers at Tangier

During their two nights with the Williams they were taken to two bull fights that, rather surprisingly, the Duchess said she enjoyed, apart from the cruelty to horses, and to a Sherry factory at Jerez. Here they were invited to smell every age of sherry. The Duchess, no connoisseur of sherry, raised a laugh when she said that the last sample she was handed seemed more like the sherry she knew - to be told that it was the oldest and choisest brand! For her however the highlight of the visit was an invitation to lunch by Miss Buck, the owner of Arcos Castle, a drive of some twenty-five miles. Arcos de la Frontera, on a pinnacle of rock with the river hundreds of feet below, was described by the Duchess as the realisation of all castles depicted in fairy tales. 'The approach up a narrow cobbled street where no two vehicles could pass did but increase the impression,' she wrote. 'Nor was the romance dispelled as one entered the castle or looked from its windows and battlements to the river at the foot of the precipice.' Before setting off for

Tangier the following day, they returned to fly past the battlements and wave goodbye. For the Duchess this visit remained one of the most enduring memories of the whole tour.

Because of the small size and rough surface of the field in which they had landed, Barnard decided to take off light and pick the Duchess up from the nearby Polo ground. The aerodrome at Tangier with its palms and cacti, contrasted greatly with those in Spain. They were met by Mr O'Brien, manager of the Cecil Hotel who had motored the fifteen miles from the town to collect them. They spent the evening in the Casino, losing a large pile of two-franc pieces that amounted in English money to no more than 8/6d.

Next morning, as Barnard had arranged for his mail to be forwarded to Tangier, they had to wait till the Post Office opened at midday before leaving for Malaga. '*I was sad to think that this is the limit of our journey,*' the Duchess wrote. '*I would willingly have spent a week here and still more willingly have gone to Fez and other interesting places.*' - but time was limited for both of them. 'Ones expenditure is limited to what one can pack,' she continued, 'and as I had not room for a hairpin more, I had to deny myself all temptation to buy mementos.'

While re-crossing the Straits of Gibraltar, Barnard suggested to the Duchess that she might like to photograph the Rock. With side-door open, camera in hand and her attache case open on her knee, she had taken a couple of shots when the aeroplane was hit by what appeared to be a minor tornado, tossing them around like a cork at sea. By the time she had managed to close the door and secure her possessions, Barnard had restored the Moth to even keel; he had flown, like many before him, into the down-draft on the lee side of the Rock.

After a night in Malaga they set off for Seville to collect the new six and-a-half gallon fuel tank that Mr Hatchett was having made for them. They refuelled en route at the military aerodrome at Granada where the Flight Commander, whose English was rather more difficult to understand than his own language, lent them his car to go down town. They rushed to the Alhambra but as it was siesta time, they were only able to see the outside so they rushed back to the aerodrome and took off for Seville. Here they found the tank ready and waiting for them but as ever, it took longer than expected to fit and next day by the time it was installed, a thunderstorm had broken and their departure for Alicante had to be postponed.

'Left 9.35 am,' wrote the Duchess, 'a very early start for my pilot.' The plan was for them to refuel at Grenada and to continue to Alicante for the night. However as they approached Grenada they found the mountains shrouded in cloud and were only able to get through by following valleys. At Grenada they were again lent a car to go to town. The Duchess wanted to take her luggage with her but Barnard still thought they could make Alicante. The Duchess wrote, *'Captain Barnard would not countenance my taking my luggage with me, but I felt sure we could not fly further that day.'* And as so often happened on a number of future occasions the Duchess was proved right. At least however this now gave them a chance to visit the Alhambra.

The hotel they stayed in was some 200 feet up and overlooked both the town and the Sierras. 'Surely no more romantic or beautiful setting could be imagined,' the Duchess wrote, 'and again on this tour of many wonders, I felt that I was seeing one of the most wonderful sights of a not uneventful life; I could hardly tear myself away for dinner. Returning later though night had fallen, it was with myriad twinkling lights, scarcely less romantic and I sat at my window till 1.30 am, knowing that I should probably never see it again. *Once again did I bless the day that I made up my mind to fly, and blessing also descended on the head of my young Pilot who had persuaded me to come on this particular flight to Spain.'* Some acquaintances from Seville who had come by train, joined them in the hotel. 'It had taken them seven hours in a dirty, dusty train,' the Duchess wrote, 'and I had taken one and three quarter hours and had arrived as clean and fresh as I started.'

Next day they left early for Barcelona, a flight of some six hundred miles calling for two refuelling stops. They left in bright sunshine but as they flew east, cloud on the mountains again forced them into the valleys. Their first stop was at Alicante where as they arrived at lunchtime, there was no one to provide them with petrol and by the time they got away, there was a strong headwind blowing and heavy rain in the mountains. As there were no landing grounds between Alicante and Barcelona, Barnard had planned to land on the sands off Valencia to fill up from their spare can. At any time, let alone in doubtful weather conditions this must have been a somewhat dubious undertaking. It was therefore not surprising that the Duchess wrote that as they approached Valencia:

'One or two rather unhappy remarks from the rear cockpit indicated that my pilot was not very happy. Fortunately however the wind was in a favourable direction and Barnard managed to make a safe landing and after filling up from the spare tin, take-off again without incident.'

By now the headwind was stronger than ever, it was raining and there were still some 200 miles to go. Shortly after leaving Valencia Barnard, who was now having doubts about whether they would have either enough fuel or light to make Barcelona, asked the Duchess to calculate one third of the distance from Valencia to Barcelona *very accurately*. This, necessitating opening a large folding map in the cramped front cockpit, was not an easy task. However, having done this to the best of her ability, she was next asked to measure the halfway point. A voice then came over the 'phones saying, 'If we get to Tarragona in half an hour we shall just do it.' For the account of the rest of the flight one cannot again do better than quote the Duchess:

'As we reached Tarragona in 37 minutes I did not ask what was coming next. An occasional remark from behind concerning wind, an animated and somewhat snappy discussion over a promontory which owing to a fold in the map I had mistaken, an enquiry as to what one did when it got dark and a few complaints that my voice was too low or too high, all tended to show that my pilot's responsibilities were weighing a little heavily. I then had to turn on the spare petrol tank with one and a quarter to one and a half hours supply and we seemed a very long way from Barcelona. At last in the very far distance I saw some lights, but still quite a long way from them we began to turn and I thought we were in for a forced landing but was surprised to see an aerodrome below. After landing it got dark very quickly and we had less than ten minutes petrol in hand. I asked Captain Barnard later what he had intended to do if the petrol had run out. 'Oh,' he said, 'you can generally crash without hurting yourself too much if you know how!' Sometime later we were discussing what chance the Moth would have of floating for a time on the sea. Captain Barnard thought 'none'. We had a very rough fifteen mile drive to our hotel over many potholes, but thus ended happily our one very narrow squeak - unless the 'Rock' was another.'

The overall journey time from Granada had been ten and a half hours, seven hours of which were spent in the air.

After his 'long day of anxiety' the Duchess decided that her pilot needed a rest so they gave over the next day to sightseeing - which included going up in the funicular to view of the town and harbour. By next day the weather was again wet and cloudy; they nevertheless drove out to the aerodrome over the fifteen-mile road of potholes and smells, where a brief flight with a military officer to check conditions quickly confirmed to Barnard that they could make no further progress that day. So it was back over the bumpy road to Barcelona. In spite of the rain and murk they decided to spend what remained of the day visiting Montserrat, the Monastery 4,000 feet up in the mountains, said to have inspired Wagner's opera *Parsifal*. Even in these conditions crowds had arrived to visit the *Black Virgin*, a statue said to have been carved by St. Luke, and to leave votive offerings. 'In a very dark chapel,' the Duchess wrote, 'the black statue of the Virgin was in a little gallery of her own with light behind her. Every minute some fresh devotee crept round from the back to kiss her face. Rooms through which they passed were filled with votive offerings of plate, jewellery, crutches and gruesome paintings of accidents and disease contributed by survivors. The precipitous mountain sides, crumbling edges and very winding road with sharp turns, made descent seem infinitely more dangerous than the Moth but for all ones qualms, Monserrat is a place to be seen and a very wonderful one too.' The nearly vertical funicular that now gives access San Jeronimo, the highest peak in the mountains, from which on a clear day Majorca is said to be visible, was at the time under construction. 'Mercifully,' wrote the Duchess, 'it wasn't finished or my companion would undoubtedly have felt constrained to go up - and I suppose I should have had to go too!'

After three nights in Barcelona the weather cleared suffi-
cientlty for them to continue to Montpellier and Lyons. As they
were leaving Montpellier the aerodrome manager's wife rushed
out and presented the Duchess with an enormous bouquet of
flowers. 'As we were already loaded to the brim,' she wrote, 'all I
could do was to transport them to a distance where they would
not blow back, and scatter them to the winds.' After all they had
seen and experienced, the flight up the Rhône Valley seemed
tame and the commercial town of Lyons with its palatial but
practically empty hotel particularly uninspiring. The following
two nights were spent in Paris where Barnard, 'by way of a
cheering evenings diversion', took the Duchess to see Les
Grands Guignols. They spent an extra night in order to visit
Versailles where, still suffering from the effects of the war,
there were neither flowers or fountains. The Duchess described
it as a 'wonderful record of Royal extravagance of a bygone day,
likely to last as long as it can be kept up.' On returning to Paris
they climbed the Eiffel Tower and in the evening went to the
Folies Bergéres, the Duchess as ever making the most of every
minute.

After landing at Lympne to clear customs, they continued to
Croydon where they ran into 'a hornet's nest of photographers'
for, in 1927, private trips such as this were news. They then
continued to Stag Lane where before landing, Barnard indulged
in some mild aerobatics, their arrival being recorded in *Flight*
thus:

> "Just before five pm it (the Moth) came over Stag Lane steadily
> at low altitude and when over the centre of the aerodrome,
> Barnard turned into a short, gentle spin, then disappeared
> behind the hangars and works and suddenly shot through to
> make a perfect landing".

For the Duchess it was now back to Woburn, X-rays, the
operating theatre and a large accumulation of correspondence.

Enormous interest was taken by the whole flying fraternity in
what at some 4,500 miles, was probably the longest 'holiday'
trip undertaken to date by a private owner. Detailed accounts of
the flight appeared in the press. A letter from the Sales
Manager of A.D.C Aircraft Ltd, makers of the Cirrus engine
summed up the general feeling with, '...your recent flight abroad

TOURING DE LUXE

On Thursday, May 12th, Her Grace The Duchess of Bedford landed in the grounds of Woburn Abbey, Bedford, having completed a tour of 4,500 miles in France, Spain and North Africa in a privately owned

"MOTH"

piloted by Captain C. D. Barnard.

The three great mountain ranges, the Pyrenees, The Guadaramas and the Sierra Nevada were all crossed at an altitude of 10,000 feet and during the three weeks that the machine was away THE TOOL BOX WAS NOT OPENED ON A SINGLE OCCASION.

The Moth—
the machine with a million miles behind it.

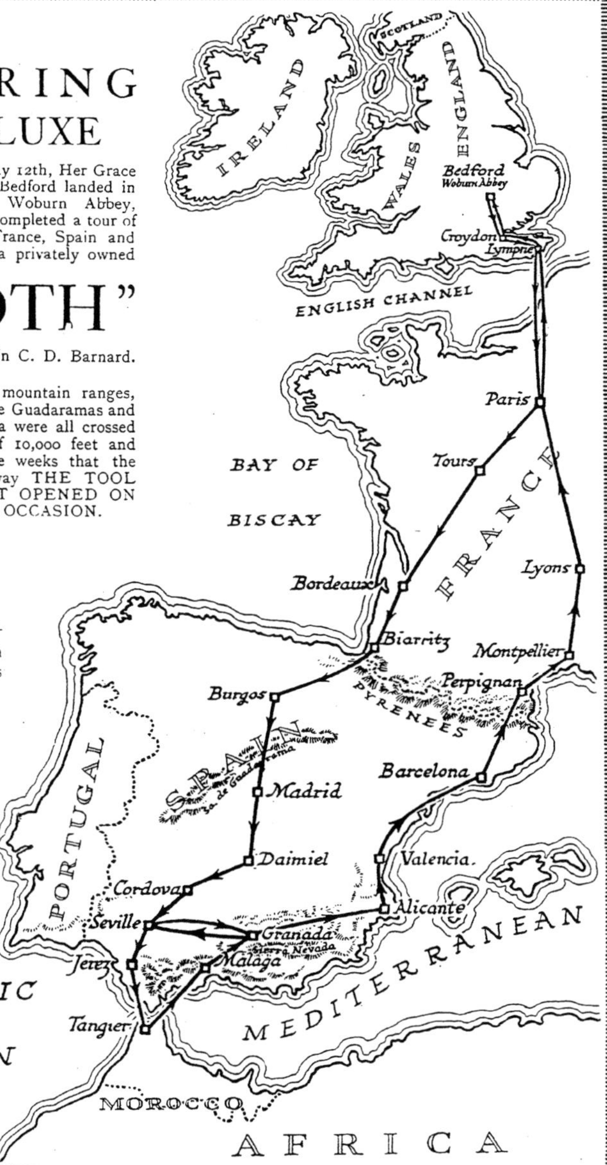

ATLANTIC OCEAN

(map showing route through England, France, Spain, Portugal, Morocco with cities: Bedford Woburn Abbey, Croydon, Lympne, Paris, Tours, Lyons, Bordeaux, Biarritz, Montpellier, Perpignan, Burgos, Barcelona, Madrid, Daimiel, Valencia, Cordova, Seville, Alicante, Jerez, Granada, Malaga, Tangier; with labels ENGLISH CHANNEL, BAY OF BISCAY, MEDITERRANEAN, AFRICA, MOROCCO, SPAIN, PORTUGAL, FRANCE, IRELAND, SCOTLAND, WALES, ENGLAND)

35

is a definite contribution to the cause of private flying and to the efforts now being made to make the Nation air minded'. The letter finished with a hope that the performance of the engine had not given her a moments anxiety. The *DH Gazette* reported the trip in detail laying emphasis on the fact that the only maintenance carried out during the whole 4,500 miles, consisted of an inspection of plugs and oil filter during their enforced stay in Barcelona. As for the Duchess, she described the trip as the most glorious three weeks holiday she had ever had and the most wonderful experience of her life. *'When,'* she wrote, *'aeroplane engines become as silent as cars, the one drawback to flying will be abolished. For the rest, in the hands of a pilot I trusted I felt far safer than on Watling Street in my car. To the pilot who persuaded me to take this flight and throughout, unceasingly looked after the comfort and amusement of his deaf passenger who at times must have been a serious drag, I here record my heartfelt gratitude.'*

The Duchess now hired aeroplanes for all journeys of any distance including visits to London. Following Woburn tradition, cars based at Woburn, in the interests of the chauffeurs, terminated their journeys at Hendon. Here passengers had to transfer to a car based at the Bedford house in Belgrave Square. Watling Street at the time was winding and in places narrow thus the first part of the journey could have taken anything up to two hours. The flight from Woburn to Stag Lane where the London car picked up the Duchess, took no more than twenty-five minutes - an appreciable saving in time apart from being, as far as she was concerned, a much pleasanter and less time-wasting method of travel.

Throughout this period Barnard was based at Stag Lane, the base also of the aeroplanes the Duchess hired. Thus it was that on 1st June, he flew to Woburn to collect her to fly to Epsom for The Derby. The Duchess described the flight thus:

'Went to The Derby for the first time in my life. I had been X-raying all the morning and Captain Barnard came for me soon after 2.30 pm. Flew to Epsom arriving a few minutes before the walk-past. Were alongside at the start and followed round to the winning post returning via Stag Lane to my X-rays. *Even Herbrand was impressed!'*

In early summer each year, the Duke and Duchess moved to *Endsleigh*, their house on the Tavistock estates near Plymouth, for the salmon fishing. This year the Duchess got Barnard to fly her down in the Moth, a journey of some three hours. In the middle of the holiday he brought her back for one night to assist at a mornings operations at her hospital, returning the same afternoon. At the end of the holiday Barnard was invited to spend the night before flying back and the following morning, the Duchess took him out fishing, her diary reading thus:

'June 20th - Got up at 5.30 am to take my pilot out salmon fishing. He hooked one but lost it. He visited his old school in the morning and we flew back to Woburn leaving at 5.15 pm. Hovered over Pauline Cockerell on Dartmoor but only saw her Sealyham. Had a look at Corfe Castle and Brownsea Island then over Bournemouth; Lyndhurst to call on Zöe but also received no recognition, then on to Stockbridge where I was born and christened and so home to Oxford where we dipped over the colleges.'

By now they had been flying for around three hours thus shortly afterwards, Barnard asked the Duchess to turn on the extra fuel tank that was fitted in the front cockpit. Try as she would however she was unable to turn the cock. Barnard, faced with an impending forced landing hastily climbed but with his usual luck, just managed to make Woburn before the fuel ran out. On the ground, much to the Duchess's relief, Barnard was also unable to turn the cock until he got a spanner. It turned out that it had been tightened by an ex-RAF chauffeur in an attempt to cure a fuel leak. 'A little joke which could have cost us our lives on some of our foreign journeys,' the Duchess remarked. During the flight a sad voice had come over the 'phones saying, 'I have been thinking of that salmon I lost all day.'

Their next enterprise was to view from the air a total eclipse of the sun. The chances of seeing it from down south were forecast to be slight so the evening before the eclipse, Barnard flew the Duchess to Harrogate where they landed on the Strays, and left the aircraft in charge of some nightwatchmen. They took off next morning at 5.30 am and climbed through fog to 10,000 feet where the sky was clear. The shadow of the moon was already showing, which ultraviolet goggles plus some fleecy clouds enabled them to see quite clearly. The shadow at first passed slowly, then rushed to totality which lasted no more than four or five seconds. There was just time to see the complete corona and a flare of light before normal daylight returned, leaving a rose and yellow dawn sky. Greatly pleased with themselves, Barnard felt his way back through the overcast and having discovered his position by swooping down over Pocklington railway station, refuelled at Malton before flying home with Ermine Street his guide. On the way they passed several derelict First World War aerodromes that the Duchess commented, might, when flying became more popular, one day come into their own. Thirteen years later many were in fact brought back into use but sadly, not for the reasons she envisaged. Of the flight the Duchess wrote: 'And here ended another of the most wonderful experiences of my life in this eventful year.' They had, it so happened, been one of only a very few who saw the 1927 eclipse. *The Times* having chartered a DH.50 piloted by Captain Olley obtained some photographs over Lancashire but down south, as forecast, clouds hid the eclipse from view.

Emerald green Cirrus Moth G-EBRI, ordered by the Duchess in May, finally obtained its Certificate of Airworthiness and was delivered, on 13th July. She had intended on her first flight in it to visit Buckenhurst, a house in Norfolk, which at the time the Duke was considering buying for her as a dower house. However it was too foggy, so instead they flew to Brooklands to collect a speaking tube that had been left in a hired Moth. Up till now the Duchess had few opportunities to fly herself as when luggage or a spare petrol can was carried, it was impossible to fit a control column in the front cockpit. On this trip however she flew part of the way and was delighted to find that in spite of the fog she was able to find her way. Other flights in her new Moth took her to Roehampton to give away prizes and to Old Buckenham Hall, another house considered by the Duke for purchase. Here they landed in a field of thistles near the house, which the Duchess described as very nice, but shut in by trees and in a terribly desolate situation. The house eventually bought for her was *Whispers* near Midhurst in Sussex, where in due course a landing ground was laid out to which she made many flights.

On 31st July Barnard and the Duchess flew to Nottingham to watch the 1927 Kings Cup, run that year from Hucknall. It was one of its less successful years as out of twenty-five entries, nine withdrew after the pre-race crash of the Bristol Type 99A Badminton in which its pilot F L Barnard (no relation) was killed, and ten retired during the race because of weather. Only six finished; the race being won again by a DH.60 Moth piloted by Captain W.L.Hope. The race was notable for being the first Kings Cup entered by women pilots. Mrs Eliott-Lynn, better known later as Lady Heath was however one of those who withdrew before the race. Lady Bailey in a DH.60 Moth started, but like many others, failed to finish.

In August, largely because of a particularly bad summer, Barnard and the Duchess set out in search of some Italian sun. Never wasting a minute, the Duchess attended the mornings operations in her hospital before leaving for Paris. Next day they refuelled at Dijon and after a night at Lyons, crossed the Alps to Turin - a flight of particular interest to the Duchess who before her marriage, had climbed from Chamonix. The Italians at this time were less than friendly to foreign aviators. Passengers on the England-Cairo run had for some years yet to spend two nights in a train between Paris and Brindisi because Imperial Airways landplanes unable to overfly, were refused permission to make transit landings in Italy. Thus landing at Turin, they were at first refused petrol, 'comforted' instead by the news that two Germans had been kept waiting three days for it. Further difficulties were encountered at Verona and at Venice Lido, Barnard's camera was confiscated despite the fact that he had a *laisser passer* signed by the Italian Ambassador. This was in due course retrieved by the British Consul. After two nights in Venice, which included a tour of the canals by moonlight in a steam launch, they left for Naples where before landing, they circled Vesuvius at fifty feet with tourists waving to them from the rim of the crater. After a further two nights they left for Nice, calling at Rome - where although they had been through only two days earlier, officials insisted on examining every detail of their papers - and at Pisa. Between

The Duchess with Captain Barnard at Stag Lane following their return from the first continental tour, May 1927. (DH Gazette)

Genoa and Nice they hit the Mistral and were given a very rough ride and at Nice, Barnard's temper was further worsened by having to wait one and a half hours for the keys of the hangar. The Duchess wrote:

'August 15th - My pilot after a very long day and much mental strain from aerodrome officials and the Mistral, was becoming highly uncomplimentary about Italian and French methods. *It has not taken me a year to find out that flying is a very good discipline for the quick tempered but at present I can bear anything with equinamity that has such tremendous compensations.*'

They left the following afternoon for Lyons, waved off by the Mayor. Shortly after take-off however they were again caught in severe turbulence, the like of which even Barnard said he had never before encountered. Tossed around like paper, they once found themselves going backwards. Barnard when he regained some control headed inland from where, looking back to the coast, they saw a waterspout travelling across the bay. Against a vicious headwind they now changed course for Marseilles, the 110-mile flight from Nice taking them three hours. It is perhaps surprising that no comments are recorded about the problems of landing a Moth in such turbulent conditions. Nevertheless, to the Duchess, even this flight had its compensations. 'The scenery,' she wrote, 'was glorious and we passed right over the great forest fires which were raging, twenty or thirty outbreaks at one moment. Sometimes houses and farms were engulfed. *Even in our encounter with the mistral I was far too interested to be frightened and had we been beaten, regret for Herbrand and disappointment that the little moth should not achieve what it set out to do were the only thoughts that occupied my mind.*' Barnard, great on publicity, reported the episode to the *Daily Mirror* thus:

"Yesterday we were suddenly drawn into the sort of whirlwind or vortex caused apparently by the wind coming down with great force over the mountains to the sea. The machine was hurled about like a piece of paper and we were hurled about inside the cockpits having difficulty in keeping in the machine. To make matters worse we were carried into great clouds of smoke caused by forest fires which are still raging in the mountains. I felt sure we would be thrown into the sea or dashed against a mountain. I fought frantically with the controls trying to keep head into wind, doing my best not to be forced out to sea. I thought that at any moment the machine would break up. After some time - it seemed a long time but was probably only seconds - we were literally thrown out of the whirlwind almost upside down. I made for the shore as fast as I was able and climbed inland over the mountains. We then saw from a safe distance a cone of water, swirling around and travelling at great speed. I calculated it was quite 50ft high. White clouds of spray were coming from the top of the cone giving the appearance of a water volcano. The Duchess although badly bruised on the arms by the terrific buffeting was not unnerved by the ordeal. I've had eleven years of continual flying but have never experienced anything so frightening or so uncanny."

They flew home via Lyons, Dijon and Le Bourget making a night-stop in Paris. The Via Dolorosa was not quite as mournful as usual the Duchess noted, as it was rather too late for funeral processions! The following afternoon they continued to Lympne

and Stag Lane where although Barnard thought he had warned
off reporters, one caught up with the Duchess and the following
erudite conversation ensued:
    'Have I the honour of speaking to the Duchess of Bedford?'
    'Yes.'
    'Are you fond of flying?'
    'Yes, very.'
    'Do you think you will ever fly again?'
    'Well as this is my own machine, I hope so.'
Because of the publicity, the Duchess was flooded with further
requests for interviews, for it was still early days for such tours.

In October, *Flight* magazine persuaded the Duchess to write
an article for them on her first years experiences as a private
owner from which she tried to excuse herself since nature had
not endowed her with the gift of expressing herself![1]

As introduction the Editor wrote, 'Not only *Flight* but British
aviation in general, owes the Duchess of Bedford a great deal
for her practical encouragement of flying. By her constant use of
her aeroplane she is setting an example which undoubtedly in
years to come, will be followed by many. What makes the
experience of the Duchess of Bedford so valuable is that having
no axe to grind, she had chosen flying because it offers the most
comfortable and quickest method of travel.' Sadly, this idyllic
age of flying in which you could fly freely round Britain, Europe
and even Africa without regulation, at heights low enough to
enjoy the view, lasted but a few years. A few days after her
return from Italy the Duchess seated in the rear seat of her
Moth, had her first flying lesson.

The Duchess had paid for new sails for Cley Mill and, in
September, flew up to inspect progress. The Mill, dating from
1713, had been bought by Mrs Sarah Wilson in 1921 from whom
the Duchess rented it. It was generally lived in however by
Sister Rachel, a Wantage Sister whose activities climbing up
ladders and over planks to reach the top balcony, sliding down
muddy boards to reach the launch and driving her car - all in
her nun's habit - seemed to the Duchess delightfully incongruous! As part of the repairs, the small Mill wheel was being

1. See Appendix I for full text

painted red and white - complained of by some although historically these were the correct colours. The sails were again replaced in 1950 and at the time of writing, an appeal is afoot for yet another set.

The year ended for the Duchess with her annual flight to Scotland. Here, instead of the field they had used the previous year at the entrance to *Cairnsmore House*, a more suitable landing ground had been prepared 'in Mrs Callendar's field near Creetown station.' It had a 'lovely hangar', to which in due course a thirty by fifteen foot extension was added for use by the Duchess as a changing room. She wrote:

'September 24th - I left (Woburn) in the Moth at 11.55, very bumpy and wet most of the way but as I was given control in spite of the bumps and managed to keep straight, I enjoyed it. Landed at Liverpool for petrol. Aviation Meeting in progress. Creetown 5.20 pm after slight diversion to wave to Cardoness.'

And of the return journey:

'November 12th - Left again in bright sunshine eleven am. Swooped down to say goodbye to Mrs Caird of Cassencary then rapid passage to Manchester. Woburn in four and a half hours including stop. *It was lovely being in the Moth again..'*

1927 had certainly been a memorable year for the Duchess. She had flown for the first time to France, Spain and North Africa; had become the owner of her first aircraft and with her pilot Charles Barnard had come through unscathed and undaunted, some hair-raising experiences. She had already accumulated over 160 hours in the air and had taken her first steps towards becoming a licenced pilot - certainly as the French might say she had received her *'Bapteme de l'Air.'*

Chapter Four

1928: Seven Weeks in Persia

In 1928 the Duchess sponsored Barnard on an even more ambitious project, to fly to India and back in eight days. Imperial Airways had surveyed the route between Cairo and India as early as 1925 but there was still no through passenger service. This was because, when the service was due to open in 1927, the Persians had, at the last minute, withdrawn their permission to overfly their territory. The London-India passenger service finally opened in April 1929 with a scheduled time for the single journey of seven days. This included flights in two types of landplane, a flying boat and for reasons given in the previous chapter, a train journey between Basle and Genoa.

The object then of the Duchess's trip in 1928 was to hurry things on by proving that with a shorter route and fewer stops - the England-India service when it opened listed some twenty - mail and even passengers could without undue fatigue, travel to India in four days. She admitted however, that if this was to become a matter of routine, a relay of pilots would be needed. As (according to Barnard) there was no suitable British aeroplane available, a Fokker VIIa G-EBTS was chosen for the flight fitted with a special Bristol Jupiter engine.

The Fokker already had a history of record attempts behind it. After two years service with KLM it had been bought by Captain R H McIntosh of Imperial Airways for an east-west crossing of the Atlantic and had been named *Princess Xenia*, after the Russian-born wife of the sponsor of the flight. McIntosh had set off from Dublin in September 1927 with Major J C Fitzmaurice of the Irish Army as co-pilot but some five hundred miles out, bad weather had forced them to return. McIntosh then teamed up with 'Bert' Hinkler for an attempt in the same aircraft, to take the world long-distance record by flying *non-stop* to India. This too failed when they were forced down by bad weather in Poland and the aircraft was slightly damaged. Repaired, it was flown back to England, put up for sale and bought by a syndicate called Air Communications Ltd, from whom the Duchess hired it for the projected flight to India. Before starting out on this venture in June however, the Duchess made a number of flights in her Moth.

On 30th March Barnard flew her to see the Grand National at Aintree and the following day, to watch the Boat Race from the air at Putney. In April they visited Frankfurt and Cologne and in May there was the usual spring visit to *Endsleigh* and several flights to Bristol to check progress on the installation of the Bristol Jupiter engine in the Fokker. By the beginning of June all was at last ready and on the 9th, the Duchess was flown to Lympne to join Barnard and E H Alliott, the other crew member, and the Fokker. The Duchess wrote in her diary:

'June 9th - After months of postponement, change of plans, etc.etc., Captain Barnard's flight to India in the Fokker *Princess Xenia* on which I am to accompany them, is to come off and I left Henlow aerodrome in my Moth with Captain Hope as my pilot. Being a somewhat stormy day and Captain Hope unacquainted with Park landings, he elected to leave from an aerodrome (Henlow) and Jemima and my two Matrons came to see me off. We had a bumpy journey and one big bump over the North Downs which my pilot subsequently made the most of to the reporters at Lympne, so that with further embellishment from them, my sorrowing friends and relations were greeted next morning with startling headlines in the newspapers: 'Duchess nearly thrown out of her aeroplane', 'nearly killed', etc. etc. I arrived however in safety at Lympne all unconscious of my 'perilous escape', and spent the night or such hours of it as our very early start permitted, at a Hythe hotel.'

For the Duchess, the night was indeed a short one as she left her hotel for the aerodrome at four am. In spite of the early hour, a small group of people including an irrepressible female reporter whose persistence made it nearly impossible for the Duchess to speak to her friends, were waiting to see them off. However, little time it would seem was wasted as they took off at 4.25 am. The longest run at Lympne, some 1,100 yards, ran northwest to southeast; the wind that morning was from the southwest. As the take-off run in this direction was less than

900 yards, Barnard with his heavy fuel load opted for a crosswind and the longer run. It was only later that they learnt that as they crossed the hedge they had hit some telegraph wires -one of the closest of a number of brushes with death the Duchess experienced in her eleven years of flying. Reports of the departure filled the press, the following being one of the more descriptive accounts:

"Dawn was breaking. A single 450 hp Bristol engine was revving slowly with a deep-throated hum. A small group of officials, friends and journalists stood waiting for the take-off. Within a few minutes the Duchess was stretched out comfortably on the luxurious easy chair in the cabin of the machine. Captain Barnard tucked a steamer rug round her and climbed into the cockpit. Mr E Alliott co-pilot and navigator sat beside him. The machine was taxied out of the hangar at once and bumped awkwardly down to the other end of the field. It turned, paused for a moment and then with a roar started up the aerodrome. It seemed to crawl. There was no impression of speed and a chill of horror crept through the watching group as each second passed and the monoplane refused to rise. Within 100 yards of a farmhouse the wheels left the ground, the aeroplane's tail went down and the machine rose slowly and painfully and skimmed over the roof. I could see the pilot give the tail another tug as he neared the telegraph wires. The propeller cleared the wires but the undercarriage tore through, the starboard wing dipped and the machine seemed to side-slip dangerously but it recovered and flew out of sight."

Some time later Barnard admitted in an article to the *News of the World* that had there not been a fall over the cliff of 500 feet, he could not have averted a terrible crash.

Another article described how with the wind gusty and from the southwest, Barnard at the last minute changed his direction of take-off heading southeast instead of into wind. The article continued:

"The machine went through a small gap between two cottages. Captain Barnard had been in tight corners before but never tighter than this. The aeroplane flew on only a few feet from the ground then when the earth fell away to the Marshes below, dropped some feet. The danger was now over. The Duchess arrived at the aerodrome a quarter of an hour before the start in her Rolls Royce, attended by her maid. She was hatless and wore a long leather coat."

To start with the weather over Europe was indifferent but as they left Belgium it cleared and following the Danube they reached Sofia, a distance of twelve hundred miles, in thirteen and three-quarter hours. As the town was some distance from the aerodrome and they hoped to make an early start, the Duchess accepted the offer of a sofa in the sitting room of a Bulgarian officer's married quarters for the night. Unfortunately this proved also to be the room in which the supper was both cooked and served, and as supper was not ready until nine pm and the officer's wife spoke no English, the evening must have been a long and trying one! The Bulgarian officer promised to call the Duchess at four am but in the event by then she was already up and dressed - something that had not taken long as the kitchen tap in the sink, which she had been invited to use for washing, provided no water. The pilots when they appeared were also unwashed and unshaven.

From Sofia, once free of the mountains, they followed the Marista river down to Constantinople. As they approached the coast, Barnard called to the Duchess to do some time and distance calculations. 'A cruel moment to do so,' she wrote, 'as it was all so wonderfully beautiful and interesting. I left my seat to get a look on the other side but was immediately called to order by, 'Have you finished that Your Grace?' I say called but all communications in the Fokker had to be in writing, so back to my sums I went and consoled myself with the hope that calculations would not be wanted on the return journey.'

'It was all a dream of beauty,' the Duchess wrote, 'over the azure-blue Sea of Marmora, then over the wonderful sandy mountains and over the narrowest part of the Gulf of Ismid.' Once in the mountains they followed the Baghdad railway climbing once to 10,000 feet, the snow line, before reaching Adana. They spent their second night at Aleppo where again because of the early start next morning, they accepted some Spartan accommodation in the French Officer's quarters. Although they had eaten little all day, they had to wait till the

47

normal dinner hour for food and as the only drink offered in the Mess was champagne, water being declared undrinkable, it was a question of drinking this or going thirsty - and the Duchess wrote, 'thirsty I went!'

Barnard had insisted that they start at dawn so the Duchess, who had an adjoining room, offered to call him. When however at first light she did so Barnard was far from pleased, complaining that by Aleppo time she had called him an hour too early - to which the Duchess as ever rightly replied that dawn is dawn anywhere, whatever clocks may say. By the time they took off the sun was high in the sky. From Aleppo, the Euphrates led them through Syria, Mesopotamia and the Iraq desert, an area of utter desolation, to the Persian Gulf. Now and again they passed trains crawling along the Baghdad railway; mirages in the form of large lakes were ever with them, receding or vanishing completely as they approached. Now and again they saw a tiny collection of mud huts and wondered how on earth the inhabitants managed to scrape a living. They also passed some extinct volcanos and near Babylon, encountered a mild sandstorm. Passing near what was said to be the Garden of Eden the Duchess remarked that had she been Eve, she would certainly have succumbed to temptation in order to be expelled from it. She added that it might not be so desolate in winter as it looked in the month of June. In excellent flying conditions, Barnard for the first time, allowed the Duchess to climb into the right-hand seat and take the controls. The fact that the Fokker handled somewhat differently from the Moth and that Alliott's seat was far too low for her made things difficult, however as she said, 'at 7,000 feet my pilot felt he could afford to leave me in sole charge once for a brief time and we remained in the air.'

After hours over desert, the last part of the flight down the eastern shore of the Persian Gulf to Bushire (Busheir) was a welcome change. Bushire had been a planned stopping place for Imperial Airways on their route to India, but a hitch in the negotiations with the Persians had caused the opening of the route to be postponed. The aerodrome was now virtually derelict but there was still a good hangar that Imperial Airways had built in anticipation of their service. On landing, only a few Persians were around to greet them but shortly afterwards, a

Barnard and Alliott (left) at Bushire on the Persian Gulf in front of Fokker VIIa 'Princess Xenia', which force-landed there during the attempted record flight to India and back. (A J Jackson Collection)

car arrived with the British Resident's secretary and some more reporters and photographers. The Duchess was immediately whisked off to the Residency where they were all invited to stay, the pilots remaining to attend to the aircraft and put it in the hangar. In the early hours of the following morning the Duchess was awakened by much coming and going of motors and a general atmosphere of unrest. Although diplomatic clearance for the flight had been obtained before leaving home, the Persians were now refusing to let them leave and at one point, Barnard had even been threatened by a sentry with a rifle if he so much as approached his aircraft. As a result, Barnard and the Residency staff had been up much of the night sorting things out. Eventually however they managed to leave without too much delay.

They had gone but short distance when the cockpit filled with smoke and spatterings of oil appeared on the windscreen. The Duchess, who as usual during take-off was sitting on the step behind the cockpit, had a map thrust into her hand as Barnard swung round to head back to the aerodrome. In spite of the 350-gallon fuel load he managed to make a good landing. 'Well,

49

that's the end of our flight.' was his first comment and, from the sight of the oil-spattered 'plane, it certainly looked like it. The engine it was found had suffered an oil blockage and while the Duchess returned to the Residency, Barnard and Alliott set to discover the extent of the damage. At first sight this did not seem too great and they entertained hopes that Imperial Airways engineers from either Basra or Cairo, could repair it for them. '*A hope I did not myself share,*' the Duchess wrote; '*From the first I wanted to get a new engine from home but my pilot, who was ever a super-optimist laughed the idea to scorn.*' As on several other occasions the Duchess's instinct proved right and after several days of delay, a new engine had to be sent for from England.

'It would be weary work,' the Duchess wrote, 'recording all the negotiations which subsequently took place and it suffices to say that it ended in a ten-week stay in Persia. *Though I should have liked to have made a record and done the flight from Lympne to Karachi in four days, the record-breaking part had not been the one and only object of my flight, as it was of my companions.* The interest in the flight concerned me most, and that was greatly enhanced by my long stay in Persia - the last place I ever expected to find myself in - and though the average tourist would not choose the months of June, July and August for a visit to South Persia, the kindness of those who were to entertain me compensated fully for the heat. Thus far we had done the journey of 2,225 miles in three days.'

On Friday 15th June the 'super-optimist' cabled the *Daily Express* in London as follows:

"Mechanic and spares will arrive on Sunday and repairs will take two days so that we hope to arrive in Karachi on Wednesday. We shall leave again on Friday and be back in London on Monday. The Duchess of Bedford is very keen on making a record flight home and is not in the least perturbed by our spectacular and hair-raising forced landing here on Wednesday. Mr Alliott the co-pilot and myself are working like slaves dismantling parts in the scorching sun. All the English here are most kind to us."

On Sunday Mr Garner, the Imperial Airways engineer, arrived from Basra by steamer - at that time the only means of

Captian Barnard and Alliott at Bushire, 1928

travelling down the Gulf. Barnard and the Duchess joined the local Health Officer in the small Persian cargo boat that met the steamer, anchored some seven miles offshore. Before returning, they took tea with the Captain. Once ashore Mr Garner quickly decided that the engine was beyond local repair and that as the Duchess had said from the first, a new one would have to be sent for. In those days before cargo flights, the only way this could come from England was by sea and a further nine weeks were to elapse before its arrival.

For the first four nights of their enforced stay the Duchess stayed in the Residency. The Howarths then left for Shiraz, the resort in the mountains frequented by those committed to summer in these parts. Before leaving, they told the Duchess she was welcome to stay on at the Residency as a skeleton household would in any case remain. Once the Howarths had departed however, the 'household' lost no time in making it clear to the Duchess that she wasn't wanted; she therefore asked Barnard to look round for a house where they could all stay on a cost-sharing basis. The bungalow he found belonged to one Robert Parkyn with whom terms were agreed but who, although they were there for some nine weeks, refused when they left to accept any contribution.

'Bushire,' the Duchess wrote, 'is accounted by those who have to spend the summer here as one of the worst climates in the world. Probably residents in the Gold Coast, New Guinea and a few other places would be prepared to dispute it but in all events, it was that most unpleasant of mixtures, heat and damp ie. sea damp. . . . Bath water is very scarce and is brought one mile in skins on the back of an ass. That means that when you get it, the bath is four inches deep and one has one jug of water in addition per day. Black ants, spiders, lizards, centipedes, sandflies and other nameless creatures of the Devil swarm in towels, sponges, bathroom mats etc. and snakes were about but only one of the latter came under my eye. The amazing thing was that though one was always wet through till clothing could be rung out, one could step into a car and motor through the night air and get dry without putting on an extra garment - chills and colds were said to be unknown. For the first few weeks of my stay however, terrible unquenchable thirst, a lack of suitable clothing, the ever wet condition of what clothing I had and lack of occupation during the greater part of the day, were all I had to complain of. Ginger beer and lime juice constituted the greater part of what I had to drink as, except at Mr Parkyn's, I found the tea in Persia quite horrible.' For the active Duchess, lack of occupation was probably the hardest thing to bear. There was a library of sorts but she had none of her own books, and writing was almost impossible as pens dried out between inkstand and paper.

Barnard too referred to Bushire as the hottest and most uncomfortable place in the world. 'Sometimes,' he wrote later, 'the temperature was over 100 degrees at night but our host Mr Parkyn did all he could to make things as easy as possible. How the Duchess managed to stand the discomfort and terrific heat was a mystery. *Her unfailing courage never flagged; in spite of the heat and discomfort she was always cheerful and anxious to continue her flight.*'

On 27th June, two weeks after their forced landing, Barnard returned from Basra where he had been to discuss the situation with Imperial Airways. He brought an invitation for the Duchess to stay with Mr Gass of the Anglo-Persian Oil Company in Abadan, a couple of hundred miles away at the northern end of the Persian Gulf. It took a good day and a half to get there. First a cargo boat to join the Mail steamer, then a 150-mile sail up the Gulf after which the steamer had to wait for daylight to enter the Euphrates. The Duchess disembarked at the confluence of the Karun river and joined an Anglo-Persian launch, the journey ending with a ten-mile drive across desert. Although temperatures still rose to 125 degrees by day, conditions in Abadan generally were a great deal pleasanter than in Bushire, not least because there was no water shortage. Water however, when it came out of the tap, was so hot that evening baths had to be drawn in the morning to give them time to cool. Surprisingly, porridge appears to have been the main dish at breakfast.

Abadan consisted of the Anglo-Persian Company works at one end and a native bazaar at the other; there were however no shops from which the Duchess could supplement her very limited wardrobe and at the European Club, her unsuitable and shabby clothes were a great source of embarrassment to her. She spent two weeks in Abadan during which she was taken to Ahwas, and from there the hundred or so miles on to the oil well settlement in the mountains, with its clubs and polo grounds as well as a very well-equipped hospital. After a fortnight the Duchess, not wishing to outstay her welcome, returned to Bushire where, as there was still no news of the engine, Mr Parkyn arranged a further visit, this time to Isfahan in central Persia. It was her great regret during this period that she had with her no camera. Before leaving home she had bought one specially for the trip but Barnard had told her that it would be no use taking it as it would not be allowed into India. 'I wondered,' she said, 'but as he was my pilot I did as he asked.' Later however she learnt that Barnard had brought his camera and that during the whole trip, nobody questioned him.

The Duchess flew to Isfahan in the prototype Junkers W.33 monoplane, D-921, the Captain of which made an unscheduled stop to drop her. Access to the four-seater cabin of this aircraft was through an opening in the roof over which before take-off, a panel was securely screwed. For ventilation, a small window let in either hot or cold air as ambient temperature dictated thus initially, the cabin that mercifully the Duchess had to herself was like an oven. As they climbed to cross the mountains however and the outside temperature dropped, the temperature in the cabin dropped also until a thick coat would not have been out of place. It was very bumpy over the mountains but at last, after some three hours flying, Isfahan came into view, an oasis in a great plain surrounded by mountains. Seen from the air it appeared as a beautiful city with its mosques, luxuriant gardens, avenues and bridges spanning the now dried up river. On the ground its attractions were modified by the dust, heat and squalor. Nevertheless the Duchess wrote, Isfahan is 'Persia of the Persians and extraordinarily interesting, and one can overlook its shortcomings even if not 'over-smell' them.' It was not, the Duchess found, easy to make a graceful exit through the roof of the Junkers, especially in a wind, and she hoped that her host Mr Moir, who had come to meet her, had not witnessed it! She had only intended to stay in Isfahan for a week but with still no news of the engine, she accepted Moir's pressing invitation to stay longer. Eventually, after a fortnight of continual social activity and visits to the extensive covered bazaars said at the time to be the finest in Asia, it was back to Bushire in the Junkers. This time she found herself sharing the cabin in which the seats were little more than a foot wide and the back-rests metal bars, with an Armenian woman, a child and an Armenian gentleman. It was intensely hot and extremely bumpy and the Duchess spent most of the four hour flight opening paper bags for the woman and child; little wonder then that on disembarking she declared that wild horses would not drag her into a Junkers again.

It was now 3rd August - eight weeks since their forced landing. The long expected steamer *Sharistan* that was bringing their engine, was due to arrive on 13th August but did not turn up. On the 14th and again on the 15th the Duchess recorded in her diary, 'No steamer, no engine.' It finally arrived on 21st August, was installed and test flown and, on 22nd August, they finally took off at 5.15 am for Karachi. They had been in Persia for just over ten weeks. The new engine had called for a new

The prototype Junker W.33 D-921 in which the Duchess flew from Bushire to Isfahan during the enforced stay when the Fokker was awaiting a replacement engine. (Woburn Archives)

propeller that reduced their cruising speed so, to save weight, the old propeller and the spare wheel were left behind at Bushire. The latter was to come in useful the following year. They landed at Dright Road aerodrome, Karachi after a thirteen-hour flight without further incident, the local paper reporting that when the machine came to rest, the Duchess stepped out, 'looking sprightly and girl-like in spite of her 63 years.' In England the *Daily Gazette* reporting their arrival said that the object of the flight, had been to demonstrate the possibility of flying from England to India and back in eight days. It said that the first half of this had in fact been achieved, because the journey from Lympne to Karachi had been accomplished in four *flying* days. The paper went on to say that the Fokker had brought to India the first *fully documented* air cargo. Other aeroplanes passing through Karachi had brought

55

small quantities of goods as a favour, but with no invoices or papers 'incidental to the movement of merchandise'. The enterprising firms taking advantage of this opportunity to send goods to India, the report continued, deserved the highest praise for encouraging an industry that was little known or understood in India at that time. Many of the named goods in that cargo are still well known today. They included Horlicks Malted Milk, Huntley and Palmers Biscuits, Waterman's Ideal Fountain Pens, Cadbury's Chocolates, Enos Fruit Salts and Booths Gin, all for local dealers. The bulk of the cargo, including a film of the Derby, had during the delay in Bushire, been sent on by sea. One can't help wondering what state the Cadbury's chocolates arrived in!

By the time they landed at Karachi it was dark and the crowd that had collected to see them arrive, had largely dispersed. The Duchess, acutely embarrassed by the state of her clothes, was immediately whisked off to Government House while Barnard and Alliott retired to deal with Customs and the Press, at the far more congenial RAF Officers Mess. Next day, inspection revealed that the new propeller had split and was unserviceable which meant a further indefinite hold up. Meanwhile at Government House, Mr Thomas was making it clear to the Duchess that he considered her whole enterprise risky and foolish and was strongly advising her to return home by boat. Had she been staying in a hotel, she wrote in her diary, she would probably have waited, although her hospital work was pressing and time for their annual move to Scotland was fast approaching. As it was, a boat was leaving for England that afternoon and a quick decision had to be made. And so it was that at 7.30 pm on 23rd August, the day after their arrival, she embarked for Bombay on what she called the, 'horrid old British India Steamship *Varena*', to catch P & O's SS *Malwa* for England. The thought of 'crawling home alone' as she termed it, depressed her exceedingly; 'I should not have particularly cared,' she wrote, 'if we had gone to the bottom.' Her thoughts at this time must have turned to those who, like Mr Thomas, would when she got back, inevitably condemn her for ever setting out. Matters were not helped by a monsoon that made the initial part of the voyage extremely rough. But in the sunshine of the Red Sea her depression lifted when she conceived the idea of having her Moth meet her at Marseilles. This way she would at least arrive home by air. Here then on 8th September she disembarked at 8.25 am and by 9.20 am, was in her Moth en route for Paris. They arrived at Stag Lane the following day. Her diary for that day ends thus:

'And so endeth my eight-day flight to India and back. *l'homme propose et Dieu dispose.*' Shall try again if I get a chance.'

Barnard and Alliott arrived home on 6th September three days before the Duchess - which must have been extremely galling for her - in a record time of four and a half days. Perhaps however it was just as well since Alliott arrived home with scarlet fever. On their return Barnard wrote an article on the flight for the *News of the World*, in which he admitted that when taking off from Lympne, had there not been a 500 feet fall over the cliff he could not have averted a crash. 'Strangely but truthfully,' he concluded, 'I can say that I was not in the least frightened.' Perhaps he should have been!

At about this time Barnard wrote an article for the *Daily Express* headed 'No Sex Equality in the Air' which included the following statement.

"Women pilots when interviewed always say 'I was not frightened at all even when . .' This means (a) that she *was* frightened but does not want to admit it or (b) the absence of fear is due to absence of imagination or experience. Imagination is only power to foresee what will be the natural consequence of a given set of facts. Nature has given us imagination so that we shall not be met by an unexpected situation. Fear stimulates the mind to its highest pitch of efficiency in moments of danger. When a woman says she is not frightened she might as well admit the absence of some faculty such as sight or hearing. She is deficient from a mental standpoint and in consequence unlikely to give that extra touch of brilliance to her work in a moment of crisis which means the difference between success and failure. Another thing about fear, it is not panic. Women I say with some experience of them in the air, tend more to panic. They lose all sense of proportion; they see danger ahead and without consideration, do something which may prove fatal. A lot of men do that too and they are of course bad pilots but panic is a thing that seems to attack women more readily. In dealing with the question it is impossible to do more than generalise."

In days when women were very much the subordinate sex he may have had a point.

The article was published with photographs of two women pilots Lady Heath, and a Miss O'Brien who had recently been involved in a crash; a photograph of the Duchess was also included. The Duchess replied to the article saying that the distinction Barnard drew between the sexes regarding fear was hard to understand. She continued, 'I read that it is mind that matters and as I'm not a pilot, my photograph was probably used to illustrate a mental deficient.' To this Barnard in due course replied that as she had never flown solo, she was right to be indignant at her photograph being included. '*She herself*,' he said, '*has shown great ability in the air and in my opinion, is one of the few examples of a woman who is quite capable of flying well*'.' - but back to the Duchess and her flying.

The Duchess had by now decided to exchange her Cirrus Moth G-EBRI for one fitted with a de Havilland designed and built Gipsy I engine. Her new Moth G-AAAO must have been one of the first as the new version had only appeared in late June. She had flown up to *Cairnsmore* for their annual Scottish holiday in G-EBRI and it was while she was there that Barnard brought the new Moth up. The following day they set off in it to Edinburgh. The weather was wet and, keeping low to avoid the clouds, they passed *under* Flores Castle and round the Bass Rock. 'How little I expected to see them thus in pre-war birdwatching days,' the Duchess commented. When they came to the Forth Bridge, Barnard asked her if she would like to fly under it. 'As there was a very strong wind blowing it did not look attractive,' the Duchess wrote, 'but as I never refuse an experience, I consented, and it looked much wider as we flew nearer - fortunately.' They returned next day, still in wet and windy conditions, to find the landing ground and hangar at Creetown flooded. History does not relate what they did about this but presumably Barnard found a dry patch somewhere to drop off the Duchess before returning with the aeroplane down south. He collected her for the return journey to Woburn on 15th November.

Chapter Five
1929: India and Back

January isn't everyone's idea of a month in which to fly in an
open aircraft, but in January 1929 the Duchess decided to go to
Holland to visit Mr Blaauw, a longstanding friend of the family
and fellow animal collector. On 3rd January therefore, Barnard
collected her from Woburn for a flight to Amsterdam. By the
time they had cleared customs at Lympne and coped with a very
strong headwind, daylight had run out and they had to spend
the night at Ostende - which the Duchess called 'a dreary spot
at this time of year.' Next morning they continued to Amsterdam from where they drove to Gooilust and Mr Blaauw.
Returning, fog over the Channel forced them to night-stop at St.
Inglevert and next day, as it showed no signs of lifting, they
abandoned the Moth and returned by boat and train. 'It was
interesting,' the redoubtable Duchess nevertheless wrote, 'seeing Holland from the air under ice and snow, but pretty cold.'
     The spring of 1929 was a poor one for flying. The Duchess
made a few short flights in February and at the end of March,
feeling in need of a holiday, decided to spend Easter at
Endsleigh. But it was not to be. They got no further than
Hungerford before explosive sounds from the engine resulted in
a forced landing and the Easter holiday had to be abandoned.
Instead a fortnight later, Barnard flew her down to Bosham
where Mr Ogilvie her surgeon had lent her a cottage and during
the stay, visited her son Hastings at Warblington House,
Havant.
     Ever since their failed attempt on the India and back record,
the Duchess had been negotiating purchase of the Fokker with a
view to another try. This was finally completed in June after
which the aircraft was sent to Holland for a complete overhaul,
and installation of a cabin fuel tank. From there it was taken to
Bristol for installation of a geared Jupiter XI engine with a
four-bladed propeller and Farman reduction gear. In view of the

60

aircraft's history of failed records, the Duchess decided to change its name from *Princess Xenia* to *The Spider* after the spider which legend has it, inspired Robert Bruce to try, try and try again. With the new cabin tank the aircraft could now carry some 400 gallons of petrol, enough for sixteen hours flying. For this trip, Alliott's place as second pilot and navigator was taken by R F Little who was well qualified for the job. He had worked as co-pilot, navigator and mechanic on Alfred Lowenstein's tri-motor Fokker VII - a job that ended when in July 1928 Lowenstein, under circumstances never fully explained, disappeared from the aircraft in mid Channel while being flown from Croydon to Brussels.

It was the end of July before the aircraft was finally ready, considerably later in the year than they would have liked. As the Park was not a suitable landing ground for the Fokker, on 29th July Barnard collected the Duchess from Henlow en route for Lympne. 'I was given control for a short time on the way,' the Duchess wrote, 'and was much surprised to find that it presented none of the difficulties I experienced last year. Whether this is due to my having done so much piloting on the Moth I do not know as the two are totally different, but I really found it easier than the Moth.' Delayed by weather, they were to spend four nights at Lympne before getting away.

They arrived on Monday. Tuesday was spent making final preparations for an early start on Wednesday, but by evening, the weather forecast was such that departure had to be postponed. For the Duchess, Wednesday therefore turned into a day of excessive boredom that she passed, for the most part, driving around in her car. By evening the weather showed little signs of change thus Thursday became another day of idleness and frustration, spent for the most part worrying about the possibilities of yet another failure, for every day lost increased the risk of running into sandstorms and monsoons. By now the Duchess, having overstayed her booking in the Hythe hotel, had been moved to a much smaller room to make way for holiday makers. She was therefore more than delighted when on Thursday evening, on returning from Littlestone where she had gone for bird-watching, she found a message from Barnard. It said that in spite of a still unpromising forecast, he was planning to leave next day. So it was that on Friday 2nd August, they finally got away. 'Left hotel in the dark at 3.45 am.' the Duchess wrote. 'The inevitable reporters and photographers awaited us at the aerodrome but the major portion had been choked off by the weather and mercifully compelled to retire whence they came.' Inside the cabin, half the starboard side was now taken up with the new fuel tank; behind this was a stool on which the Duchess was to spend many hours, pumping petrol from the cabin tank into the wings. What remained of the starboard side was filled with a table and a shelf on which any odd jobs from preparing pilot's meals to cleaning plugs was carried out. The port side was for the most part taken up with tools, boxes, luggage and coats; in front of these was the deck chair which, as on the previous trip, formed the Duchess's seat. 'This time,' she wrote, 'we took off successfully at 4.50 am *and removed no telegraph wires!*'

The weather looked none too promising, being thick, rainy and rather cold and to Barnard's disgust, they found that the hotel cook had put cold soup in the Thermos bottle. But as they flew east the weather improved to an extent that when over the Danube, the Duchess was allowed to take the controls. They covered the 1,400-mile distance to Sofia in eleven hours thirty minutes, the Duchess announcing after landing that she didn't feel a bit tired! This time the Duchess was put up in the house of the Commanding Officer, not luxurious but a distinct improvement on the accommodation of the previous year.

They left early next day for Aleppo. The weather was less good than when they came last year and, approaching the Sea of Marmora, they were forced down by low cloud and fog. After following the tortuous course of the Baghdad railway through the Taurus Mountains, as required by the Turkish authorities, they reached Aleppo in nine and a half hours. Since leaving England they had now covered some 2,400 miles in twenty-one hours flying. Although it was very hot, the Duchess was given no opportunity for rest as the Armenian Deputy British Consul, who met them at the aerodrome, insisted on taking her round the Citadel and the Bazaars which, in the opinion of the Duchess, did not compare favourably with those in Isfahan. When at last he dropped her at her hotel, he said that a very

*The Duchess at Aleppo in Syria, where they stopped for refuelling
during the successful record flight to India and back.*
(Woburn Archives)

nice French dance was being given that night and he would be
delighted to get them invitations. From this they managed to
excuse themselves, but did not entirely avoid it as the dance
took place opposite their hotel and the resulting noise continued
until dawn, by which time they were just leaving. The pilots
meanwhile, having had difficulty in getting oil for the aeroplane, didn't get back to the hotel for dinner until ten pm by
which time, the Duchess, who never ate until her crew joined
her, declared she was more than ready for it!

After another ten-hour flight in poor visibility, following for
the most part the Euphrates, they reached Bushire, the scene of
their prolonged stay in 1928. Here their friend Robert Parkyn
with whom they had stayed the previous year, met them with
his newly acquired wife bringing much appreciated drinks and
sandwiches. A tyre had punctured on landing; luckily Parkyn
had kept the spare wheel, abandoned the previous year to
reduce weight, thus averting what would otherwise have been a
serious delay. Again after changing the wheel, Barnard and
Little were very late for dinner. With an eleven to twelve-hour
'against the clock' flight to Karachi in front of them, this left
them as ever, with a very short nights rest.

They were now into the season of sandstorms and visibility that had been poor ever since leaving Aleppo, continued to be bad down the Persian Gulf and along the Gulf of Oman. At times Barnard had to descend to two hundred feet to keep the coast in sight and at Karachi, the weather was so gloomy that it was compared to a foggy day in England. They landed on the new Imperial Airways aerodrome at 14.25 GMT - around seven o'clock local time - with only a few aerodrome workers to see them arrive. 'At least we have flown to India in four days,' the Duchess commented, 'whatever is in store for us on the homeward flight.'

The Hudsons who had been on leave when they arrived in 1928, whisked the Duchess off to Government House. 'Here,' she wrote, 'with an efficient electric fan, a lovely big bath, a comfortable bed and the knowledge that I should be awakened by a sentry, I had a sound three and a half hours sleep, which was all we ever had on this flight - but one gets used to it.' The pilots who had to overhaul the aeroplane had even less rest - Little getting only an hours sleep. Early next morning they set off on the return half of their record-breaking flight.

In spite of the early hour a few people had collected at the aerodrome to see them off including the inevitable reporter. With the weather still unfavourable and heavy cloud over the coast, Barnard was forced to route inland. This was a bonus for the Duchess as it took them over marshes teeming with bird life about which she wrote, 'Though it is indiscreet to comment on the interest of low flying to ones pilot who would prefer a clear sky and an altitude of 7,000 feet, one is permitted to enjoy oneself in private. What look like spots and patches at 9,000 feet become palm-trees and mangrove swamps. One can identify men, dogs, camels, buffaloes and birds and even species of the last if they are of conspicuous plumage like Flamingoes, of which we saw hundreds; storks, cranes, waders and gulls were also disturbed by the mighty insect invading their haunts. The only drawback to low flying as far as I am concerned was that the two pilots had to be outside, so that most of my time was spent in the cabin. I did not however lead an inactive existence as on this flight, I did nearly all the pumping of petrol from the big extra tank into the wing tanks. At first I found it hard work

Robert Parkyn in Bushire to whom the Duchess left £2,000 as a
recognition of his 'great kindness in 1928'.

especially with the left hand, but afterwards it became almost
mechanical.'

The Parkyns, as had become their habit, met them at Bushire
and next day they continued to Aleppo. 'The one perfect day of
the whole trip,' the Duchess wrote, 'visibility wonderful and I
was given control for a considerable time. Very good view of
Abadan, Basra and others.' At Aleppo where they had landed
only three days previously, the Commanding Officer commented
drily that they had not lost much time. With a reputation
behind them they were now greeted at the hotel with smiles,
baths and assiduous attention as opposed to the somewhat
offhand way they had been treated previously. Sadly this did
not extend as far as next days breakfast. Overnight they had

ordered an early breakfast of coffee and rolls. Barnard and the Duchess were the first to come down to a gloomy dining room lit by a single light. With a view to the long day in front of them, they reluctantly embarked on the stale rolls and flyblown jam that had obviously stood on the table overnight. Little, when he joined them, switched on a second light and shortly after, was seen to be scrutinising his plate intently. He had discovered that the rolls were swarming with black ants. 'I can say that I felt none the worse and that the black ants did not actively disagree with our digestion' the Duchess wrote, 'I only suffered mentally!'

The Duchess described the next leg of the flight thus:

'The Taurus mountains looked rather ominously cloudy and matters did not improve as we drew near them. We found the Baghdad railway, but to follow it was another matter. Time after time we were compelled to turn, and from the cabin window it looked as if we had some unpleasantly near squeaks of being caught by cloud in narrow valleys where there was no room to turn. With the one-sided view which was all that I had from the cabin window, it was difficult to see what was going on, but when I imagined we had made some progress, I was always finding we were back at the same Viaduct.'

Eventually Barnard was forced to climb through the clouds to the sun and an Arctic landscape above, relying on Little's navigation. But once clear of the mountains the clouds broke and, as they descended, they flew into a flock of Egyptian vultures which split in the slipstream and passed within feet on either side of the aeroplane. 'Had one hit the propeller,' the Duchess remarked, 'we would probably have had a Parsee burial!' Weather problems had resulted in the flight from Aleppo to Sofia taking twelve and a quarter hours instead of the nine and a half hours it had taken on the way out. This time instead of accepting offers of accommodation on the aerodrome, they drove out to a local, if third-rate hotel, which at least relieved them of the pressures of being guests.

There were further diversions for weather on the final leg from Sofia to Croydon which, with a flight-time of thirteen and a quarter hours, proved the longest leg of the whole trip. Initially Barnard set a direct compass course for Calais but

England to India, 1928 and 1929

Date	From		To	Time
10/6/28	Lympne	-	Sofia	13hr 45min
11/6/28	Sofia	-	Aleppo	11hr 30min
12/6/28	Aleppo	-	Bushire	10hr 00min
22/8/28	Bushire	-	Karachi	13hr 00min
2/8/29	Lympne	-	Sofia	11hr 30min
3/8/29	Sofia	-	Aleppo	9hr 30min
4/8/29	Aleppo	-	Bushire	10hr 00min
5/8/29	Bushire	-	Karachi	11hr 30min
6/8/29	Karachi	-	Bushire	11hr 40min
7/8/29	Bushire	-	Aleppo	11hr 20min
8/8/29	Aleppo	-	Sofia	12hr 15min
9/8/29	Sofia	-	Croydon	13hr 15min

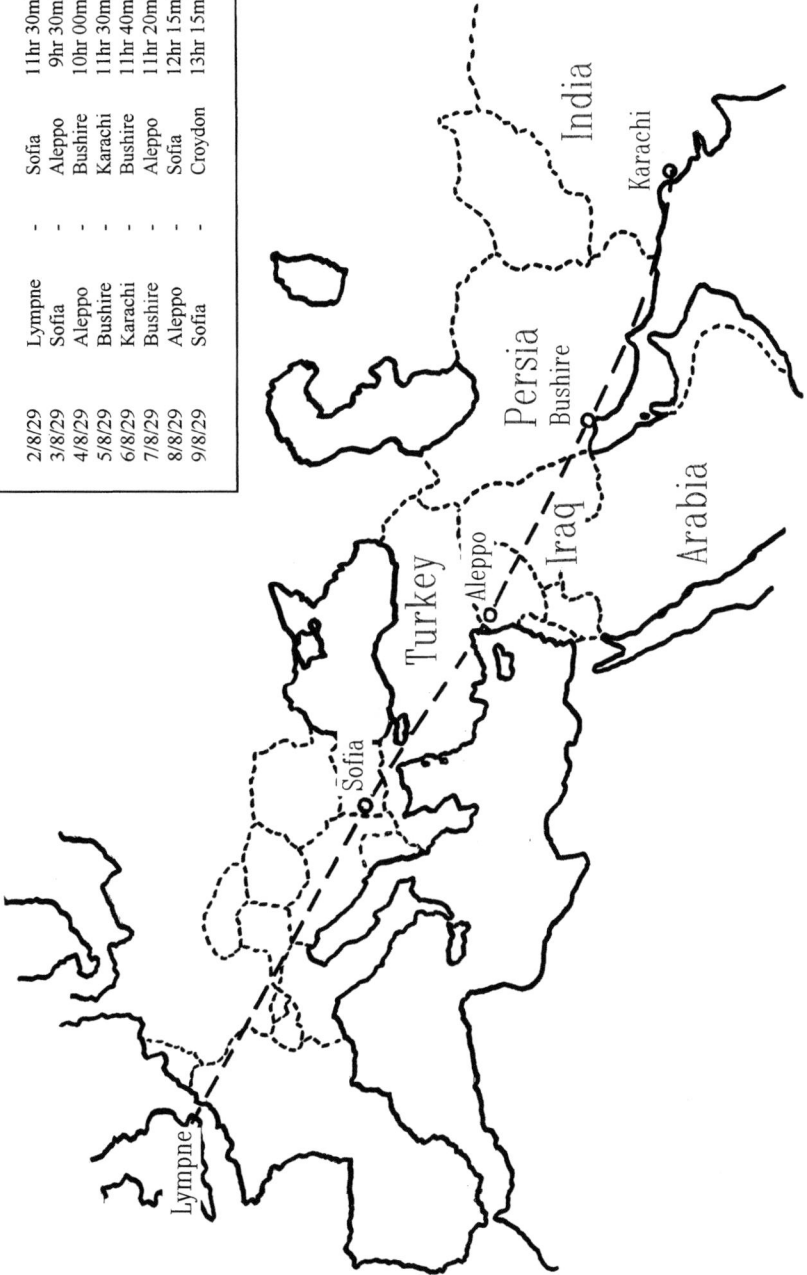

India

Karachi

Persia

Bushire

Iraq

Arabia

Turkey

Aleppo

Sofia

Lympne

mist, cloud on the hills and pouring rain soon forced him down into the valley of the Danube. Over eastern Europe the weather at last cleared and they crossed the Channel in good visibility. After circling Lympne to report their arrival, they continued to Croydon where they landed at 17.30 hours on the afternoon of Friday 9th August. They had made India and back in under eight days, showing Imperial Airways as one paper put it, what could be expected of them in the near future. The flight had been of technical significance, the report continued, because of the long stages and the good average speed that had been maintained on both outward and homeward journeys. The Duchess reckoned that had the weather been better they could have made India and back in an even shorter time but that, if she was ever to do it again, she would choose to start in early June.

'Flying over England a few minutes before landing,' the Duchess wrote in her diary, 'I was feeling a little depressed that our flight had come to an end. The early starts, the long hours in the air, the pleasant but irregular and rather sparse meals had all become a matter of routine.' All who have undertaken adventures of this kind will know how quickly such a routine becomes a way of life. She added that she was speaking for herself, and not for her crew who, 'had had such an anxious time that I think both had enough of it.'

Before they left for India, the Aviation Press had taken little interest in their proposed flight not least perhaps because in April, a nonstop flight from Cranwell to Karachi had been made by two RAF pilots, in just under fifty-one hours. The reception they got at Croydon on their return was therefore all the more unexpected. Warned of their arrival by Lympne, Press and photographers turned out in force to greet them. Representatives of aviation bodies, including the Air Ministry and the Royal Aero Club, were there and among the telegrams of congratulation, was one from the King. Overnight, the Duchess had become a celebrity. The public were intrigued, as they would no doubt still be today, by the 64-year old woman who had survived this long and exhausting journey without even appearing tired. As a passenger, she had not had to share in servicing the aircraft each evening but like the pilots, she had to

Charles Barnard, the Duchess and Bob Little at Croydon on their return from India in 1929. The Fokker had now been bought by the Duchess and renamed 'The Spider'
(Richard Riding Collection)

endure uncomfortable and cold conditions in the aircraft, very long days and some extremely basic overnight accommodation.

On the weekend following their return, Barnard broadcast an account of the flight from Savoy Hill; in this he expressed his regret that no British aircraft was capable of making such a flight. The Fokker, he said, could have carried 1,000 pounds more weight, a statement subsequently hotly challenged, but he stuck to his point. Later in the month the Duchess too was persuaded to speak on the wireless and from all reports, this went down well, especially her quotation from Jeffery Day's *Poems and Verses* which read:

Have you seen the narrow riband, unimportant half forgotten
    that tells you that the Thames is far below?
Have you glanced with smiling pity at the world's most
famous city, a large grey smudge that barely strikes the eye?
Would you like to see things truly and appreciate them duly?
    Well then, do it, damn you, do it, learn to fly.
Have you chased the golden sunbeam down a gold and silver
    alley with pink and orange jewels on the floor?
Have you raced a baby rainbow round a blue and silver
    valley, where purple caves throw back the engine's roar?
Have you seen the lights that smoulder on a cloud's
    resplendent shoulder, standing out before a
        saffron-coloured sky?
Would you be in splendid places and illimitable spaces?
    Well then, do it, damn you, do it, learn to fly!

She was heard by friends from Scotland and even by an old lady
from Woodbridge, Suffolk using an ear trumpet who wrote to
say that she heard the Duchess as if she were in the room. A
member of the BBC wrote thanking her for 'one of the most
charming talks we have ever had.' 'So many people,' he
continued, 'have told me how much they enjoyed it and I only
wish we could more often find speakers with your vigour and
enthusiasm.' The *Daily Express* however took her to task for
saying 'damn' on the wireless.

Before this, the Duchess and her crew attended a lunch given
by the Bristol Engine Company, to celebrate their return.
Barnard and Little flew to Bristol in the Fokker, picking the
Duchess up en route. In his speech the Lord Mayor of Bristol
said the flight from England to India and back in a week had
been a striking record of courage and endurance, which opened
a new era in the history of communications between Britain and
India. It was a matter for congratulation, he continued, that the
engine used for the record had been both designed and
manufactured in Bristol. Speaking of the Duchess, he said that
the record had called for physical endurance that many young
men might have shirked. Throughout the flight she had been an
active, useful and efficient member of the crew. In her reply, the
Duchess said that while for her two companions the flight had
been a strenuous one, for herself it had been a pleasure cruise.
She had the best of pilots, the best of mechanics and the best of

engines, and nothing but weather conditions could have robbed them of success. Like Robert Bruce they had taken their lesson from *The Spider* and though at first they had not succeeded, they had tried again and spun a web across the Continent. The lunch was attended among others by Roy Fedden designer of the engine and Cyril Uwins the company test pilot who afterwards escorted the visitors round the Filton factory. The Fokker was left at Bristol for engine overhaul, Barnard and the Duchess returning to Woburn in her Moth.

For many weeks, letters of congratulation, requests for talks and articles, and for her attendance at various events poured in for the Duchess. Among the invitations she accepted was one on 29th August to open The London Air Park, better known as Hanworth aerodrome, an event that included a garden party laid on by its owners National Flying Services Ltd. A week later she flew to Hamble to board the 20,000-ton steamer SS *Orford*, for a three-day cruise laid on by the Royal Aero Club in conjunction with the Orient Steam Navigation Company, for the 1929 Schneider Trophy Air Race. There were three British and three Italian entrants for the race, which was won by Flying Officer Richard Waghorn in a Supermarine S.6 at a speed of 328.6 mph. The Trophy was handed over at a banquet held on board the *Orford* on the evening of the race. This was attended among others by Ramsey MacDonald, General Balbo and the Under Secretary of State for Air Sir Philip Sassoon. 'I should have enjoyed it more,' wrote the Duchess, 'had I not been pestered all the time by reporters to give an account of the race, which a Sunday newspaper had proclaimed the previous week without the slightest authority, that I was going to do.' When she quite rightly refused to undertake something she was ill qualified to do, the paper offered Barnard 1,000 guineas to persuade her to give just a short message, but as the Duchess said, Captain B. had to go without his 1,000 guineas and the Manager of the newspaper excused himself next day, by saying that the account of the race by the Duchess of Bedford that they had hoped for was not available.

On 9th September they collected *Spider* from Bristol and flew it to Croydon, which was now to be its home. 'It was lovely being in her again,' the Duchess wrote, 'and I piloted her most of the way. It now seems easier than the Moth.' For three years the Duchess had taken the controls of aircraft in the air, but had as yet received no formal instruction. On 11th September Barnard at last volunteered to give her a lesson in 'taxying and landing' and a week later, the Duchess recorded in her diary that she had a lesson in spins and side-slips, and had *looped her first loop*. 'I have been longing to do this for two years and had been promised it for ages,' she wrote, 'but as I prefer to leave 'stunts' to my pilot to propose, it has only come off now. It is very strange seeing the earth above ones head for the first time without any of the apoplectic sensations one would expect if one did it on earth. I prefer 'looping the loop' to 'spins.' I had done these before but only at long intervals, and have not yet arrived at being able to contemplate my progress throughout with open eyes.' However, after four lessons the time came for the family move to Scotland so for the time being, that was that. Her log book records a flight to *Cairnsmore* on 24th September and her diary shows that on 30th September she opened Palnure Hall, the first new building in Palnure since they came there 41 years before.

This year, no return flight is shown so one must assume that on this occasion, she had to return with the Duke by train, possibly because Barnard was not available. By the end of 1929 her log book showed a total of 496 hours in the air.

Chapter Six.

1930: Cape Town and Back

By the end of 1929 plans were already afoot for a further record attempt in *The Spider*; this time it was to be to Cape Town and back with the crew the same as before. In January therefore they flew the Fokker to Woodford to be overhauled by Messrs A.V.Roe and afterwards, took it to Bristol for a new engine to be fitted. Barnard's time was now divided between supervising preparation of the Fokker, and attending to the affairs of his own new company, Brian Lewis and C D Barnard Ltd. Based at Heston, the company offered to supply 'every aspect of service to the private owner', from teaching people to fly, to making fuel arrangements and providing maps etc. for anyone contemplating a special flight. It was in the name of this company that all arrangements for the Cape flight were made.

Towards the end of January, the Duchess flew up to Woodford in her Moth to check progress on the Fokker. 'Piloted myself all the way there,' she wrote, 'and nearly all the way home.' She also paid another visit to *Whispers* where extensive alterations were being made, noting that the gale of last month had made 'awful havoc.' She saw, however, that the building of the new part of the house was complete as far as the exterior went and that the garage was practically finished. Considerable progress had also been made on the power house and laundry. During February and March the Duchess resumed her flying lessons, at first with Barnard and when he was not available, with Sidney St. Barbe from the London Aeroplane Club. Meanwhile, on 5th February the Royal Aeronautical Society, Royal Aero Club, Air League and the Society of British Aircraft Constructors joined to host an Awards dinner at the Savoy Hotel at which The Duke of York as Guest of Honour, presented the awards. The dinner was attended by some 400 people and, among the awards, the Royal Aero Club's Gold Medal was presented to Charles Barnard for his flight to India and back in eight days. The

Britannia Trophy, for the most meritorious performance of the year, was awarded to Lady Bailey for her flight to South Africa and back via the West coast. The Duchess was presented with an illuminated address for her part in the India flight. But to Robert Little, who had played a part equal to that of Barnard in this venture, no recognition was given. C G Grey writing in *The Aeroplane* castigated the organisers of the banquet for this pointing out that Little was the engineer, navigator and relief pilot on whom the success of the flight depended - just as an Army's success depends on its Engineers and Service Corps. He also wrote:

"There is a certain humour in the fact that two noblewomen should have given us the finest lessons in the possibilities of aviation for the Empire. If Lord Trenchard is to be known hereafter as the Father of the Royal Air Force and if Lord Wakefield is to go down in history as the Patron Saint of British Aviation, then Her Grace the Duchess of Bedford and the daughter of the Rossmores (Lady Bailey) deserve to become historic characters as the Mothers of Imperial Communications. There is biological authority for the statement that great men owe their characters to their mothers rather than to their fathers. So let that be a happy omen for the future of Civil Aviation within the Empire. And anyhow, they are a fine argument against those who regard our best families as an effete aristocracy."

Permission had been obtained from the owner for the use of a field at Lewsey Farm between Luton and Dunstable for practice take-offs and landings, and it was from here that on 8th April 1930, the Duchess made her first solo flight. Barnard was to write later:

"The owner of the land was kindness itself and several times we were invited to tea - sometimes to breakfast. Whenever the Duchess had an hour or two to spare she would telephone me to fly the Moth to Woburn. At first she was much too rough and jerky with the machine but I gradually managed to persuade her that it was absolutely essential to be smooth and gentle in the use of the controls. She had infinite patience and I never had a keener or more willing pupil. It will be readily understood however that her deafness was a great handicap, the only contact between instructor and pupil being a telephone system consisting of tubes and headphones, with the noise of the wind and the engine by no means perfect with people of sound hearing. For some time she had considerable difficulty in keeping the machine straight when taking off, a common fault to most beginners, but after ten hours instruction I could tell that she would prove to be a safe pilot without having perhaps, the hands of an expert. Take-off after take-off we made, landing after landing. I wished to make quite certain that the first solo flight would be perfect in every detail. In view of the Duchess's age I was I suppose, erring on the side of safety in not sending her off alone before she ultimately did go. I know she was disappointed but I insisted on ten at least, perfect take-offs and landings made consecutively. Unfortunately at this period I had to go to Bristol to superintend the installation of a new engine in Her Grace's big Fokker so, without my knowledge, she obtained the services of a well-known instructor Mr Sidney St. Barbe, who promptly sent her solo after less than two hours dual. He told me afterwards that he would never be able to understand why I had not had the courage to send her off myself. If the truth be known I had intended to do so on the first suitable day. The day following we made our first non-stop flight from England to Africa, Lympne to Oran, Algeria, on our way to the Cape."

Of her first solo flight the Duchess wrote:

'.....I did a very good take-off and approach, a little bound on first landing but not a serious one, and was mightily pleased that I had done it, and so I think was my instructor as he was very keen to teach me.'

The Aeroplane recorded the event with the following words:

"Her Grace is 64 years of age and must therefore be the oldest woman to reach the solo stage. She is to be congratulated on her pluck and energy not only on learning to fly at her advanced age but also on her persistence in making these long flights . . .Mr St. Barbe likewise deserves congratulations on his painstaking and thorough instruction."

Barnard's standard of ten consecutive 'perfect' take-offs and landings was a virtually impossible target for any learner and one can well understand the frustration and inevitable sense of failure that the Duchess must have felt in taking so long to 'solo' - the first landmark in a pilot's life. Achievement when it came therefore would have been all the sweeter and she must have set out for Africa with a real sense of achievement and a great load off her mind. On the day following her solo flight St. Barbe collected the Duchess in her Moth and, stopping at Croydon to check that all was well, followed the Fokker to Lympne. The next day Barnard, Little and the Duchess left shortly after five am amid much photography, St. Barbe in the Moth following them over the Channel until he was outpaced. Their first leg took them to Oran, a distance of some 1,600 miles, in twelve hours and fifty minutes. The weather over the latter part of the route had been wet and cloudy to an extent that over the Pyrenees, Barnard had even thought of turning back and it was still raining when they reached Oran. 'To breakfast in Lympne and dine in Oran,' wrote the Duchess, 'is in these comparatively early days of flying, rather an achievment!'

A short leg to Tunis was followed by an eleven-hour flight to Benghazi. Here they were met by the British Consul who, while the pilots checked out the aeroplane, took the Duchess for a drive. In the evening when invited to dine with them, the Consul told them that a well known lady pilot, who had passed through recently with her companion, had been rude to the Italian Commandant with the result that he now refused to meet any English pilots. Notwithstanding, they found the Italian officials at Benghazi a great deal more helpful than those they had encountered in Italy.

From Benghazi they followed the coast to Alexandria, then flew down the Nile to Assuit where they had special permission to land. By now the Duchess was taking long spells at the controls and on this last leg piloted for some one-and-a-half hours, being left alone she wrote for a considerable part of the time. At first she had some difficulty in controlling the aircraft's trim when Barnard went aft, but soon got used to it. At Assuit they stayed with a Colonel Haseldine and dined with the Egyptian Pasha Governor of Assuit who spoke no French or English. However, his son spoke English and his daughter

In August 1930, with the same crew of Barnard and Little, the
Duchess made a record flight to the Cape and back. The Duchess is
seen here at Juba, in southern Sudan, during a refuelling stop on the
outward journey.

(Woburn Archives)

French, so all went well. The following morning they left at
05.40 hours local time and followed the Nile most of the way to
Khartoum. Here they stayed at the Grand Hotel, in later years
if not then, the only place in the town with waterborne
sanitation. The Governor sent his ADC to enquire after their
welfare and apologise for not coming in person, but the Prince of
Wales was staying with him. All lights in the hotel were

77

extinguished after dark in an attempt to keep a plague of sandflies at bay; Frederick Tymms from the Civil Aviation Department of the Air Ministry, was one of a small group who joined them for dinner. It was then on to Juba. So far the flight had gone well and apart from over the Pyrenees, the weather had been good. All this was to change when they entered the rain forests of equatorial Africa.

Barnard had been told that he should on no account follow the Nile to Juba, but must stick to a compass course. This no doubt was because following the Nile would have taken them over them over the Sudd, the vast area of inaccessible swamp from which rescue in the event of a forced landing even if possible, would have called for vast effort and expense. The settlement at Juba had only been going some two years and the aerodrome was a new one. There had been heavy rain shortly before they landed with the result that one wheel of *The Spider* got bogged - luckily not too seriously. They were now in tropical Africa and it was hot but not disagreeably so. The Duchess described Juba as a delightful place, with scrub up to the station and hills all around. 'I walked back late in the afternoon towards the landing place to look for birds,' she wrote, 'and it was strange to consider for the first time the possibility of meeting a lion, though I imagine it can only be after dark that they would come anywhere near the station.'

They were warned that the airstrip at Tabora, their next scheduled stopping place in what is now Tanzania, was completely waterlogged. When Alan and Lois Butler had landed there two weeks earlier in the Gloster AS.31 Survey 'plane which they were delivering to the Cape, the aircraft had sunk in mud up to the undercarriage struts. It had taken a hundred men of the African Rifles to haul them out. The only possible alternative to landing at Tabora was Dodoma, 200 miles to the east, lengthening their journey significantly and with the added disadvantage that they had no arrangements for petrol. As they crossed Lake Victoria the clouds got lower and lower; 'unpleasant for my pilot and navigator,' the Duchess wrote, 'but if one has nothing to do but pump petrol from the tank in the cabin to the wing tanks, it is better to forget the danger part of it and think of something else, and when you see Equatorial Africa for

Barnard and an Askari guard at Dodoma, Tanganyika. This was not on the original itinery, but the intended landing place at Tabora was water-logged. (Woburn Archive)

the first time from the treetops there is plenty of diversion for those who desire it.'

On and on they flew over miles of forest, scrub and swamps which offered no possible landing place for *Spider*. To the Duchess, peering through the windscreen between the pilots, visibility seemed practically nil and she was glad she said that she was not piloting. At last the ground dropped away, the cloud base lifted and visibility between the torrential local rainstorms became good but there was still nothing below them except forest and swamp. It was with considerable relief therefore that at last, Barnard came to the Tabora-Dodoma railway and was able to follow it to Dodoma. The flight from Juba had taken ten and a half hours - a long time in which to endure adverse conditions over completely unknown country. Unfortunately the only hotel available to them at Dodoma was undescribably awful. It was dirty, the food was terrible and the mosquito nets that had only been let down after moths and mosquitos had collected inside, were filthy. Electricity was turned off early leaving them to go to bed - and get up again next morning - by the light of a single candle; an advantage the Duchess said as it prevented her from seeing the colour of the bedclothes.

It was with considerable relief therefore that they left early next morning for N'dola in Northern Rhodesia (Zambia). Here the Duchess was immediately whisked off to the District Commissioner's house. No sooner had she got there however, than a message arrived from Barnard to say that the landing ground was too small for take off with a full fuel load, and they would have to land again at Broken Hill. Broken Hill in Northern Rhodesia, named after its namesake in Australia, was the original mining colony in what became known as the Copperbelt. Its aerodrome, surrounded by the huts of miners and their families, had been opened by the Air Ministry in 1919 as part of a plan to provide landing grounds every 250 miles from Cairo to Cape Town. Many of those there came from Britain and whether they were miners, hotel proprietors, District Commissioners or other officials, all agreed that although they would like to see again their relatives, they did not want to return to Britain to live. The hotel at Broken Hill was clean and comfortable but the Duchess wrote, '. . as I am rather tired of being hustled off as soon as we arrive, and waiting for hours for my pilots who often do not return for dinner till ten pm or later, I made off for a walk before I was caught.' Early next morning they left for Palapye Road in the Bechuanaland Protectorate (Botswana), a leg of some 550 miles. This on the Salisbury - Cape Town railway would leave them within a thousand miles or so of their destination, which in their terms, was a comfortable one-day flight.

Within a short time of leaving Broken Hill, they were again flying in and out of cloud at treetop height. At times they were so low that the Duchess could identify water-lilies in the pools, and the plumage of quite small birds as they flew from tree to tree. 'Tremendously interesting for me,' she wrote, 'but not so nice for pilot and navigator, but even Captain Barnard who saw a lion immediately below us, could not refrain from saying later that it was wonderfully interesting.' To see out from the cabin, the Duchess had to sit either on the hard pumping stool or on the luggage. In order not to miss anything, the Duchess spent most of her time there. From time to time they crossed railways and when drivers waved to them, them the Duchess waved back. Towards afternoon Captain Barnard passed the *Printator* slate to the Duchess saying that they might after all be going to Livingstone and to look out for the Victoria Falls. However 'a great deal of communication between Captain Barnard and Mr Little went on for a long time and it became pretty evident to me,' the Duchess wrote, 'that though we might be going to Livingstone, we might quite equally be going somewhere else, and as petrol was getting low, if that landing place did not happen to be one adapted to *Spider's* needs, that 'somewhere else' might be a place nobody knows very much about.'

'We crossed a big river,' she continued, 'which I was told was the Zambesi, but we came to the real article a good deal later on. We wound about through valleys and cut across railways, but with nothing whatever under these conditions to tell us where we were. However just when, as I afterwards learnt, Captain Barnard was considering the best place to crash, we came across a railway station on the line to Bulawayo, and to Bulawayo we went, landing there in the afternoon.' As there is only one railway between Broken Hill and Bulawayo and this continuously winds and turns, they must, it seems, have been crossing and re-crossing it. I am told by someone who knows the area that severe tropical rainstorms that occur at the tail end of the 'rainy' season can badly affect the compass, so this may have added to Barnard's problems.

It was streaming with rain at Bulawayo and, as this was not one of their planned places of landing, no petrol awaited them. Moreover as it was Easter, all the best hotels were full and they had to make do with the very indifferent Carlton. The Duchess, as ever, waited for Barnard and Little to join her before eating but by the time they arrived, the cook had gone to bed and the pilots were too tired to do anything but follow suit. The Duchess spent the night in an icy and fireless bedroom with inadequate bedding; it was with no regrets therefore that they left early next day for Cape Town. 'If it had been sunny and warm, the shops open and some dinner available after having lived on Brands Essence for the day, I might have liked Bulawayo better.' the Duchess wrote. 'I have no desire to return.'

81

It was still raining when they left but after a couple of hours, the weather cleared enough to enable Barnard to climb to 9,000 feet and thus reduce fuel consumption. Landing at Bulawayo instead of Palapye Road had added 200 miles to their last leg and Barnard was now doubting whether they could make Cape Town without a further landing. This in the event they managed to do, arriving after the best part of twelve hours at Maitland aerodrome, only to learn that large crowds awaited them at the RAF aerodrome at Wynberg. They had flown 9,000 miles in 101 flying hours and nine and a half days and the last 1,250 miles from Bulawayo was said to be the longest nonstop flight yet made in South Africa. When two years later Imperial Airways introduced a weekly service to the Cape, the scheduled time for the journey from England was eleven days.

From the time they landed on Saturday afternoon until they left again on Easter Monday, Barnard and Little spent the bulk of their time working on the Fokker. The Duchess meanwhile dealt with reporters, visitors and telegrams - a task no less demanding - but she also managed to fit in some sightseeing. 'I did too much in the time,' she wrote later, 'to take in *where* I went, but it was all beautiful and interesting and I was sorry that my stay had to be so short. It has been such a contrast to the rather dreary afternoons I generally have to spend on these long flights, when I am hauled off to hotels by some Samaritan who offers a lift, and have nothing particular to do except wait for the late dinner when my companions turn up. However, this is the only drawback to long flights for a single passenger and there is more than enough to compensate for it.'

After barely 36 hours at Cape Town they set out on the return journey, their first stop Palapye Road. When they left Cape Town clouds hung ominously over the mountains but once above them they were in sunshine and had a good journey. As will be seen the next leg was to bring them to within an ace of disaster. They left Palapye Road in bright sunshine, heading for Broken Hill via the Victoria Falls and in the clear air, the spray from the Falls could be seen from far off. As the engine was not running too well they were unable to fly low over them, somewhat to the disappointment of the Duchess. As they crossed the Kafue River clouds started to appear and shortly afterwards, the Duchess found herself struggling to keep awake. 'Nothing of note on this journey,' she wrote, 'except that I found it quite impossible to read even a paragraph of my book without falling asleep. As I did not wish to miss anything it was rather a painful struggle to keep awake for the whole flight. I did not at the time know that not only were my companions equally sleepy but were feeling ill also, and were compelled to keep handing the controls over to each other. As they had been having the most restful days of their flight they were at a loss to account for it.' The explanation came at Broken Hill where it was found that because of two broken exhaust pipes, they had been inhaling carbon-monoxide. Had they been anywhere else than Broken Hill the necessary repairs would have caused a serious delay, but willing helpers from the mines adjoining the aerodrome made two new pipes the same night; fitting them, however, again made the pilots very late for dinner.

Barnard later gave the press his version of what happened:

"We had been in the air flying on dead reckoning for possibly five hours when I suddenly felt an overpowing drowsiness which increased with every minute. After a while I touched Little on the shoulder and asked him to take over the controls to enable me to go to the back of the machine and bathe my head in cold water. He told me that he was in the same sleepy state as myself and said that he couldn't possibly carry on at the controls for more than a few minutes, would I come back as quickly as possible? I stumbled through the cabin and noticed that the Duchess appeared to be fast asleep which was very unusual for her as she always took a great interest in the country over which we were passing and took her turn with us at the controls. I shook her gently to awaken her but she still slept on. In my dazed state I did not attach much importance to this and after one or two more efforts to rouse her, I left her to sleep undisturbed. The feeling I had is most difficult to describe but it was like being overcome by an uncontrollable, inexplicable desire to sleep. We had had of course very little opportunity for a good rest since leaving England, and this was the only reason I could suggest at the time for the extraordinary sensations which we were experiencing. We were over country where it was absolutely impossible to make any sort of landing, impenetrable and uninhabited jungle with no open spaces whatsoever. It was only by exerting all our will-power and by changing places at the controls at frequent intervals and by holding our heads outside the cabin windows, that we were able to keep awake and reach Broken Hill in safety. After landing I found that the Duchess was completely unconscious and it was impossible to awaken her, so we had to carry her from the cabin into the open air where she revived after about half an hour. B.H itself is a copper mining district and we were able to procure medical aid. By this time we all felt very sick and ill and the doctor suggested that our symptoms were those of some form of poisoning. In our dazed state we were unable to attribute the cause to anything; the machine was running perfectly and we could not think of anything we had eaten or drunk that could have this effect on us. However I suddenly thought of the heating pipe which ran from the exhaust pipe to heat the carburettor and also the cabin. This was a form of muff which carried hot air from the exhaust manifold. We discovered by dismantling these parts that a large hole in the exhaust pipe was causing the exhaust fumes to be driven in upon us. We had of course been poisoned by carbon-monoxide fumes from the engine. The doctor's opinion was that we could not possibly have stood another hour of the fumes, particularly the Duchess who was sleeping in the fume-laden cabin. The Duchess was not in the least bit upset by her unpleasant experience but treated the whole thing as a joke. Personally I do not know whether similar instances have occurred but it was one of the most unpleasant experiences I have had in the air."

The weather was still good when they left Broken Hill for Dodoma. 'All forest and no landmarks,' the Duchess wrote. 'Passed N'dola, Bupula River, Chesi Lake. Saw Rhinos and Hippos and, after Abercorn (now M'bala) and Lake Rukwa, big herds of elephants. The lakes must have been a great relief to my pilot and navigator whose nerves were getting very much on edge. The engine, which had never worked well since Khartoum, gave them additional cause for anxiety. Both B and L refused to feed or be fed and thereby greatly added to their nervous exhaustion. However we arrived at Dodoma in safety but in a perfect deluge of rain and the whole place was flooded. Arrived

Aerial view of the Broken Hill mining camp, northern Rhodesia, where a leaking exhaust was repaired on the return flight.
(Woburn Archives)

1.55 pm.'

With the rain, the hotel was in even worse condition than before. 'The corridors,' the Duchess wrote, 'were deep in mud and I was wet through myself. I could not venture upon a bath (I was cleaner without), and I was glad when darkness prevented my seeing the colour of the bedding and mosquito curtains. I packed all I could before dark and awaited the dawn with one miserable candle, which I lit every hour to see how the time was going. Mosquitoes added to the general horror of things; however 'everything comes to him who waits' and on April 24th we left Dodoma at 4.05 am with a lot of heavy cloud about and not at all a promising outlook. It was an amazing experience to see all this great zoological collection fleeing before us in every direction. Unfortunately just as we were passing them Mr Little indicated that pumping was urgently required. My special task was to pump the contents of the big extra tank of petrol into the wing tanks daily, an operation which meant a quarter-hours pumping every hour until it was empty, 270 gallons I believe. A thousand pumps took just about a quarter-hour.'

They were over the shores of Lake Victoria when the Duchess was passed a note on the *Printator* slate which read, 'There is a leak in our oil supply and we shall have to make a forced landing to examine it. Do you think it was hard ground where we saw all that game?' The Duchess replied that where there were zebras and ostriches the ground *ought* to be hard but although she saw no splashing, she wasn't very happy about it. Meanwhile, Barnard continued to hold his course until after a period of some suspense, another note came through with the message that they might just make Kisumu. 'It is rather interesting to experience just how one feels when one knows that the end may come at any moment.' the Duchess wrote. 'My own experience is that with a little determination panic can be lived down if one has no responsibility on ones shoulders. It would be a different business if one had; also probably, if one knew one's fate rested in unreliable hands; but knowing as I did that if a crash was to occur it could not have been avoided, it is possible to divert the thoughts to other channels and accept *Che Sera Sera*. It is more easy if there is as much to interest oneself in as there was on this occasion. Beyond the ordinary anxiety of forced landings in England, of which I have had my share, the worst time I ever had was in the Mistral on the Riviera and for actual test of one's principles of refusing to be seized by panic, I give this the palm.' Landing at Kisumu they found, no doubt with considerable relief, that they had in fact plenty of oil and that it was the gauge that was at fault. Having satisfied themselves as to the oil and with only four hours daylight left, they took off on the 400-or-so-mile leg for Juba.

But they had not gone far before they again ran into heavy storms and bad visibility. 'I wondered what was going to happen,' the Duchess wrote, 'but the luck which failed us in the matter of weather in this flight seemed to be playing with us, and when it was made sufficiently uncomfortable always provided a way out. The N'mule landing ground was not far off and to that we went.'

Later Barnard wrote of the flight from Dodoma, omitting reference to the landing at Kisumu:

"We reached Dodoma without further trouble and set out on the 1,000 mile flight to Juba in the Sudan. We left Dodoma in squally weather and thick fog and I could see we were in for a sticky trip. The climax was reached at a point very near the junction of the Blue and White Nile[2] when we ran into a very violent thunderstorm. It is mountainous country and we were forced to turn back rather than take the risk of flying through the valley of the Nile to Juba. Through pouring rain and blinding flashes of lightning I found a clearing at a place called N'mule which I believe is now used as an emergency landing ground by Imperial Airways. Despite the rain the noise of the engine had attracted about fifty natives of all ages and both sexes who were crowding round the machine which was probably the first they had seen. It was a little embarrassing at first as none wore a stitch of clothing. After giving them chocolates and cigarettes we were marched triumphantly to the native village of mud huts about two miles distant from the scene of our forced landing. The pathway from the clearing led through very tall elephant grass possibly twelve feet high and at both ends of our cavalcade, a native carried a flaming torch. Only one native spoke a smattering of French picked up in the Belgian Congo and he explained that it was very dangerous to walk through the pathway as lions lay in wait for the unwary traveller, hence the flares. We were given the Chief's hut and two chickens were boiled for us which we ate with our fingers. We tried to sleep but were kept awake all night long by the inevitable tom-toms which however familiar, still have an eerie sound in the dead of night in a strange native village. Consequently we were up and away at five am. The men, women and children gave us a wonderful send-off, their most cherished possessions being apparently, the lids from the tins of cigarettes we had given them which several had already hung round their necks."

---

2. The White Nile and the Aswa River; the Blue Nile joins the White Nile at Khartoum.

The Duchess recorded the stopover in greater detail:

'We were immediately surrounded by a weird collection of natives dressed in girdles and beads only, very black but very cheerful looking and apparently quite as much amused by my appearance as I was by theirs. The pilot's book of directions said that shelter might be obtained through a native doctor. So I wrote a note which Captain Barnard managed to dispatch to this official. After a long wait a man who spoke English and dressed as an Englishman appeared and said that the doctor had left two years ago but that there was a hut, apparently intended for sheltering stray astronauts, to which he would conduct us. So by the light of an electric torch we followed a native guide for over a mile along a path with many pitfalls, with long grass crops on either side. Our guide told us that it was not safe to walk after dark without a lantern, as there were lions about which were wont to spring out on foolish virgins and others who had none. They were not likely to attack those carrying lanterns, but merely roared to instil proper respect. At last after what seemed a long mile, we reached our shelter - a stone hut which had neither doors nor windows (ie only frames) and was thatched with grass or reeds. Some little camp bedsteads, a table, and some chairs were unearthed from somewhere, and as each little bedstead was erected, my exhausted companions flung themselves down upon them. The hut had two compartments, but no door between. Our supper was to come from four-and-a-half miles away so there was no prospect of seeing it for some hours. The bedsteads were provided with mosquito curtains but no other bedding, and as the hut was but dimly lit by three candles, I followed my companions' example and rolling up my skirt as a pillow, crawled under the mosquito curtains hoping to get some sleep. I had dozed rather fitfully till eleven pm when supper arrived. It consisted of two chickens, which I imagine must have been captured and cooked after our arrival; at all events knives would not penetrate them, so we resorted to fingers and teeth. Supper over, we crawled on to our charpoys once more and I watched the fireflies dancing up and down outside, and only longed to hear a lion roar to complete the romance, but they were not broadcasting that night.'

They rose at the first signs of dawn and were ready to leave before anyone could be roused to carry their cases and by day, the long path leading to the landing area seemed less formidable. As this was an emergency landing ground with no facilities, there was nothing the pilots could do by way of maintenance - which was lucky as they were both dead tired - so they set course for Juba less than an hours flight away. The weather fortunately had now improved for which as the Duchess remarked it was indeed time, for it was difficult enough navigating over this type of country in clear weather; the weather they had been having had put a great strain on the pilot's nerves.

N'mule was but a short distance from the Nile to which they now clung ignoring previous advice, until they reached Juba. Despite their restless night, two hours later after refuelling and tidying up, they set off for Khartoum. 'I could wish our weather had been better for more reasons than one,' the Duchess wrote, 'as it is very difficult to see the big game well from the cabin windows. Sitting in the one and only chair I could see practically nothing and it meant perching on top of the luggage or on the pumping stool. In bad visibility both pilot and navigator have to be in the front cockpit, or indeed at any time when navigation is difficult; but as we fly too high to identify most game when circumstances permit of my being up front, I saw more on the whole from the cabin. But I would never travel in a closed machine if I could help it. Arrived Khartoum and stayed at the Grand Hotel. Seems very deserted since last there. Fortunately sandflies and midges seem to have taken their departure.'

After a good nights rest they left for Cairo, where Barnard planned to give the engine a thorough overhaul before embarking on the last stages of the flight back to England. It took them twelve hours and fifteen minutes to cover the thousand-odd miles to Cairo, slow going but, at that time of year, the wind would have been against them. In good weather over the desert the Duchess could again share in the flying; 'it was a great joy to be outside again,' she wrote, 'and I love flying over desert.'

Forty-two years had elapsed since the Duchess was last in Cairo. She was then on her way home from India with Herbrand, shortly after their marriage. Tom Russell (Russell Pasha), a cousin of the Duke who was working with the Egyptian police in what would now be termed an anti-drug squad, called on the Duchess soon after her arrival and took her to dinner at his house in Gezireh. This after so many dreary afternoons spent in unattractive hotels waiting for the return of her pilots, she very much enjoyed.

Meanwhile Barnard had decided that instead of returning as they came via the North African coast, he could save a day by taking the more direct route through Turkey and the Balkans. They left Cairo for Aleppo on 27th April in bright sunshine passing over the Suez Canal and Ismailia, then flying low along the coast of Palestine past Joppa (Tel-Aviv), Tyre, Sidon and over Mount Carmel. As they approached Aleppo, however, cloud and rain in the mountains forced them to climb to 10,000 feet. By now they were well known at Aleppo and unusually speedy refuelling enabled them to drive to their hotel in town together.

The Duchess described their experiences of the next two days in some detail and one cannot do better than to quote directly from her diary.

'April 28th - Left at 3.50 am (GMT) in sunshine but heavy clouds over mountains. By 4.25 am had reached the Mediterranean and were skimming over them at 9,000 feet and then 10,000 feet. At 5.30 we passed over the Viaduct where we had such a bad time last year. It was uncommonly cold and there was a great deal of snow on the mountains. The poor pilots were making vigorous efforts to instil some life into their fingers. The cabin is almost as cold as the cockpit, as the draught comes in everywhere, particularly from the luggage compartment below the cockpit, where ones legs receive the full blast from the soles of the feet upwards. After some little diversions caused by uncertainty as to the route, we arrived over the sea once more, and again passed over beautiful Constantinople. After that we had a rough time in very bad visibility and strong headwind but came through alright and landed at Sofia. Dined with the Cowans at the British Legation.

'April 29th - Weather forbidding in the extreme, especially over the mountains we had to cross; however nothing would have deterred Barnard at this stage of the journey, after all we had been through of a similar nature, so we took off full of hope that this was to be the last stage of our record-breaking flight. We had not been flying for more than twenty minutes and were just entering the lower hills when I heard the engine give some ominous thumps. In a moment Barnard whisked round to the flat fields we had just left, the engine stopped, and he made as perfect a landing as if it had been intentional. Quite apart from the fact that we were as heavily laden as when we made our forced landing in Persia, he had no time whatsoever to choose his landing and most of the ground was a swamp from heavy rain. 'Flat' is rather a figure of speech as far as the surface was concerned, for the whole place was honeycombed with glorified potholes and it looked as if it would be impossible to take off again.

'Then came the inspection to see the cause of the engine going on strike. It was very evident that the oil supply was choked and as nothing seemed out of order on the surface, they came to the conclusion that the oil pipe must have broken in an inaccessible part of the engine. The only thing to be done was for Barnard to get in touch with Sofia and assistance, so he made off to a small railway station which was fortunately not far off. Poor Little was in the depths of dejection.

Little was to recall later that at this bitter moment, the Duchess had no words or thoughts but for him and Captain Barnard's disappointment after so much hard work. They had been over everything the previous evening and been very late getting back to the hotel in order to ensure that all should be well on this our last stage. Not long after Barnard had gone, an aeroplane flew over and reported us to Sofia. They soon sent an officer with a small machine who landed in an adjoining field. He spoke no English and very little French, but the first question he asked was whether our undercarriage was broken and when we said 'No', he shrugged his shoulders by way of expressing that it ought to have been! We made him understand that we wanted a car and the mechanics who had helped the previous evening, so he made off in his aeroplane, but *L'homme*

propose et Dieu dispose and when he reached it, nothing would induce the engine to start. So he too went off to the station to ask for assistance.

'A good-natured cheery-looking crowd of rustics collected round the *Spider*, but were rather an anxiety to Little and me. I am afraid I had hitherto had a feeling at the back of my mind that all lower class Bulgarians were graded brigands. Probably because in pre-war days one heard little of anything but their brigands and their petty wars; but on this visit I rubbed off a layer of insular prejudice, and was very much attracted by all those with whom we came in contact. Both here and at the

(Above and opposite page) On the return flight from the Cape, a blocked oil pipe led to a forced-landing in the Dragoman Pass, near Sofia, Bulgaria. Inevitably a crowd of onlookers was soon on the scene. After on-the-spot repairs, the Fokker was flown back to Sofia, where, with the help of the Bulgarian Air Force, the aircraft was repaired. (Woburn Archives)

aerodrome they did everything they could to help us and make themselves generally pleasant. After a long wait Barnard returned in a car with a Member of the British Legation whom he had met at Dragoman, and just as they arrived, another aeroplane landed to succour us. I was then driven back to the hotel by Mr Peto and left to battle with the depression of the situation alone.

'My surroundings were not of a cheerful order; it was raining hard and horribly cold and my window looked out on to a derelict churchyard. I had no clothes to get wet and muddy in so could not go out. Barnard and Co. were about twenty-five to thirty miles away, so I had no chance of hearing what was going on. *The Times* reporter captured me in the afternoon, and I felt less inclined to murder him than most of his kind, at least he was someone to talk too. I had been up at 3.30 am. Towards evening I received a note from Barnard scribbled on a scrap of paper, saying that the trouble had been located and that nothing was broken, but owing to our having come suddenly from a very hot climate to a cold one the oil was like rubber, and would not circulate (Ed. a condition known as 'coring'). They had cleaned it all out, taken everything they could out of the aeroplane to lighten it, and he hoped to get back to Sofia aerodrome and start again for home in the morning. Never in my life was I so pleased to get a scribbled note. The world seemed a pleasanter place altogether, and it was with a very light heart that I once more repacked my luggage. Captain Barnard told me that the French mechanics who worked like slaves for us had had similar trouble themselves and at once suspected what was wrong with the *Spider*. The pilots did not get back till ten pm.'

The following account of their delay, almost certainly emanating from Barnard, appeared in the edition of *Flight* dated 2nd May, 1930.

"Having successfully accomplished a record flight out from England to Cape Town in ten days, the Duchess of Bedford has experienced an eleventh-hour mishap which has marred an even better record return flight home. It was expected to be able to make the return journey in nine days - and therefore the 18,800-mile out and home return flight in nineteen days - and it looked as if this would be accomplished, when a minor mishap brought the machine down on the last stage. None the less, the flight as it stands is a most remarkable achievement, and the matter of one day delay in no way affects the establishment of a flight record. . ."

"They left Sofia on 29th April for the final stage to Croydon, where they were expected in the evening. Unfortunately however, twenty minutes after starting, a broken oil-pump forced them down in a field at Fliunitza, near the frontier. Captain Barnard proceeded to the railway line nearby and stopped the Simplon express, boarded the train, and reached Dragoman whence he telephoned to Sofia for assistance. A Bulgarian aeroplane forthwith flew from Sofia to the stranded *Spider* and on the extent of the damage being ascertained, returned to Sofia with Mr Little for the necessary spare parts. These were eventually dispatched with three expert Bulgarian Air Force mechanics, and the *Spider* was taken to Sofia for more repairs."

In England, the news that Barnard had forced landed in the Dragoman Pass was received with disbelief since a landing in the cutting, looked upon as the worst deathtrap for aeroplanes

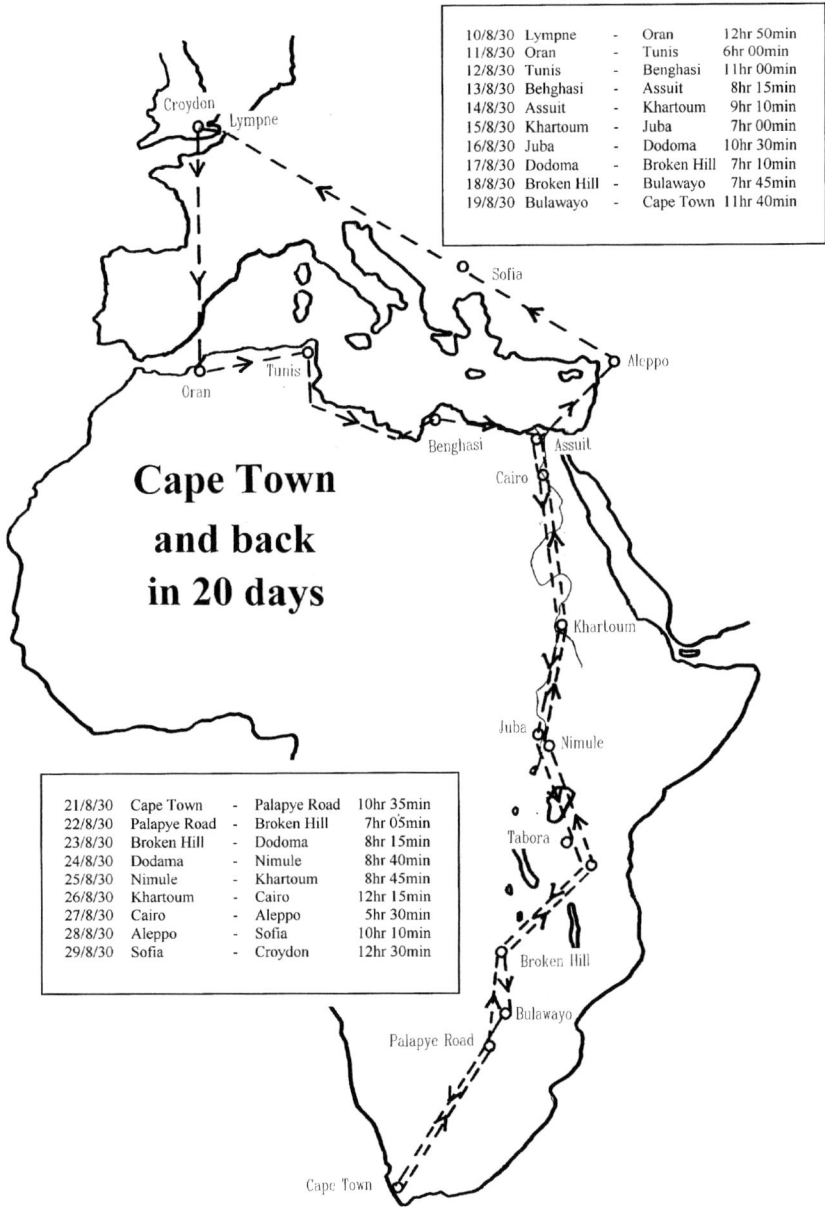

10/8/30	Lympne	-	Oran	12hr 50min
11/8/30	Oran	-	Tunis	6hr 00min
12/8/30	Tunis	-	Benghasi	11hr 00min
13/8/30	Behghasi	-	Assuit	8hr 15min
14/8/30	Assuit	-	Khartoum	9hr 10min
15/8/30	Khartoum	-	Juba	7hr 00min
16/8/30	Juba	-	Dodoma	10hr 30min
17/8/30	Dodoma	-	Broken Hill	7hr 10min
18/8/30	Broken Hill	-	Bulawayo	7hr 45min
19/8/30	Bulawayo	-	Cape Town	11hr 40min

Croydon
Lympne
Sofia
Aleppo
Oran
Tunis
Benghasi
Assuit
Cairo
Khartoum

Cape Town
and back
in 20 days

Juba
Nimule
Tabora
Broken Hill
Bulawayo
Palapye Road
Cape Town

21/8/30	Cape Town	-	Palapye Road	10hr 35min
22/8/30	Palapye Road	-	Broken Hill	7hr 05min
23/8/30	Broken Hill	-	Dodoma	8hr 15min
24/8/30	Dodama	-	Nimule	8hr 40min
25/8/30	Nimule	-	Khartoum	8hr 45min
26/8/30	Khartoum	-	Cairo	12hr 15min
27/8/30	Cairo	-	Aleppo	5hr 30min
28/8/30	Aleppo	-	Sofia	10hr 10min
29/8/30	Sofia	-	Croydon	12hr 30min

in Europe, was not thought possible. Added to this, at the time of the engine failure a following wind of some 40 mph it was said, had been sweeping through the Pass and with cloud covering the hills on either side, visibility had not been good. Yet with no room to spare on either side, Barnard had somehow managed to turn into wind and against all odds, land successfully on the rough and marshy ground.

For a description of their flight home after the aircraft had been repaired, it is back to the Duchess's diary:

'April 30th - In streams of rain dawn found us once more making our way to the aerodrome. Only a couple of mechanics who had been working all night were there to see us off. I had to paddle through a sea of mud from the car to the aeroplane, and the floor of the cabin was so slippery with it that I could hardly stand up. There was just a small rift in the clouds when we took off at 3.55 am but before we reached the Balkans, there was an appreciable amount of blue sky which increased as we flew on so that the dreaded Dragoman Pass was flown through in bright sunshine, with only lumps of fleecy cloud floating about here and there. It was a wonderful change from yesterday, when I very much doubt whether we should have got through, even if the oil supply had not stopped us. We passed over Belgrade and followed the Danube for a time and as long as we were in the Balkans, and the plains of Yugoslavia beyond, all was sunshine and easy navigation. The mountains of Austria and the forests of Germany were another matter. Once more pilot and navigator had to battle with rain, hail, snow, and almost impenetrable cloud. The cold was horrible and we were nearly frozen, but needless to say, those who had the piloting to do came off the worst and Captain B. whose burnt hands always suffer in cold weather from bad circulation, was about as thoroughly miserable as he could well be. In spite of it all he got through, and when we reached Western Germany and Belgium we were once more in bright sunshine. B. and L. had had about enough of it and were greatly cheered by the 'White Cliffs of Dover'. I too was glad that we had accomplished the record flight we had set out to do, *but these long flights are such a joy to me that I always feel sad when they are at an end. For me they*

are the one perfect rest I get in the year, though at present the
non-flying public cannot realise it.

'The pilots had had a very nerve-racking time. Only on four
days since leaving Lympne had we flown entirely without rain
or very low cloud, and that over country which was absolutely
unknown to them and where for the *Spider* there were no
landing places for hundreds of miles, other than those we took.
Landing-grounds are being made, but most are still too small for
the *Spider*. A great deal of the country is featureless as far as
flying is concerned, being nothing but endless forest. We always
knew that we must meet the rains somewhere, but we were
assured that it was quite phenomenal coming in for them
everywhere but in the desert. Seeing that we came through
safely, I cannot but feel glad that we were compelled to go low
over those wonderful tropical forests and the big game as, quite
apart from the fact that the engine was giving anxiety for a
great part of the flight, no pilot in his sense would have risked
flying the *Spider* just over the tree tops, and at a nominal
height of 7,000 to 8,000 feet I should have missed everything
but the pleasure of being in the air, the record, and a very
general view of the country.

'Passing over Lympne aerodrome to report ourselves, we saw
them waving to us, and it did not take us long to get to Croydon.
In England we had bright sunshine all the time.'

They arrived at Croydon at 5.30 pm on 30th April, after
completion of a twelve and a half hour flight from Sofia, and
195 flying hours in all. Here the welcome they received was
even greater than on their return from India the year before. As
they landed, Sidney St. Barbe, a sky-writing expert, climbed to
10,000 feet in his S.E.5a and wrote 'Bravo' in the sky. On the
ground, representatives from every branch of aviation were
there to meet them. Sir Sefton Branker, Director of Civil
Aviation, in a speech of welcome, thanked them on behalf of the
Air Ministry for the example they had set. The flight, he said,
was the best thing he had known in civil aviation in the past
three or four years. Lord Thomson, Secretary of State for Air
(killed later in the year with Sir Sefton Branker in airship
R-101) sent a telegram on behalf of the Air Council saying that
the journey of 19,000 miles in less that twenty-one days,

afforded an illustration of the many benefits air transport held in store for the Empire, by way of speeding up communications. 'We regard with admiration,' he continued, 'the spirit of enterprise which prompted you to embark on the undertaking which you have today, brought to so successful an issue.' The Duchess again received a personal telegram from the King.

Meanwhile, 'smothered with bouquets', the Duchess accepted invitations to dine, to lunch, to speak etc. most of which, made in a hurry, she repented at leisure. Later when she was attempting to leave by car from the Aerodrome Hotel she was besieged by an army of autograph hunters. Tired as one would have expected her to be, she stood for a considerable time, it was reported, smiling and signing, so as not to disappoint 'the importunate multitude'. The Duchess wrote in her diary that she was so little tired on arrival that she could easily have flown back to the Cape next day; the hard work, she said, was to come. This consisted of coping with shoals of letters, telegrams and invitations on top of the inevitable accumulation of business and hospital work which had built up while she was away.

Manufacturers were not slow to latch on to the record. KLG Plugs, Bendix brakes, Dunlop wire-type tyres and patent wheel discs all claimed to have played their part, while Titanine claimed that their paint had been unaffected by tropical heat and heavy rains. Barnard, writing to map-makers Edward Stanford Ltd, said that their maps, 'so neatly made', had helped considerably towards their success. Shell Mex, who had organised the supply of special petrol and Golden Shell Oil, now arranged for *Spider* to be displayed outside Bush House in the Strand. They also laid on a lunch at the Savoy Hotel in their honour at which the Chairman Mr S Samuel MP, said that he hoped their example would be followed by many others. He also congratulated Roy Fedden, designer of the Jupiter engine, on having achieved 'almost the impossible'. The Duchess, in her reply, paid tribute to the efficiency and courtesy of the Shell representatives; only those who had made long flights could, she said, appreciate how much it meant to be able to start refuelling as soon as one landed. Barnard too spoke of the company's excellent organisation and told how with prohibition in Cape

The Duchess is welcomed at Croydon after their record flight to the Cape and back by F D Bradbooke of 'The Aeroplane' and Flora Green, who is holding the Duchess's Pekinese, Tu Fu.

(Richard Riding Collection)

Town on a Sunday, Shell had come to his rescue when he had got extremely dry working on the Fokker. He also told the story of how when they were over Cairo, he decided to make a detour to photograph the Pyramids. On asking Little to pass him the map he got the surprising reply that as the map was an old one, they probably wouldn't be marked! Sir Sefton Branker, on behalf of the Air Ministry, said that the Duchess, a quiet unassuming and businesslike woman, possessed of the qualities of quiet energy and iron determination, was exactly what they wanted in civil aviation. Barnard was a pilot who, besides skill, possessed that divine thing called *luck*, while Little had upheld the highest traditions of ground engineers. They had asked the Air Ministry for no financial help. They simply did it and they filled his heart with joy. The flight, he continued, was the best thing in civil aviation for many years. They had rendered immense service to the Empire and he hoped that the *Spider* would go on building up the Empire's communications. These hopes were not to be fulfilled, as shortly afterwards Barnard and the Duchess parted company.

Barnard had always had close associations with the Press and was now also heavily involved with his new companies. As a result the Duchess could no longer rely on him to be available when needed. Since she was particularly anxious at this time to continue with her flying lessons in order to qualify for a pilot's licence, she told Barnard that he had 'too many other engagements allied to the Press fraternity' to please her and she would have to look for another pilot. 'This is goodbye,' she wrote, 'to my long flights which I have enjoyed so much and it will not be easy to find so good a pilot, but his alliance with modern reporting is too much for me.' Her last flight with Barnard, a flying lesson, took place on 14th July.

Taking over *Spider*, Barnard now set up a company called Barnard Air Tours Ltd., which inaugurated the country's first Air Circus. The 'air circus' had its origins in the Unites States. After the war, because it was the only available form of civil flying, numbers of ex-Army pilots banded together to 'barnstorm' the States and even Lindberg started his flying career in this way. It was from these circuses that the first airmail pilots were drawn before passenger services had been established. In England too there were plenty of experienced civil pilots eating their heart out for flying jobs; Barnard therefore had no problem finding pilots. The main purpose of the Circus was aviation education at a time when farsighted people like Alan Cobham and Captain Harold Balfour MP, were desperately

trying to make the public air minded. During 1931 Barnard, heavily sponsored by the *Daily Mail* with both editorial and financial backing, was to tour some 150 towns 'preaching the gospel'. The Fokker that led the circus was used principally for joy rides for which, as a high-wing monoplane, it was ideally suited, giving passengers a far better view than was enjoyed from the currently used biplanes. Other aircraft in the circus included an Avro Avian, a Potez cabin monoplane that, unlike the Handley Page variety, had fixed slots, a Spartan three-seater fitted with 'wireless receiving apparatus', a Sports Avian biplane used for high-speed aerobatics and a Cierva autogiro flown by R A Brie, Cierva's test pilot and flight manager. John Tranum made parachute descents with an Irvin Airchute (£72 new and £45:5s:5d used) for which he was paid £25 a drop for the first year and an extra £5 for wing-walking. After 1931 however, the latter was banned by the Air Ministry who considered fabric wings unsuitable for walking on.

Barnard's Circus opened at Luton in April 1931. The Fokker, which had received considerable publicity because of its record flights, was of interest as it had not yet been seen around by the general public. Other references in the aeronautical press to the use of this aircraft by Barnard include one for July 1932 when he was engaged by the British Navigation Company to run a temporary eight-day service between Bristol Whitchurch and Cardiff. Four flights, it was said, were flown each day and in all, 1,160 miles were flown and 199 passengers carried at a rate of 15s single, £1:7s:6d return. In September 1932 he is recorded as flying the Directors of Plymouth Argyll football team to Stoke, one presumes to watch a match, and on 11th November, as leaving Heston for Paris with eleven passengers. But to go back to the Duchess.

After the Cape Town flight the Duchess found herself in constant demand with social engagements extending many weeks ahead. The Air League took the opportunity to combine their anniversary dinner with one honouring the flight. From this the Duchess left early to fulfil and engagement to broadcast from Savoy Hill. The Bristol Engine Company again laid on a lunch at Bristol to which Barnard and the Duchess flew in her Moth, the wind being such that it took them one and a half

Fokker VIIa G-EBTS at Croydon on its return from the Cape. The restricted view from the cabin is evident from the small sliding window. (Richard Riding Collection).

hours to get there from Woburn but only 55 minutes to return! Among other less formal invitations was a tea-party laid on by Lady Elibank for her to meet among others, Princess Victoria, Princess Louise and the Lord Mayor of London, and one to the preview of the Chelsea Flower Show where she was to meet the King and Queen. On this occasion the Duchess elected to fly to Heston in her Moth where she was picked up by a 'London' chauffeur. Unfortunately, however, shortly after leaving Heston the car broke down and by the time alternative transport had been arranged, the Duchess arrived at Chelsea to find that the King and Queen had left and that the place was practically deserted. The same evening the Duke and Duchess dined with the Prince of Wales - an invitation the Duchess attributed to the fact that the Prince was to lunch with them at Woburn before the coming Agricultural Show at Ampthill. As the Prince was himself both pilot and aircraft owner, much of the conversation must have revolved one feels around the Cape Town flight. After yet another dinner, this time at the College of Nursing, the Duchess wrote, 'I have not dined out so often for thirty years, but all are on account of the African flight.'

There were 101 entries for the 1930 Kings Cup Air Race that was run on 5th July. The course this year consisted of eleven legs beginning and ending at Hanworth and with 88 starters, probably had the largest entry in its history. It was also the first time the race was won by a woman - Winifred Brown. The Duchess, watching the return from Dunstable Down, noted that the male experts who did not win, were all grumbling at the refuelling arrangements, which the perceptive Duchess surmised, with so many competitors probably *were* pretty bad!

At the end of August the Duchess resumed her flying lessons at Hatfield with Sydney St. Barbe, the instructor who had sent her solo the day before they set out for Cape Town. At the same time she made some trial flights with pilots who had applied for Barnard's job. Among these were a Mr Wayte and a Flight Lieutenant Walker, but none suited until an application arrived from one Flight Lieutenant J B Allen.

Aged 33, he too was an ex-Royal Flying Corps pilot. He had transferred to the Royal Flying Corps from the Gloucester Regiment in 1916 and had remained in the RAF after the war. Although recommended time after time for a permanent commission he had always been turned down at top level. C G Grey writing in his magazine *The Aeroplane* said, 'I think the reason was that he was slightly deaf as a result of his war service and the Treasury influence at the Air Ministry was afraid that he might go completely deaf and then, invalided out, claim a pension for life.' In 1927, therefore, he transferred to the RAF Reserve and took an administrative job with Brunner-Mond in Liverpool. Flying, however, was in his blood and when the Liverpool and District Flying Club advertised for an instructor, he applied and got the job. It was from here that he joined the Duchess. For her Bernard Allen proved to be an ideal flying companion. A careful and reliable pilot who sought no publicity and was popular wherever he went; but above all he loved aeroplanes and flying. He arrived at Woburn on 6th September and, unlike his predecessor, took up residence in Paris House in Woburn Park. Two days after his arrival the Duchess had her first flying lesson with him at Hatfield and afterwards they flew down to *Endsleigh*, making a forced landing en route in a field where they waited an hour for fog and rain to clear. A fortnight later when the time came for the annual move to Scotland, the Duchess flew up with her new pilot, Allen remaining with them at *Cairnsmore* for the first two weeks of their stay. During this time they took daily flights using the sands at Luce Bay for practice landings and here, before the Moth returned south on 8th October for its annual overhaul, the Duchess made several solo landings.

When Allen returned with the Moth on 14th November, the Duchess declared it 'very lovely' in its new emerald green and silver paint. The following day they returned to Luce Bay but after the first landing the Moth got bogged by the incoming tide and went on its nose. Fortunately in the soft sand the propeller was not damaged and after Allen had dug it out, they were able to fly back to Creetown. Next day, instead of landings, the Duchess practiced figure-of-eight turns, as had to be demonstrated at that time for a private pilot's 'A' licence.

They set out for Woburn on 17th November, but fog at Preston forced them to land at Blackpool where they spent the night. The following day as it was still too thick to continue, the Duchess returned home by train - the first train journey, she wrote, that she had made for a year. Her diary for Christmas Day noted that there had been almost incessant fog since their return from Scotland and that they had to light candles for luncheon. With a pilot on the spot to look after it, the Duchess now moved her Moth to Woburn where, by the end of the year, a hangar had been built. This had a large room at the back, which included a comfortable office in which she would have spent many a happy hour. To maintain the aeroplane she now needed a ground engineer licensed to Air Ministry requirements and for this job, she chose J W Todd, one of the chauffeurs. Before World War I the Woburn garage had run an apprentice scheme and on leaving school, Todd had worked there as an apprentice. During the war he joined the Royal Naval Air Service returning to Woburn afterwards as a chauffeur. To obtain the necessary licences the Duchess now sent him to Gravesend for practical training, after which he completed his exams by means of a postal course. In Allen the Duchess had found not only a pilot but a companion and friend and backed up by Todd, they became a very happy team.

Chapter Seven
1931: A Change of Pilot

John, 13th Duke of Bedford writing about the three years during which Flight Lieutenant Bernard Allen was his grandmother's private pilot said, 'Together they flew here, there and everywhere; this period was probably the Duchess's happiest time.'

With no more record flights to draw the attention of the public to her, a new pilot with no allegiance to the press and with ever increasing numbers of private owners making overseas flights, the Duchess's flying activities ceased to be headline news. However, during the three years Allen was with her, she not only completed over 100 hours solo flying but, after a long battle with the Air Ministry over her medical, was finally granted a private pilot's licence. Without this, her flying was by law restricted to the aerodrome circuit. Thus on all cross-country flights, she had of necessity to be accompanied by a pilot and could never fill in her log book as 'pilot in charge'. But back to 1931.

During February and March that year, her practice landings and solo flights were carried out for the most part from Weston-on-the-Green, between Bicester and Oxford. With Allen she also made many cross country flights taking in visits to Cley Mill and to *Whispers*, her house near Midhurst. There were also special trips such as that on 7th March when they flew down to Bristol to see the Severn Bore. The Duchess recorded that it was a bitterly cold day with an east wind, and that when landing at Whitchurch the throttle-rod broke causing them a delay of several hours. On another occasion they flew to Stonehenge landing on the site of the old World War I aerodrome alongside the monument, entries in her diary over this period are however few and far between. She did record that on 1st April, when Barnard brought the *Spider* to Luton for his first air circus, she flew to Dunstable and from there

*After the Cape flight Barnard bought the Fokker from the Duchess
and inaugurated Britain's first Air Circus. This opened at Luton in
April 1931. Barnard, his wife and several members of his team are
seen at Luton with the Cierva Autogyro and the Fokker, which he
used to give joyrides. (Airman Friday)*

motored over to see again her one-time pilot and aircraft. It
was, she wrote, a cold and windy day with few of the public
around. She sat in on two ten-minute joy rides during which
Barnard allowed her to take the controls and leaving her with a
longing to be off again on tour.

On 23rd April she set out on the first of her continental tours
with Allen, the last of such trips in her open Moth. As
throughout the sixteen days they were away it rained virtually
every day, it is perhaps hardly surprising that later in the year
she bought a cabin machine for future continental excursions. It
is probably appropriate here to pause for a moment to recall the
conditions under which this 'holiday' was made - ones which
today all but the very hardy would find totally unacceptable but
which the Duchess, at the age of 66, took in her stride.

For a start, with dual control and an extra fuel tank there would have been only room in the Moth for small cases and the extra fuel would have limited weight. Warm clothes, before the advent of synthetics, were both bulky and heavy; shoes and no doubt suitcases would have been made of leather contributing significantly to the overall weight. The amount of spare clothes they could carry must therefore have been limited to an extent that makes it difficult to visualise just how they coped with the rain against which the open cockpits afforded little protection, shoes wet through from soggy grass aerodromes and hotels which probably offered little in the way of drying facilities.

The spring and summer of 1931 were exceptionally cold and wet and the weather on this trip bad from the start; even when crossing the Channel at the regulation height of 5,000 feet the Duchess wrote, it was very cold. They spent the first night at Cologne and the second at Basle from where they continued to Lausanne where at the time, the small aerodrome was being enlarged. At Geneva, their next port of call, it poured with rain. They had to abandon their projected plan - one of the Duchess's ambitions - to fly over the Alps, setting course instead for Nice and Italy where in early May, the Duchess felt confident they would find some sun. But at Pisa it was still cloudy, the hotel horrible, the food bad and, the Duchess asserted, the sheets smelly. Nevertheless before leaving for Naples they delayed long enough to climb the leaning tower and to visit the church and Baptistry about which, bearing in mind her deafness the Duchess somewhat surprisingly wrote, 'At latter, man sang a few notes with wonderful voice creating wonderful echo which sounded like organ and choir.' At Naples they were blessed with their first day of real sunshine and visited Pompeii. The following morning the rain was back again, in spite of which before setting course for Rome, they flew round the crater of Vesuvius, trying to take photos. By the time they reached Rome it was again pouring. They stayed three nights in Rome paddling round the Colosseum, St. Peter's, the Vatican and various churches. The Duchess wrote in her diary, 'Never imagined that weather could treat us thus in Italy in May. Brought summer dresses. Never worn.'

Naples, April - May 1931

Date	From		To	Time
23/4/31	Woburn	-	Heston	4hr 05min
	Heston	-	Lympne	3hr 55min
	Lympne	-	Cologne	1hr 55min
24/4/31	Cologne	-	Basle	35min
25/4/31	Basle	-	Lausanne	2hr 40min
27/4/31	Lausanne	-	Geneva	1hr 00min
28/4/31	Geneva	-	Marseilles	2hr 35min
	Marseilles	-	Nice	3hr 55min
29/4/31	Nice	-	Pisa	1hr 20min
30/4/31	Pisa	-	Naples	1hr 20min
2/5/31	Naples	-	Rome	2hr 40min
6/5/31	Rome	-	Pisa	3hr 40min
	Pisa	-	Nice	3hr 45min
7/5/31	Nice	-	Lyons	2hr 45min
	Lyons	-	Paris	1hr 30min
8/5/31	Paris	-	Lympne	
	Lympne	-	Woburn	

Cologne · Basle · Lausanne · Geneva · Lyons · Paris · Woburn · Heston · Lympne · Marseilles · Nice · Pisa · Rome · Naples

Coming home they had to land again at Pisa to refuel. Here the weather was so bad that the officer in charge of the aerodrome refused to let them take off without prior clearance from the Commandant. The Duchess decided that another night in the hotel was a worst prospect than the weather. The Commandant having by now washed his hands of them, they took off, hugging the coast until nearing Nice, where they at last ran into somewhat better weather. But it was rain again up the Rhône valley to Lyons and Paris. They 'did' Notre Dame and the Louvre in the rain before setting out on a cold and foggy flight to Lympne and Woburn, where they arrived on 8th May in time for dinner. Even the Duchess admitted that the trip had been, 'almost utterly spoilt by weather.' It was still raining at the end of the month when the family left for *Endsleigh* for the salmon fishing. 'Rained daily,' the Duchess wrote, 'river never settled then flood. Such floods in May quite unprecedented - so was rain Rome, Naples.' Later having flown home earlier to her work at the hospital she wrote:

'June 9th - Herbrand still on banks of Tamar waiting for river to subside. His patience did not hold out; came away fishless on 10th.' At the end of June they returned to try again and this time Herbrand, the Duchess, and Allen each caught a salmon - Allen's first. By then the Duchess had passed her 'A' licence flying tests at Henlow, the observer one Flight Lieutenant Massey. She could not claim her pilot's licence until she passed the Air Ministry medical and, until this was cleared, her solo flying continued to be confined to the aerodrome circuit.

In July 1931 the Duchess took delivery of Puss Moth G-ABOC. Although she much preferred flying in an open cockpit, the experience of her tour in the spring had convinced her that a cabin aircraft that carried more luggage, and by carrying more fuel allowed them to fly greater distances without refuelling, was a better proposition for holiday trips abroad.

The DH.80 Puss Moth, a high-wing, strut-braced monoplane had first flown in September 1929. The original version was of conventional wooden construction but the later DH.80A, had a tubular steel fuselage and was fitted with an inverted Gipsy III engine, forerunner of the ubiquitous Gipsy Major. The standard Puss Moth carried 34 gallons of fuel - a substantial increase on

The Duchess with Flt Lt J B
Allen, who joined her as her
pilot in September 1930.
(Woburn Archives)

the nineteen gallons carried in the DH.60 Moth. Two passengers
could be carried in staggered seats behind the pilot but the
aircraft was more often fitted with one, leaving room for a dual
control column. Since any view of the instrument panel from the
rear seat was blocked by the pilot's back, only limited flying
could be undertaken from this seat; but of this, more later.
Impetus for the design of the Puss Moth had come from an
earlier trip made by Geoffrey de Havilland (later Sir Geoffrey)
and his wife Louie in their open Gipsy Moth. They had made a
number of short trips to the Continent, but had now decided to
venture farther afield. So with an extra five-gallon tank fitted in
the front cockpit, they set off on what de Havilland later
described as one of the most fascinating journeys in his life, to
France, Spain and Morocco. 'It is hard to describe,' he wrote in
his book *Sky Fever*, 'the pleasure, satisfaction and sense of
independence to be found in flying a light 'plane over the

111

Continent in fine weather, dropping in for a meal or a night's
sleep at almost any town or village that takes your fancy.'
Inevitably the weather wasn't always fine and, on the return
journey, they had a particularly 'hairy' crossing of the Pyrenees.
'After the cold and buffeting we had endured on that trip,' de
Havilland later wrote, 'I was more keen than ever to design a
light cabin aeroplane which would do away with the draughts
and discomforts of open cockpit flying.' Thus was the Puss Moth
born and the Duchess, two years later, bought one for similar
reasons.

The Puss was delivered to the Duchess on 28th July and she
lost little time before setting off in it on her first continental
tour. They left on 2nd August for Cologne, continuing to Berlin,
which the Duchess considered a thoroughly well-managed and
thriving city in great contrast to Paris; in the afternoon they
visited the Zoo. From here they went on to Vienna where they
spent two nights and where with good shops and well-kept
galleries, they were somewhat surprised to see no signs of
poverty. They spent a further two nights in Budapest visiting
the tomb of the Hapsburgs with its enormous silver and gold
Sarcophagi. It was then on to Belgrade and from there to the
Lido for which they left early 'because Italian officials had to be
coped with.' and true to expectations, this was the only place
where their luggage was examined by customs. They spent a
day there going over to Venice in a steam launch and round the
canals in a gondola, and although the evening was wet and
stormy, they returned to Venice for dinner. After this they left
for Lausanne, refuelling at Milan as they had planned to fly
over the Alps - which in the event they did with some difficulty.
'When passing Mont Cenis,' the Duchess wrote, 'and in most
undesirable situ., heavy snow storm and things looked distinctly
unpleasant as in twisting gorges of which we knew nothing. My
pilot made a dive for it and we got clear. I have never had a
really clear and sunny crossing of the Alps, but this year one
does not expect to find fine weather.'

From Lausanne they took the train to Zermatt and, the
following day, went up by train to the Gornergrat Hotel.
Walking back, they passed an hotel with a magnificent view of
the Matterhorn. As the hotel in Zermatt that had been booked

for them by a courier had no view, they rushed back as fast as their legs would carry them, cancelled their rooms and caught the last train up to the hotel overlooking the Matterhorn. But by the following day, as the brief sunshine had gone, they decided to return to Lausanne. The Duchess wrote:

'August 15th - Intended to return to Zurich as told not possible to land at Lucerne as race meeting on Military Ground. As weather unpleasant intended taking valley route but soon after leaving, cloud so low not possible. Sunshine appeared to be in mountains so tried that way. Beautiful flight over Thuner See and Lake Lucerne but at Zug very low cloud. Tried to find way through to Lake Zurich which was not far, including following railway which went into tunnel and we could not find where it emerged. Had to return to Lucerne and land on Race Meeting. Expected to be very unpopular but Swiss race-goers most sympathetic to extent of breaking down fence to let Moth through to hangar. Poured with rain all afternoon.'

Next day they took a long drive, lunched on top of Furka Pass and viewed the Rhône glacier. On the flight home the Duchess had her first experience of the back seat of a Puss in rough weather. Thrown out of her seat, she hit her head on the overhead longerons. 'Immense amount of building over the war area,' she wrote, 'but trenches still visible. Obliged by headwind to land at St. Inglevert.'

'*My first impressions of the Puss Moth,*' the Duchess wrote at the conclusion of her first trip, '*are that it is very convenient in that one takes more luggage and if not beset by headwinds, would be an advantage in that one can take longer flights in shorter time. Probably too for pilot in front seat, pleasant enough.. For passenger in rear who likes fresh air and not abominable draught and likes amusement of controlling and navigating the machine, it is a detestable conveyance. The dual control is a farce as one can neither see the instruments nor where one is going and holding the joy-stick under these conditions is more conductive to sleep than to pleasure. So to bed the Puss will go until I want it once more for a flight abroad.*'

On 19th August the Duchess flew to Hanworth to watch from the air, the *Graf Zeppelin* land on its return from a cruise round Britain. In spite of a very strong wind, Dr Eckener, head of the

German Zeppelin Company, managed with the assistance of a 200 strong landing party from the nearby Underground Railway workshops, to dump his water ballast and make a good landing. Because of the conditions he remained on the ground only long enough to unload his British passengers and take on 26 others for the return flight to Germany. A celebration dinner laid on by Colonel Shelmerdine for the German crew at the Dorchester hotel in London, had therefore to be cancelled. The wind was so strong that in their Moth, the Duchess and Allen virtually hovered alongside the airship, giving them an excellent view of the proceedings. Like all things done well by an expert she commented, the whole operation looked easy. Two days later they flew to Aldergrove to watch some motor-racing, spending a night at *Cairnsmore* en route. The 12th and last of the Schneider Trophy races was scheduled for 12th September 1931. Due to bad weather the French and Italian entries failed to arrive and the race was postponed till the 13th. When on the 13th they still hadn't appeared, Flight Lieutenant, later Air Marshal Sir John Boothman, piloting an S.6B, went round the course on his own in good weather, to win the Trophy at 340mph and set up a new 100 km closed circuit record. The Honorable 'Freddie' Guest, former Air Minister and Secretary for State for Air, had invited the Duchess to watch the race from his house at Wittering and, in spite of the weather, she flew down with Allen for lunch. Because his private aerodrome was in an area closed for the race, Allen had to land in a stubble field at Hunston. After lunch, with the race postponed, they set out for home but were forced down by fog in Windsor Park, where a Mr Copeland Griffiths gave them tea while they awaited the arrival of a car in which to complete their journey.

A week later they flew to Sywell, Northampton where the Duchess had undertaken to open and distribute the prizes at the first British flying meeting organised, to the scepticism of many males, entirely by women. In spite of an overcast sky and poor visibility the show was well attended and some seventy aircraft flew in. Jim Mollison even arrived in his Moth from Dundee where he had been flying for Barnard's Circus, which in the prevailing weather, was considered a good effort. On the other hand Amy Johnson, whom he was to marry a year later,

The 'Graf Zeppelin', piloted by Dr Eckener, head of the Zeppelin Company, landing at Hanworth in August 1931 after a round-Britain flight. The Duchess flew with Allen to Hanworth to watch it land.
(Richard Riding Collection)

failed to make it because of a cold and heavy rain at Bridlington. Other well known women pilots unable to attend included Winifred Brown, winner of the 1930 Kings Cup, who had sprained her ankle, Winifred Spooner, who was scheduled to give an aerobatics display but was at the time in a liner in mid Atlantic, and parachutist Delphine Reynolds, who had recently dislocated her hip in a riding accident. In her absence an aerobatic display, somewhat limited by weather, was put on by Miss Doreen Tyzack. Well known women pilots attending included The Hon. Mrs Victor Bruce who the previous year had been the first British pilot to fly from England to Tokyo, The Hon. Mrs Richard Westenra, who later in the year was to hit the headlines after flying with R H McIntosh to the Cape and back, Pauline Gower and Lady Bailey. Lieutenant-Colonel Shelmerdine, Director of Civil Aviation at the Air Ministry, was flown in with his wife by Gordon Olley.

During the opening ceremony Miss Tyzack took off in a Moth, nearly blowing the ceremonial party away in the process, to

115

drop a bouquet for the Duchess. This attached to a parachute, was in due course retrieved by a car and presented. Both the Arrival competition and the Ladies Race consisting of two laps of a 22-mile course, were won by Susan Slade, a private pilot from Heston who was killed during World War II while ferrying a Wellington bomber. The Duchess recorded that she found this event, quite the cheeriest of the generally depressing aviation meetings she had attended, also that the fog at one time was so thick that they had doubted whether they would make it home. On 24th September the Duchess flew up to Dumfries to pay a final visit to Barnard's Circus which, as it was being wound up at the end of the season, she felt might be her last chance to see the Fokker. Barnard told her that during the summer, he estimated that he had flown more than 30,000 joyriders in it. He was now planning to use *Spider* for charter work and by October, was offering it for tours to Italy, North Africa, Palestine and Egypt. On these he planned to take eight passengers instead of the usual sixteen. The fact that he still had record-breaking in mind is shown by a letter dated 7th January 1932, which he wrote to the Duchess from his home at Grasmere, The Avenue, Radlett and which read thus:

> "I'm afraid I am always bothering you but I know you will be interested to hear that Hinkler and I have arranged to attempt together a record flight to Australia and back. I want to ask you whether you would care to join us on the flight. We should not ask you to put up much money. We are keeping the whole thing secret but propose starting about the beginning of March."

The flight never came off, perhaps because of competition. Charles Kingsford Smith arrived at Croydon from Australia on 16th December 1931 carrying Christmas mail. He left again on 8th January 1932 with a 700 lb load arriving at Darwin eleven days later, a record for an aircraft carrying a useful load. During February and March there were two more attempts on the record, both in Moths and both ending in failure. In April, C W A Scott regained the England - Australia record with a time of eight days and twenty-one hours, a record that would have been hard to beat. But back to the Duchess. From Dumfries they continued to *Cairnsmore*, where they spent the night, returning to Woburn next day owing to the forthcoming General

The Duchess with Gipsy Moth G-AAAO, used extensively by her from
1928 until July 1932. (A J Jackson Collection)

Election that had caused the family visit to Scotland this year to
be postponed. It was not therefore until 6th November that the
Duchess flew to *Cairnsmore* in her Moth for the annual autumn
shoot. For this they must have had a particularly strong
tail-wind as it took them only two hours and twenty minutes - a
ground-speed of some 105 mph. 'In the Puss Moth we would
have done it in one hour fifty minutes.' was the Duchess's only
comment.

By 1931 the 1929 Wall Street crash was having its full effect
in Europe. In Britain no immediate action had been taken by
the government to counter the effect. Thus by 1931, with
unemployment and government expenditure rising and revenue
from taxes falling, economies had become an absolute necessity.
When proposals were made to cut unemployment benefit, the
Prime Minister, Ramsey MacDonald, was finally forced to
resign. The King, refusing to accept his resignation, sent instead
for Stanley Baldwin and Sir Herbert Samuel, leaders of the
opposition parties. Having ascertained that they would be
willing to serve, he initiated the setting up of a National
Emergency Government in which Ramsey MacDonald remained

117

Prime Minister, Baldwin became Lord President of the Council and Sir Herbert Samuel, Home Secretary. In the General Election of October 1931, which gave authority to the National Government, Neville Chamberlain replaced Snowdon as Chancellor of the Exchequer, with the specific task of bringing the country back into credit. This inevitably meant large increases in taxation, causing serious problems for among others the Duke of Bedford, one of which was whether he could afford to continue leasing *Cairnsmore*.

There was little shooting that year. An exceptionally wet autumn had left floods and waterlogged ground. The Duchess's return was also delayed when, due to fog, Allen waited two days before he could fly up for her. They eventually flew back on 5th December in thick weather and a strong headwind. Two days after their return they flew to Hanworth to join in the welcome to 'Bert' Hinkler, who landed there in his Canadian-built Puss Moth CF-APK, on completion of his record-breaking flight from Canada to England via New York and the South Atlantic. This was not only the first west-east crossing of the South Atlantic but the 1760 mile leg from Port Natal to Bathurst, which he made in 22 hours, was the longest nonstop flight by a light aircraft so far made. To minimise the effect of the northeast trade winds on leaving Port Natal, Hinkler had flown just above the water until it got dark when, unable to see the sea, he was forced to climb. Navigating solely by dead reckoning, with no dashboard lighting, his only visible instruments a turn-and-bank and a compass that had luminous figures, he had crossed the African coast within ten miles of Bathurst, his planned destination. He seemed, people said at the time, to be able to judge drift by instinct. The Duchess, seeing Hinkler besieged by Press and cameramen, described him as a merry-looking person who looked as if he would call a spade a spade but whose nerves must have been far more sorely tried by his welcome than by his lone voyage. Sadly his career ended two years later when, in an attempt to break the record set up by C W A Scott from England to Australia, his Puss Moth went missing. Some weeks later the wreck of his aircraft was found in the Appenines.

Before the end of the month the Duchess managed to fit in a further hours solo flying; she also had some instruction in side-slips and forced landings and had made a cross-country flight to Wittering. By the end of 1931, her total flying amounted to 1,170 hours, which included over thirty hours of solo.

Chapter Eight
1932: Birdwatching

On 31st January 1932 the Duchess wrote in her diary, 'we have come to the end of an amazing January; much fog for flying but always clear enough for shooting.' The month has been the warmest, she wrote, that she had ever known, with only short breaks of frost. During the month she managed to put in a number of flights including over two hours solo at Henlow. Meanwhile, on 19th January she wrote:

'Yesterday evening I flew to Fairyland. After doing three-quarters of an hours solo at Henlow, Flight Lieut. Allen suggested that we should go above the clouds to see the sunset. We climbed to 4,000 feet and came out in an Arctic landscape. The moon was behind us but high in the heavens. In front a very bright Venus was making her way to the western horizon. Below her was the sunset sky, shading from palest primrose to pink and blue. On our right was a blue 'sea' with a 'coastline' of grey-blue hills and islands (we were between Henlow and Woburn!), but only those who have been in Fairyland know how indistinguishable this can be from the real thing. All around us were snow-covered hills and plains, tinted on the horizon with pink shading to deepest carmine. Just now and again we came to a dark hole in our solid-looking snowfield, through which twinkled the electric lights of the world below. They seemed more like fireflies though I have not hitherto associated them with Arctic regions, but ones fancy may take flight above cloudland. I longed to stay up till the last rays of the sunset had faded but the time had come to plunge into the snow below and to leave our Fairyland for the gloomy end of a cloudy day.'

There must be few even in the sophisticated world of today who are unmoved by the sight of a magic sunlit world from just above the clouds.

In February the Duchess flew with Allen to Cley Mill for some bird-watching and while there, discovered in the Mill some old

Cley Mill at Cley-Next-The-Sea, Norfolk, where the Duchess was a frequent visitor and from where she would indulge in her other passionate interest of birdwatching.

papers dating from 1711 AD. One of these described a frost that, in the 14th century, lasted from September to April. 'I trust it may not recur in my lifetime,' the Duchess commented. She also spent a few days at Sarrat Mill, complaining bitterly of the 'vandalism' carried out at Chenies - one of the most beautiful villages in England - where the elms had been lopped, the road widened, trees cut down and hedges replaced by wire fences. The Parish Council had started it by erecting an unsightly notice-board on the Green, she wrote, which might well have been placed elsewhere, but now, 'they have surpassed themselves in acts of vandalism.' Despite this, in the bushy hedges, sedgy meadows, thick undergrowth, commons and running water, there was still much she noted, to attract birds.

In April with the longer days, their cross-country flying started in earnest with flights among other places to Lincoln, Ripon and Cranleigh. At the end of the month Allen and the

Duchess set out for the Continent on what was becoming for her an annual spring outing. They were away from 29th April till 22nd May doing a 'grand tour' of Spain, and calling at the North African towns of Fez, Oran and Algiers. 'As much of the flight was over the same route that I took in 1927,' she wrote, 'it is not worth recording in detail. *This time unfortunately it had to be in the Puss Moth which I do not like, as it is a closed machine. But it has the great advantage of enabling one to take more luggage and carries more petrol than the 'Gipsy'.'*

They spent their first night at Orleans instead of the usual Paris, 'a very much better arrangement,' the Duchess wrote, 'as there were no delays at Le Bourget, and it is only a short drive to town. Moreover, Paris in these post-war days seems to have greatly deteriorated. On my last visit to the Claridge Hotel we were put to dine in a sort of Grillroom restaurant underground, with a *very* queer lot of people - because they could not apparently, afford to keep the dining room open all the year round. That decided me not to try this once-best hotel again.'

The weather as might be expected thus early in the year, was not all sunshine. They had an unpleasant crossing of the Pyrenees and at Burgos, where they landed for petrol, it was cold, cloudy and windy. Nevertheless, they left the aerodrome to take a look at the Cathedral, but as even Cathedrals in Spain closed for midday siesta, they were turned out three minutes after they arrived. Most of the Galleries were also closed in the afternoon - 'a great nuisance for the tourist and leaving one,' as the Duchess put it, 'rather at a loose end.' They continued the same afternoon to Madrid.

Here they spent three wet and cloudy days 'doing' the Galleries in the morning and for the most part, walking in the afternoon. There was little sign, the Duchess wrote, of the revolution in which during the previous year, King Alfonso XIII was dethroned and Spain declared a republic - a situation that remained until the outbreak of the civil war in 1936. There were a few statues with their heads knocked off and some defaced inscriptions, but at least outwardly, everything seemed quiet and normal. There had been a marked deterioration in the standard of service at Spanish aerodromes since her visit five years previously. Then refuelling had been carried out promptly

North Africa, 1932

29/4/32	Woburn	- Lympne	1hr 05min
	Lympne	- Orleans	2hr 45min
30/4/32	Orleans	- Biarritz	4hr 30min
2/5/32	Biarritz	- Burgos	1hr 45min
	Burgos	- Madrid	1hr 55min
6/5/32	Madrid	- Seville	4hr 05min
8/5/32	Seville	- Malaga	1hr 05min
12/5/32	Malaga	- Tangier	1hr 10min
13/5/32	Tangier	- Fez	2hr 30min
14/5/32	Fez	- Oran	3hr 00min
	Oran	- Algiers	2hr 20min
16/5/32	Algiers	- Tetuan	5hr 05min
17/5/32	Tetuan	- Granada	1hr 45min
18/5/32	Granada	- Barcelona	4hr 15min
21/5/32	Barcelona	- Cannes	3hr 25min
22/5/32	Cannes	- Le Bourget	4hr 50min
	Le Bourget	- Lympne	2hr 15min
	Lympne	- Woburn	1hr 00min

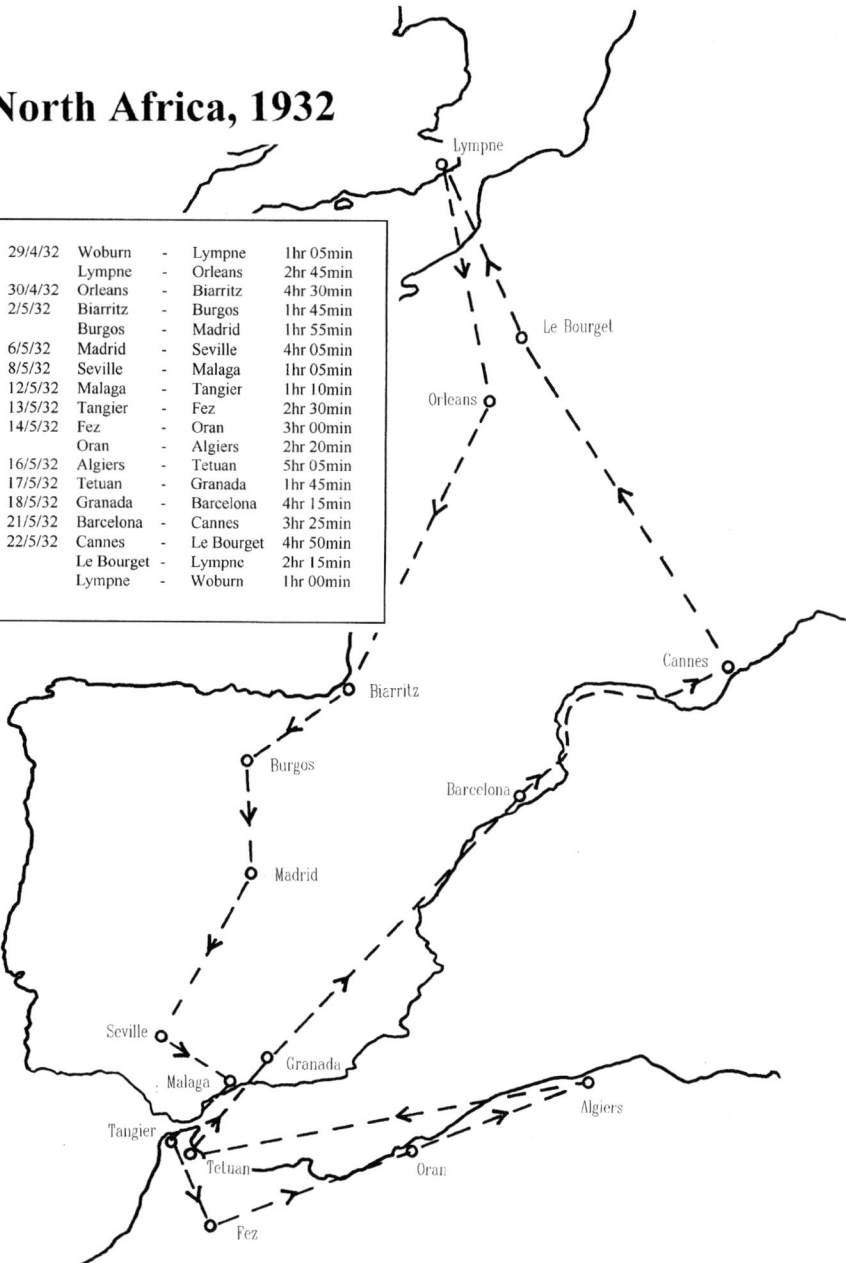

Lympne

Le Bourget

Orleans

Cannes

Biarritz

Burgos

Barcelona

Madrid

Seville

Granada

Malaga

Tangier

Algiers

Tetuan

Oran

Fez

and efficiently, hangarage for the Moth had always been available and people generally had been friendly and helpful. By 1932, with over 400 private aircraft in Britain and a much larger number on the Continent, the arrival of a light touring aircraft would no longer have been a novelty - so the deterioration in standards may not have been solely due to the change of government.

After spending Whitsun in Algiers they set out for Grenada but landing for fuel at Spanish controlled Tetuan, the Duchess was so taken with the look of it that they stayed the night. On their return they spent three nights in Barcelona and while there, visited Montserrat, which again the Duchess found much changed since her visit in 1927 with Barnard. On the last day of the tour they left Cannes at 10.55 am, reached Le Bourget in three and a half hours without refuelling and after clearing customs again at Lympne, continued to Woburn where they arrived at 8.25 pm in time for a late dinner. 'In the Gipsy Moth,' the Duchess wrote, 'this journey would have taken us two days.' But once back at home, the Puss Moth was again relegated to its hangar and two days later, they set off in the open Moth to join the family at *Endsleigh*.

On 17th June the Duchess wrote in her diary:

'Flight Lieut. Allen and I took a moonlight flight from the Park over Bedford, London suburbs and Tring. *It was my first experience of night flying and a wholly delightful experience.* As we had no lights I am not quite sure that my companion thought so as though there was a full moon, it was not ultra clear and clouds at times came over it. However, we met no other adventures and I managed to find my way home from the farthest point west.'

The latter comment confirms the extent to which the Duchess was now flying herself although as she had not passed her medical, solo flying had still to be restricted to the aerodrome circuit.

On 26th June the Duchess attended a Civil Air Display at Brooklands, organised on behalf of the Guild of Air Pilots and Air Navigators of which she was an honorary Liveryman. She had entered both her Moths for the *Concours d'Elegance* in which prizes were offered for both open and cabin aeroplanes.

J W Todd, a Woburn chauffeur, who in November 1930 became her ground engineer. He was responsible for the maintenance of her aircraft until the time of her death in 1937
(Mrs Audrey Taylor)

In the event the judges awarded first prize and the Tatler Cup to the Puss Moth, the 'Gipsy' coming second in its class. Afterwards the judges admitted that in their view the Gipsy Moth had also won its class but that they felt it would be wrong to award both prizes to the same owner. They had therefore given first prize to the Puss because it was way ahead of any other entry in that group, and had given the prize for open aeroplanes to one that had run the 'Gipsy' a close second. The Duchess couldn't help feeling that it was the Gipsy Moth that should have got the first prize because it had done over 700 hours flying, and yet looked every bit as smart as the Puss. She had been asked to give away the prizes and was delighted to be able to present the Tatler Cup to Bernard Allen as a reward for three strenuous days spent cleaning and polishing.

But Gipsy Moth G-AAAO's days were now numbered. In July the Duchess bought a new Gipsy I Moth G-ABXR. Strangely there is no mention of this in her diary but her log book shows that on 19th July, her first flight in it took her to Ratcliffe, Lindsay Everard's private aerodrome near Leicester. The following day she flew down to Shanklin 'for a breath of sea air', lunched at an hotel and sat among the holiday crowds on the beach.

This year, because of the financial depression, the Duchess forwent her holiday abroad and returned instead to her old hobby of bird-watching. Her diary reads:

'August 10th - As the migration seasons always make me long for my old bird-watching haunts, and foreign travel in these difficult times is discouraged, I decided to give Radiography and Theatre work the go-by for a brief space, and try for a bird-haunt. *Some day when aeroplanes require less space to land and take off in, or every town has its aerodrome, it may be easy to combine my two hobbies but at present it is difficult to get 'far from the madding crowd'. The golfing resorts give the best chance as there is the probability of a good hotel and bird resorts left in peace.* So to St. Andrews I went for the first time for some twenty years to find, after all the seaside places I have visited at home and abroad lately, that St. Andrews was just the same as a pre-war holiday resort. Everyone suitably, quietly, and adequately dressed in the sea and out of it. The painted lips and fingernails of the Southern Jezebels were conspicuous by their absence.

'Golf is not allowed on Sundays, which would be enough to kill any holiday resort in the South, and though I am by no means a strict Sabbatarian myself, it was strangely restful to experience a pre-war Sunday. The rush of motors was practically non-existent and all seemed strangely peaceful. I did not see anything out of the ordinary in the way of birds, but it was delightful to be prowling about in lonely places, watching and renewing acquaintance with the sea birds again. I stayed till the 22nd and then went back to work.'

Her log book shows that they landed at Leuchars and that two days later, they flew to Meikleour to visit friends. As no more flights are shown until the 22nd it seems likely that Allen returned south and came back later to collect her.

On 30th August the Duchess went north again, this time to investigate the prospects for bird-watching on the Yorkshire coast, just north of Spurn Head. They selected a field some five miles south of Withernsea where she hoped they would be undisturbed but at the sight of the aeroplane, a number of people appeared from nowhere as is their wont, just to stare. Before doing anything else therefore, the Duchess and Allen sat down and had their lunch in the hope that in the meantime, the spectators would get bored and go away. But as the Duchess wrote, 'inspecting crowd having seen you land, are prepared to wait indefinitely to see you take off again, so I walked off leaving my pilot in charge.' She had been gone no more than twenty minutes when she was buzzed by Allen in the Moth, obviously trying to attract her attention. He then dropped a note scribbled on a fragment of paper out of his note book and wrapped in less than a quarter of front sheet of *The Times*, saying that he was going to inspect the Withernsea Hotel. The note had dropped on the road and some bystanders watched her pick it up; after reading it she threw it away together with the piece of *The Times*, and went on her way.

From the sand dunes she had just seen an interesting wading bird when a man who looked like a merchant seaman, walked close in front of her with a terrier running alongside. As he had disturbed the bird, the Duchess sat on the breakwater until the man was out of sight. She then strolled on only to meet the man again, and again he passed without speaking. The Duchess wrote,

'As he had utterly dispersed every bird within a mile of me I walked over to the Humber shore where I again found him dogging me, so as time was getting short, I returned to the aeroplane and as he was only a few yards behind me and I was getting pretty exasperated, I turned round and said, 'Good Morning'. He then informed me that he was a customs officer and that I had been seen to pick up a *parcel* dropped from an aeroplane and that he had the right to demand to see it. I told him what it was and that I had thrown it away in spite of which he informed me very unnecessarily three times, 'Well, I've taken the number of yer aeroplane d'ye see and shall report yer.' - which trouble I saved him by reporting *him* for dogging me for two hours without speaking, but it did not reward me for having my hardly earned birdwatching completely spoilt.'

A week later, with her surgeon Mr Ogilvie on holiday, Herbrand, struggling with financial matters and not yet ready to go to Scotland, the Duchess decided to precede him and fill in the time with more bird-watching. She arrived with Allen at Cairsmore on 5th September and as the weather was wet, foggy and muggy, she took the opportunity 'to get away on the remote chance of finding a landing place near Machrihanish.' So off they went to the Mull of Kintyre, which she said she had for a long time hoped to visit. By good luck they found a suitable field between Campbelltown and Machrihanish and after a certain amount of argument with the owner concerning the possibility of leaving the aircraft in safety for the night, he agreed to put his cattle elsewhere. Meanwhile, 'the poor little Moth' had been left to the mercy of a crowd of small children who swarmed around. 'To their credit,' the Duchess wrote, 'though they appeared to stand and gaze at it for the best part of two hours, they left no traces. The worst part was to come. The whole of the occupants of the Hotel and neighbourhood appeared to have deserted their golf links etc. and gathered in the hall of the Hotel to stare at the two poor lunatics who had ventured to fly to the Mull of Kintyre. I can stand a crowd of village children but to be thus inspected by ones own equals seems to me to be a refinement of cruelty.' The Duchess then recounted the story of the only occasion on which she had managed to get even with an inquisitive member of the public. In the summer she often drove over the grass drive that crossed the main Woburn to Hockliffe road at Ivy Lodge, to her hospital on the Leighton Buzzard road. On these occasions the Lodge Keeper, warned of her coming, would open the Abbey gates on either side of the road in anticipation of her arrival. When this happened passing cars often pulled up, waiting to see who or whatever it was for which this ceremony was being performed. When, as often happened, she was in her open horse-drawn carriage, the Duchess found this particularly trying but on this occasion, she was in a car wearing her nurse's uniform. As she reached the road, a car with a male driver who must have been watching her for some time, started up and drove off in front of her with a look of disgust on the driver's face - but not before the Duchess, an excellent lip-reader, saw the driver say to his companion, 'It's only a nurse!' But to return to Machrihanish. Having found overnight accommodation for both themselves and the Moth, they flew back to *Cairnsmore* to collect their luggage.

There are few references in the Duchess's diary to her son Hastings, now rising 44 years of age, whose house at Glen Trool was within easy reach of *Cairnsmore*. But on 9th September she records, he took his first flight in her Moth and afterwards lunched at *Cairnsmore*. A few weeks later she quotes a letter from him that includes, 'How very energetic of you to climb Craig Nedler. It is a stiff, long pull from Dallash that would defeat many pairs of legs that had only carried their owners for twenty years.' Had Herbrand been there, the visit to *Cairnsmore* would almost certainly not have taken place because of the rift that had developed between them. The Duke, a professional soldier in the Grenadier Guards and in the First World War, a Colonel in the Bedfordshire Territorial Regiment, expected his son to join the Army also. Although initially, Hastings joined a Territorial regiment he hated the life and found that he had little in common with his fellow officers. Resigning, he became a pacifist and during World War I, a conscientious objector, after which he hardly saw his father again. The fact that the Duchess kept in touch with him at least from time to time, is evident from the occasional reference to him in her diary.

The Duchess and Bernard Allen made further visits to Rothesay and Machrihanish but for the most part, it was too wet and blustery for bird-watching. The day before the arrival of the household therefore, they flew to St. Andrews, where the Duchess spent most of the time on the pier in the hope of seeing some long-tailed Harold Ducks. Next day they flew on to Montrose, dropping a note, 'with great success for Ethel Southesk at Kinnard Castle as she had been pressing me to stay, but I had felt too deaf to face the large party I was likely to meet.' Landing back at Leuchars, they took a short walk before returning to Cairnsmore where they found Herbrand, Jemima, Miss Thorpe and Tu Fu (her Pekinese) who had just arrived.

The arrival of the household put an end to flying and two days later, as Allen took off for the south, she wrote: 'Took final flight round Mull before saying goodbye to my dear Moth for some weeks.'

On 15th November the Duchess wrote, 'Today Herbrand and Jemima left *Cairnsmore* for perhaps the last time. It was our first country home after we married and we have had forty-four very happy years here. It is very, very sad although sometimes the climate is very dreary in the persistent rain and fog to which this part of the West Coast is so subject; in fine weather there can be few places more beautiful. The sunsets here seem to me to be more wonderful than in any place I know; I do not know why as the sun sets in the same way everywhere but there is a peculiar vividness in colouring in this clear atmosphere, and the combination of high and low hills, estuary and moors, makes it all indescribably beautiful at this season of the year. *Heavy taxation is of course the main cause of our leaving.*' After the 'family' left, the Duchess drove out alone to enjoy, for what she feared might be the last time, the glens and waterfalls off the New Galloway road.

In the event this was not their last visit as Sir Keith Stewart, from whom they rented *Cairnsmore*, was also in financial difficulties. Unable to find a new tenant, he petitioned the Duke to renew the lease at least for one further year - which he undertook to do by reducing expenses elsewhere.

On 25th November, Allen arrived back at *Cairnsmore* in the Gipsy Moth and two days later, they left for Woburn. 'Left *Cairnsmore* blowing a gale and had a rather tempestuous passage home, two hours thirty minutes,' the Duchess wrote. '*Would have been quicker if I had not made an involuntary diversion in thick weather after Fleetwood.* A slight doubt as to whether we are to return or not made the leaving of *Cairnsmore* less of a wrench than it would otherwise have been, but it will come very hard on our landlords and as far as we are concerned, it depends on a possible reduction in taxation which in its turn depends on world affairs. Anyhow, the doubt was worth having at the time.'

It was a good December that year for flying and the Duchess made a number of cross-country flights during which, one can be sure, she did most of the flying.

Chapter Nine
1933: Petra, Egypt, and
a Pilot's Licence

Although the Duchess made many flights during January and February 1933, it was not until March that she restarted her solo flying and on 18th March was able to record in her diary that she had completed her first fifty hours 'solo'. Two days later they left in Puss Moth G-ABOC for what was probably the most relaxed and enjoyable of all her trips. They were away over a month and put in over 82 hours flying on a tour that today even if possible, would call for unlimited paperwork, permits and planning.

The Duchess, unlike Allen, was by now an experienced traveller; she could also take a full part in both the planning and in the air, the navigation. The detailed account she gives in her diaries of this trip reflects, often with considerable humour, the happy relationship that had grown up between herself and her new pilot. For the most part therefore one can do no better than quote directly from her diaries:

'March 21st - Left Woburn for Frankfurt in the Puss Moth G-ABOC in very fine weather which was not maintained on the Continent, and on the last part of the flight we flew through thick snowstorms. Since Captain Barnard ceased to be my pilot, my conscientious present incumbent has always flown straight by compass through Rhineland and at a height of 2,000 to 3,000 feet. Having learnt that my flying scruples were not of as high a standard as his, he followed the Rhine this time at 1,000 feet and though it was very cloudy, I once more enjoyed seeing its beautiful old castles. Stayed in Frankfurter Hof.

'March 22nd - Our start was delayed by fog and we spent the morning at the aerodrome, leaving at 1.50 pm. It was then lovely but rather cold. My original plan had been to go to Vienna but having read in the Press that there were rather serious revolutions going on there, which like many 'revolutions' I have read about in previous years were for the most part confined to the Press, we went to Saltzburg instead, the change being influenced by my having very pleasant recollections of the place when I visited it many years (thirty?) ago. I was not disappointed as we were travelling early in the year, and snow on the mountains was almost down to Salzburg and the view of the Dolomites was lovely. No trippers but I; the hotel almost empty.

'March 23rd - We left in glorious weather but as we approached Budapest it began to snow, and by the time we arrived it was snowing so fast and thickly that we could not find the aerodrome and after flying round and round very low over the town, were compelled to land on the old racecourse. The inevitable crowd immediately gathered and in spite of the cold and heavy snow, showed no inclination to disperse. Flight Lieut. Allen went off to telephone to the police, leaving me in charge, an unpleasantly anxious job guarding the more vulnerable parts of the aeroplane. However a very rough-looking party of somewhat criminal appearance constituted himself guardian of one side and by the conciliatory permission to peep inside given to some of the children and adults, they were all very pleasant and nice but I was relieved when my pilot returned after what seemed a long half hour. Of course nobody spoke English and only one man French. As we were very loath to leave the aeroplane where it was to the mercies of the crowd, Flight Lieut. Allen thought we might try and find the aerodrome as we were shown where it ought to be. With our rather heavily loaded machine we had a rather near 'squeak' getting off and missed the fence by a small margin. Again we flew round and round but it was impossible to find the aerodrome and it said something for my pilot's orientation abilities that he again located the race course. So once more we landed and once more, the crowd returned. However by the time we had drawn up under the doubtful shelter of a 'jump', a good Samaritan in the shape of a Hungarian pilot appeared who offered to go up with Flight Lieut. Allen and find the aerodrome whilst the luggage and I were shed to go to the hotel by car. I learnt later that not even he found his way direct. As we had not intended to stay in Budapest we had no Hungarian money and Flight Lieut. Allen had nothing but German coins to offer the self-appointed guardian when we first took off, but to his credit be it said, in spite of his criminal appearance he returned to help me at our second landing.

'It had been definitely cold work in the Moth trying to find the aerodrome as owing to the snow, both front windows had to be open and in the back seat, one would have been better off outside as the draught was awful. We stayed at the Hotel Hungaria wither I was escorted by the French-speaking Electrical engineer.

'March 24th - We left the aerodrome at twelve noon and for one-and-a-half hours flew over dead flat country, all cultivated, but not a wood, grass field, or hedge to be seen anywhere. There was a great deal of snow, except for a short stretch of mountains, which would probably have been pretty had the weather been clearer; this deadly flat and uninteresting country continued to Bucharest but as we crossed the hills, thick snow came on again and we had the same difficulty in finding the aerodrome as yesterday. As there had been nothing whatever for Flight Lieut. Allen to check his course by since we left the Mountains, he could not even be certain that it was Bucharest till we saw big power-stations and railway junctions. Finally, after much low flying round the town, we at last sighted an aerodrome and landed in a sea of mud. It happened to be an Air Force one, and the Officer in Charge was not at all pleased to see us and warned us to take off again as the Civil Aerodrome was quite near. Flight Lieut. Allen told him we had no petrol, and after ascertaining from the other aerodrome that we could not possibly find them, he allowed us to stay, or rather the 'Moth'. We had to make off to the Civil Aerodrome for Customs etc. where we encountered about the roughest and most disagreeable specimen of Customs Officer that it has been my misfortune to meet. I had only two suitcases in all but he was so persuaded that I wished to sell the contents in Bucharest, that he wanted me to leave one of them at the aerodrome for the night - which naturally I refused to do. A gold and black broche handbag, homemade by Bailey, aroused his special concern; also my silk under-linen and dresses, all much worn!

'We were pretty hungry when we reached the Grand Hotel as we had had nothing but a bit of omelette at 8.30 am, and this was 8.45 pm. The hotels were just like an oven, not a breath of air anywhere; all the aerodrome offices are the same; how these people survive going out from these hothouses into the snow without, I cannot imagine.

'March 25th - Flight Lieut. Allen had to go and fetch the Moth whilst I was shut up in the Civil Aerodrome oven guarding my luggage. On arrival my car sank deeply into the gutter, fortunately just at the door, as I should not have relished walking in the deep mud before a long flight. It was pulled out later by a tractor. Fetching the Moth and more particularly conforming to all the regulations, getting log books, etc. having taken three-and-a-half hours, we left at 1.45 pm as the weather looked better and the forecast was favourable.

'However, we had not gone far before we found that there had been far more snow than at Bucharest, and soon it became foggy. In the low hills snow commenced again, and as it was too thick we were obliged to return. The officials tried to shut me up in the hot waiting-room again but having already had three hours of it this morning, I left our luggage to its fate and escaped to the hangar, where I had rightly guessed that Flight Lieut. Allen would be investigating the cause of the engine 'coughing' just before we landed, due to water getting into the carburettor yesterday. He also cleaned up our poor dirty little 'Puss' after its mud bath last night at the Air Force Aerodrome.'

'March 26th - The Authorities assured us that we could not leave today, being Sunday, because they could not get a weather forecast. But as it was perfectly useless yesterday and the weather was much finer, we risked another try. Unfortunately, as soon as we reached the foothills it became foggy again, doubtless due to evaporation from the snow. But Flight Lieut. Allen persevered and hoping to get above it, he climbed to 4,000 feet where we saw a dim sun, but soon lost it and snow once more began to fall. Hoping for better things on the coast, he flew blind over the mountains for about an hour and then we once more saw patches of earth as we neared the coast and guessed our troubles were over. Owing to the long strain of blind flying, I had been giving a little assistance with the rudder when I found it erring unduly from its course. As I have done this at home, I thought Flight Lieut. Allen would know I was helping,

134

but afterwards learnt that he thought the rudder was getting jammed with the frozen snow which was forming on the struts and other parts of the machine, because whenever he turned round to see if it was me he saw me quietly knitting, and did not realise that I had one and a half eyes on the compass and only half a one on the knitting. It is easy to help anyone else keep straight when one has no responsibility and only the rudder to look after. His alarms were not quite at an end even when his mind was set at rest on this point, for as we decreased our altitude something seemed to fly off the front of the machine and bang the windows. But when the performance was repeated a few times without any untoward results, we found it was the frozen snow flaking off. There was also a little shock over one petrol tank having completely emptied itself and the other being quite full. However as we still went on when he shut off the empty tank entirely, this too must be attributed to freezing.

'Before leaving home, having read and heard much of the troubles we might expect to encounter with Turkish officials, we had provided ourselves with every possible thing they could ask for and hoped for the best. On arrival at Constantinople (Istanbul) Aerodrome they greeted us very civilly and invited me as usual into the frightfully hot waiting-room with a huge stove in the middle, whilst Flight Lieut. Allen put the Moth in the hangar. They gave a very cursory examination to my luggage and after a very long wait, informed us that the nephew of the Chief of Police had come for us in his car and was going to drive us to Constantinople. The young man on being introduced to me, said he had been told to convey expressions of regret from the Governor of Constantinople that he had been unable to meet me in person.

'On our way to the City, Flight Lieut. Allen asked him if the banks would be open.

N.C.P. 'What do you want the bank for?'

J.B.A. 'To get some Turkish money.'

N.C.P. 'What do you want Turkish money for?'

J.B.A. 'To pay our hotel bills and other expenses.'

N.C.P 'But you will have no expenses; you are the guests of the Turkish Government, and all your expenses will be paid.'

'And so they were, and moreover the young man took us all over the place sightseeing the following day, and back to the aerodrome next morning. So much for the Turks! I afterwards learned that Tom Russell (Russell Pasha of the Cairo City Police, a cousin of Herbrand), was a friend of the Minister of the Interior and had mentioned my probable advent to Constable but even so, it was a measure of civility he can hardly have expected.

'March 27th - Flight Lieut. Allen spent the morning at the aerodrome cleaning up for tomorrows flight. Last time I visited San Sofia we were only allowed to see it from the Gallery. Now one is allowed to go all over it with sandals on, but such is the difficulty of keeping them on that I fear my infidel feet touched the sacred carpets more than once. One cannot but feel glad that it has remained Turkish, for all its Christian history. We also went to the Sista Basilica again, the entrance to which had been greatly improved from the tourist's point of view of access. But here once more improvement has destroyed the weird effect of entering through a mere hole in the earth and peering into the gloom (now lit by electric light), where the unwanted were said to have been thrust to perish in the waters!

'When I dined with British Ambassador Sir Nicholas O'Connor in 1899, I remember he was much upset because the Sultan's valet had 'died suddenly' that day. He told me he was really much more than a valet, and was a very valuable man who gave the Sultan much wholesome advice. Apparently too wholesome, as like many others whose advice was not palatable, his illness was sudden and brief. It was said that others were given a cup of strong(?) coffee and dropped quietly into the Bosphorus. From the windows of his Palace I saw the Salamik procession, and the Sultan sent his Chamberlain, Emir Bey, to tell me he was pleased to hear of my arrival and later would receive me, but Sir Nicholas got out of this as he said it meant bestowing a Turkish Order on me, which at the moment was not very desirable. We were warned before dinner at the Embassy not to say anything that could not be repeated to the Sultan, as it was known that the butler was his spy. But Sir Nicholas said that he was a most charming and efficient servant who had been a very long time at the Embassy, and it was much better to know who was doing the spying.

'And so once more I left Constantinople - last time in a scorchingly hot train with a couple of pariah puppies which I took home to be christened Per and Galata - this time by air, fully appreciative of the improvements in the methods of travelling, but a little sad that all the romance had gone out of Constantinople. *Sic Transit Gloria Mundi*, or perhaps it would be more accurate to write *Sic Transit Impietas Mundi*, if my Latin is correct.

'The Governor's Secretary came to see us off and in fine weather, we left for Aleppo. We crossed the sea of Marmora and at first it was somewhat cloudy but it soon cleared off. The mountains were thickly covered with snow above 2,000-3,000 feet, indeed there had been snow at Constantinople the day before we arrived. Before Konia we had a little more blind flying but soon came out of it as we left the hills. We landed at Konia for petrol. The aerodrome is somewhat difficult to find on account of there being little to locate it but it is quite good when found. There was a most picturesque caravan of camels, tiny ponies and donkeys passing at the moment of our landing. Though the aerodrome is five miles out of Konia town, some kind personage of importance brought us out some very welcome coffee and biscuits; we then continued to Aleppo.

'We saw Tarsus and Alexandretta (Iskenderum) a little way off and near them great flocks of Flamingos in the Marshes. Later we flew over weird mountains and most curious rock formation flying at 7-8,000 feet above sea level but not much above the mountains. It has been a most interesting and beautiful flight all day of 640 miles. As we cut off a good bit of the usual course to shorten it, it is probable that few have flown over the best part of Alexandretta. We occasionally took short cuts away from the prescribed flying routes, as not only did we save time and thus ensure having plenty of petrol, but there is a fascination about flying over country which may never have been seen by man before. One is warned against taking these short cuts, because ones 'remains' would never be found if one came to grief. But it would make little difference to us, or indeed to our relatives, whether we were found or not, as a forced landing on prescribed routes would inevitably end in 'remains' only. So it is worth exploring a little when there is anything really worth seeing and economy of petrol is important. As it was we landed at Aleppo just before dark and the Moth's toilet had to be performed by electric torches as there was so little twilight. This is my fifth visit to Aleppo. Driving to town we had a very good view of the eclipse of the moon. The Hotel (Barron) seems to have been much cleaned up to its advantage. There were many English people in it going home from farther east for the hot weather. Flight Lieut. Allen was much pleased to find a copy of *The Times* as we had seen no newspaper since leaving home but on opening it, discovered that it was published a fortnight before we left!

'March 29th - Left Aleppo at 12.15 pm after spending much of the morning between bank and money changers and for the last, had to walk a long way through covered bazaars which were much more interesting than they are now at Constantinople. The country was at first flat and uninteresting but we passed enormous flocks of storks, one single bird of which swept close under our wing.'

At Baal'bek northwest of Damascus, once a city of great size, wealth and splendour, they flew low to inspect the famous ruins of the Great Temple of Baal. 'Damascus from the air,' the Duchess wrote, 'with its flat roofs looked like a child's box of bricks; we then passed within three miles of the Sea of Galilee and Tiberias and I had my first view of the River Jordan. The Sea of Galilee (L. of Tiberius) is prettily situated with high hills all round it. Had a distant view of the Dead Sea.'

'We landed by mistake on a prohibited aerodrome,' the Duchess continued, 'where there was no shelter for the Moth or telephone available, and we were told the only thing to do was to stand on the main road and stop a passing car and ask them to send us a taxi (five miles). We tried this with poor success as far as the first car was concerned, even though this was Jerusalem and not England, where we have highwaymen. The Pharisee passed by on the other side and disregarded our appeal. After some time a second car came with three men and a chauffeur inside but in spite of this, not only did they pull up, but offered to take us to Jerusalem and moreover to wait until the Moth had been pegged down and we had collected out luggage. Thus on arrival at Jerusalem did we meet the Pharisee and the Good Samaritan. Our Good Samaritan spoke very good English, but I think was a foreigner though Flight Lieut. Allen thought Lancashire, but having regard to his name, H Vitelos, I put him down as Greek.

'Flight Lieut. Allen reported on arrival in Jerusalem to Squadron Leader Soden, who was not only kind enough to forgive our landing on his prohibited aerodrome, but arranged for a guard to look after the Moth all night. He dined with us and brought an album of beautiful photographs of Petra taken by himself, and persuaded us to go there. Jerusalem stands 2,000 feet above sea level and is surrounded by high hills, which makes it a much prettier place than I had ever anticipated from pictures. The 'Good Samaritan' had lived there for six years and said he never wished to live anywhere else. We stayed at the beautiful King David Hotel, as good a hotel as I have found anywhere.'

The following morning they collected the Moth and flew via the Dead Sea and Jericho to the Royal Air Force aerodrome at Ramleh near Lydda, the position of which had been wrongly marked on their AA maps. On passing near the Mountain of Temptation the Duchess commented that the Devil might well still be in possession of it as it looked a most god-forsaken spot. Having deposited the aeroplane in the safekeeping of the RAF, they drove back to Jerusalem and spent the afternoon sightseeing.

'We went to the Holy Sepulchre, Mount of Olives and Gethsemane.' the Duchess wrote. 'This last I thought the most impressive. It is in charge of the Franciscan Monks who have built a church there, the interior of which is sombre, but serves to intensify the solemnity of the place and show up the large and impressive picture of Christ praying in the Garden (*If it be Thy will, let this cup pass from me. Nevertheless, not as I will, but as Thou wilt.*) which is placed over the Altar. There was nothing tawdry about the church and none of the glare and glitter of gilt which destroys the solemnity (to me) of the Church of the Holy Sepulchre. There are some wonderful old olive trees in the Garden. We looked at the War Cemetery on our return, which is all that one can wish for. In a beautiful situation on the hillside, bright with flowers, and every 200 headstones enclosed by a low hedge of rosemary. It is all simple, dignified and beautiful and one trembles to think what it might have been, had individual taste been permitted to choose the memorial stones.'

On 31st March they left Jerusalem for Petra. This involved an hour and a quarters drive to the aerodrome and then one hour forty minutes flight to the Air Force Station at Ma'an. The Duchess wrote:

'The scenery the whole way was the acme of desolation. I piloted most of the way, and though we were 4,000 feet above sea level and Flight Lieut. Allen said, 1,000 feet above the earth, I appeared to be uncomfortably close to it. It was awfully bumpy and we both got a most unpleasant crack on the head from the steel bars supporting the roof of the fuselage. I was ordered to keep low on account of the bumps and am certain that at one moment I cannot have been 200 feet from the ground, but Flight Lieut. Allen professed not to have been looking just then. All along the railway line we saw the remains of huts and trenches occupied during the War. This was the scene of Col. Lawrence's exploits and any European troops quartered here during the summer - his of course were Arabs - would certainly have deserted to go to Heaven. On arrival at Ma'an we were assured that the car ordered for us would be there in a few minutes, but we ended by waiting two hours in the Officer's Quarters. We had one-and-a-half hours drive over desolate country, which reminded me very much of my drives in Persia except that it was cool and pleasant.

'After the motor drive with many perilous bends but fortunately no other traffic, we disembarked at a small village where two scraggy ponies with men's saddles were waiting for us on which to ride to Petra. As I had not been on a horse more than twice since the War, I rather mistrusted my ability to stick on, but a few minutes in the saddle reassured me, and except for stumbling I cannot say I was in any way tired while the ponies were led by Arabs, armed guard walking in front and behind. By Government order every tourist has to have an armed guard, though rifles were so antiquated I should have been sorry to have depended upon them had we been attacked, just exactly by whom I do not know but I suppose Bedouins. The track was exceedingly rough and the ponies none too sure-footed, and as mine had been compelled to leave a very young foal behind in the village, it was always looking back and neighing instead of looking where it was going. As we neared the camp we came to the wonderful gorges and rock dwellings which have made Petra famous. The effect as one views this marvellous city of the past, is beyond my powers of description, and those who would know what 'Petra' is must read the works of Sir W Kennedy and others and not the impressions of a one-day visitor. Suffice it to say here that I gathered on the spot and from those who have written about it, that its first-known inhabitants were Troglodytes some 19,000 years ago, who left their implements in the natural caves where they are occasionally found. The caves have been successfully inhabited by Edomites, Nabataeans, Romans, Byzantine Christians, Crusaders and Arabs and are still today the refuge of a few families of a primitive people, it is said without laws or religion; waifs and strays who have drifted into holes and corners to escape the notice and taunts of their Arab neighbours. About ten families of these, some with one or two children and a goat, move from cave to cave and are the only permanent residents of Petra today.

'The wonderful dwellings all up the face of the rocks, the great area of the city, its intricate system of canals, cisterns and pipes, its flights of steps by which only could the upper dwellings be reached, its theatres, altars etc. must represent centuries of ceaseless labour and then apparently, all left suddenly and no man knows why! Cook and Son have established a very comfortable little camp of twelve visitors tents and a Mess tent for four months of the year. Only pity is that one's armed guides do not speak more English or French as one can learn little from them.'

Over fifty years have passed since the Duchess's visit and inevitably things have changed. Buses now bring tourists down from Amman, branching off the desert highway before Ma'an. Many ponies led by Arab children and even the occasional camel, wait to take visitors down the still rough and stony path to the 'rose-red' city. The Bedouins, no longer allowed to live in the caves, have their own village and armed guards to protect visitors are no longer needed. Instead of the Cook and Sons tented camp, visitors now stay either in a large modern hotel or a Government resthouse, both within walking distance of bus-stop and ponies. But in spite of earthquake and flood, inside the thirty-five square miles that is Petra, much of the magic remains. As John Burgon, the Dean of Chichester wrote in 1845,

Match me such marvel save in Eastern clime.
A rose-red city half as old as time

'There were only two other visitors,' the Duchess continues, 'one an obvious German or Austrian professor (Dr Emil Baer), with black hair standing straight on end for some four inches and a black beard, who wrote up his notes all the evening with the aid of a Baedeker and was not heard to utter a word, and a bright little lady who had obviously travelled a great deal and made herself very pleasant.' This lady was in fact none other than the famous traveller, writer and Arabist Dame Freya Stark, who later recalled the Duchess sitting in the Mess tent knitting a black sock!

After a rather cold night - for Petra is high and March is early in the year for tourists - they went down for a last view of the city before breakfast; it is by the light of the rising and setting sun that the sandstone rocks can take on their famed rose-red hue. 'We had a two-hour pretty stiff climb up the Hill of Sacrifice,' the Duchess wrote, 'stiff because it is not only rough and steep but, as mentioned, one had to climb up and down boulders.' After breakfast they drove back to Ma'an where the RAF Officers confided in them that they had an expensive time entertaining people en route to Petra - luckily Allen and the Duchess had accepted nothing from them but water. From Ma'an they set off on a roundabout route to Cairo, refuelling at Gaza where as they landed, the spring on the tail-skid broke. This resulted in them having to stay the night while a new one was sent up from Cairo. Meanwhile they got the old one mended in the Bazaar. Although a little out of perpendicular, they thought it would probably have got them to Cairo. In the morning, the Fokker arrived, bringing a new one from Cairo so it was never tried out. While in Gaza they stayed in the

Imperial Airways quarters, which although they got a good dinner, the Duchess considered both expensive and dirty.

'Left for Cairo,' the Duchess wrote, 'and scored one over my pilot - a rare event where it concerns navigation - but I told him that if we steered the course we were going, we should be south of Ismailia, which I wanted him to see. He said 'No' he had made allowance for that, but we arrived at the Canal considerably south of Ismailia and he had to be humble!'

The following description by the Duchess of flying a Puss Moth from the rear seat is both accurate and ageless, as anyone who has tried it will know. The only dual controls in the rear were a control column and rudder bar; the only instrument a compass. There was not even a fore-and-aft trimmer and the view of the front instrument panel was inevitably blocked by the back of the person in front. Moths were equipped with an elementary wind-operated airspeed indicator fixed to a wing-strut that, in case of failure of the dashboard instrument, gave the pilot some general indication of airspeed but was not accurate enough to be use for height-keeping. The rear compass was, as the Duchess describes, fitted hard up against the leather back of the pilot's seat making it both difficult to see, and the locking clamps difficult to reach. But to continue with her Diary:

'Navigation from the rear seat of a Puss Moth is not entirely the sinecure it might be supposed to be. Times were when the control was handed over to me for a short time where mistakes could easily be remedied. But now it is handed to me over deserts and mountains for hours at a time, and my pilot at least affects that he is then at liberty to study scenery, maps, etc. As I found navigation over uninteresting country too strong a sedative without any other instrument than the airspeed meter on the wing, he has been kind enough to install a compass at the back of the seat. But those two are all that I have, for normally his person clad in a heavy pilot coat, often undone and with flaps sticking out and sometimes a felt hat as well, not only obscures the instrument board but most of the landscape.

'I am unfortunately deaf and have to use special speaking-tubes which remain in my ears very well when I can wear a helmet. But when it becomes too hot for that in a Puss Moth, the ear-pieces can only be relied on to stay in place in my ears when I am looking straight ahead. I therefore greatly prefer to look at the instrument board rather than the airspeed meter on the wing. However as I have said, these are generally denied me except for the reflection of the clock in the window pane and the engine-revolution speed meter, both of which require some consideration (being reversed) by this means, and have little interest seeing that I have no throttle to control. About once in two hours my pilot gets a sudden inspiration that I have this partiality for seeing the instrument panel and shifts himself entirely to one side and leans against the fuselage. But this consideration for my comfort has been known to last precisely one minute (the record) when one by one airspeed meter, Reed turn indicator, and the altimeter suffer eclipse, and I return to the clouds, mountains and woods as substitutes. Sometimes when I have some really nice pet cloud or other object in view which relieves me from the necessity of too strained attention on the compass, my pilot is getting a little bored, and leans over to one side to study the surrounding country, and so 'Good-bye' for the time to all observation of the landscape for me.

'Occasionally the compass, placed low at the back of the seat, requires a little adjustment and I bend down to do it, an action of which the Moth takes advantage and dips or rises according to fancy. 'About 105 miles per hours please,' is at once ordered down the speaking tube, so a momentary glance at the pet cloud or landscape has to be made to readjust matters. But the compass cannot be left 'all anyhow' and the adjustment must be done. But it is so placed that when Flight Lieut. Allen is sitting in his seat, the leather presses very hard on the compass and it is exceedingly difficult to move one of the clamps. However, it has to be done, and as I have no tail trimmer in the back seat, the Moth again soars and dips according to pleasure. The speaking tube is again seized, '105 miles per hour, please,' is shouted down a little louder. I do not remonstrate, because the compass was installed to please me and was unasked for, so I take it meekly and say nothing, but turn my head to see the airspeed meter on the wing and out drops an ear-piece. Once more that speaking tube is seized and even with only one ear, and that probably the deafest, I hear *'105 miles per hour please your Grace.'*

'Now and again I feel pressure on the control column, an indication I presume that I am letting the nose go up too much or am wanted to go lower, so I finger it very lightly for the moment or even give it up to him altogether to see what is required of me. But the Moth then plunges into the abyss and I have to resume control. He was only leaning a map heavily against it. This may last for a quarter-hour, but I learn to adjust myself to the engine taking on a few extra pounds weight. The only occasion when I am not called upon to regulate the airspeed are when, with a good old desert bump, our skulls are nearly cracked against steel bars supporting the roof of the fuselage, and he looks round to see if I am still conscious. For the belts in the Puss Moth which fulfil all Government requirements, do not meet across one's knees within about four inches. *But they are there, which is all that matters for the Air Ministry inspector!*

'There is an unwritten law against wearing a helmet in a Puss Moth, because it is supposed to be silent and free from draught! At least it is not *comme-il-faut* to wear one. So it is in the pilot's seat, but in the rear I have reason to know, you can be nearly blown out of your seat or perish with cold. At present the only phones are connected to the helmet as far as Flight Lieut. Allen is concerned, my special phones fit into my ears. As he is somewhat deaf all my remarks have to be shouted till I become voiceless and my timid remonstrance is met with *'105 miles per hour please.'* We arrive in Cairo to be met by Tom Russell's car and later by Tom himself at the hotel. We filled up most of the afternoon by a visit to the Museum to see Tut-ankh-amen [sic] treasures.'

The Duchess spent the morning visiting the Pyramids with the wife of the Chief of the City Police. The Sphinx, she observed, had been greatly excavated since her last visit on her return from India after her marriage, and she now appreciated why Herbrand, never an ardent sightseer, did not want to take her up the Pyramid. 'However,' she wrote, 'I have done it now and enjoyed it 45 years later.' They left next day for Luxor, at

March - April, 1933

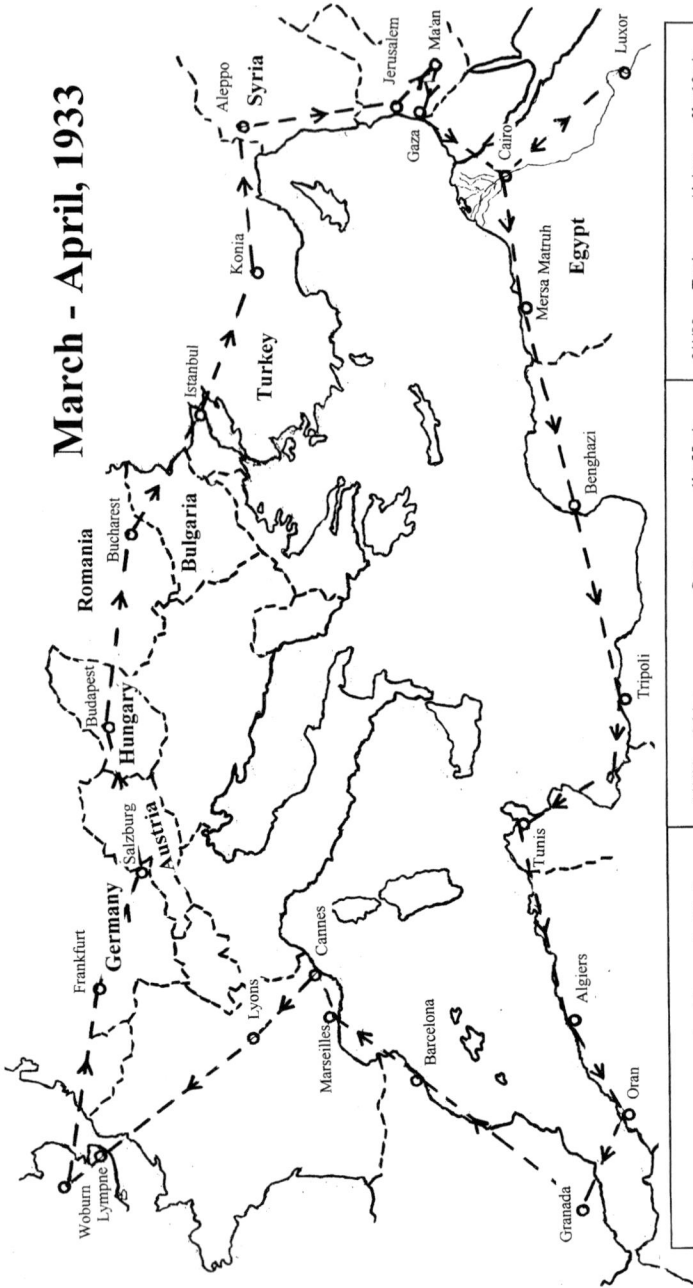

21/3/33	Woburn	- Frankfurt	4hr 35min
22/3/33	Frankfurt	- Salzburg	2hr 25min
23/3/33	Salzburg	- Budapest	4hr 00min
24/3/33	Budapest	- Bucharest	4hr 50min
26/3/33	Bucharest	- Istanbul	3hr 05min
28/3/33	Istanbul	- Konia	3hr 10min
	Konia	- Aleppo	2hr 45min
29/3/33	Aleppo	- Jerusalem	3hr 55min
31/3/33	Jerusalem	- Ma'an	1hr 45min

1/4/33	Ma'an	- Gaza	1hr 55min
2/4/33	Gaza	- Cairo	2hr 25min
4/4/33	Cairo	- Luxor	3hr 25min
5/4/33	Luxor	- Cairo	4hr 05min
6/4/33	Cairo	- Mersa Matruh	2hr 25min
7/4/33	Mersa Matruh	- Sirte	2hr 55min
	Sirte	- Tripoli	2hr 40min
8/4/33	Tripoli	- Ben Gardamme	1hr 30min
	Ben Gardamme	- Tunis	3hr 10min

9/4/33	Tunis	- Algiers	3hr 10min
10/4/33	Algiers	- Oran	2hr 10min
	Oran	- Granada	2hr 40min
11/4/33	Granada	- Barcelona	4hr 15min
	Barcelona	- Marseilles	2hr 30min
12/4/33	Marseilles	- Cannes	50min
	Cannes	- Lyons	2hr 35min
13/4/33	Lyons	- Lympne	4hr 40min
	Lympne	- Woburn	55min

first following the Nile and then as it curved westwards, cutting across the desert. The Duchess wrote:

'We visited the Temple at Karnak in the afternoon which leaves one speechless with amazement at the stupendous amount of labour which must have gone to the making of this marvellous building. It was a cruel earthquake which destroyed so much of it nearly 2,000 years ago, and but for this, time must have left us an amazing record of what labour then achieved without all our modern mechanical appliances. On our return we visited the Luxor temple. Luxor is a lovely place and the lights at dawn and sunset *most* beautiful. Here one can appreciate that one is really back in the heart of Africa again and, being so late in the season, the hotels are empty and one escapes the disturbing element of fellow tourists. As with Petra we had seen it all very sketchily but unfortunately, *not only do I fly but time also.* There had been a very strong wind in the morning and as our little Moth had no shelter I was relieved to find it intact. Had strong headwind for return to Cairo which we only reached after lights were lit, in three-and-a-half hours.'

Next morning they visited the Tombs of the Kings, a 'nice old Dragoman, the head of his clan' taking them round. 'I do not know how much he may have imposed on us,' the Duchess wrote, 'but anyhow he was very interesting, and the wonders of the tombs are such that there can have been little need for inventing fables about them. Having read Howard Carter's *Tut-ankh-amen* a year or two before coming, it was immensely interesting seeing his (Tut-ankh-amen's) tomb, though owing to his early death it is less decorative than others. We were also told that the Kings began the decoration of their tombs as soon as they were crowned.'

Her diary continues:

'April 6th - Hotel Semiramis where we are staying closes today and we are off to Benghazi. The deep blue sea of the Mediterranean alongside the coast is such that anyone seeing the underside of our wing would find it impossible to believe it was not painted deep blue, such is strength of reflection even at 3,000 feet. Have now flown over a good deal of desert and it has great fascination for me. The lights and shades, morning and evening are so soft and beautiful from the air. As a rule there

147

are rocks and hills but the Libyan desert is deadly flat and one can imagine, could have same fatal soporific effect on the aeronaut as the Atlantic, if one had too much of it.'

At Benghazi they were met by a particularly affable British Vice-Consul who as usually happened, tried to hustle the Duchess off to the hotel instead of allowing her to stretch her legs after being compressed in the aeroplane. This time she was more than usually loth to be whisked off as having visited the hotel before, she knew that it was little more than a restaurant - and a poor one at that. She therefore dug her toes in and insisted on remaining with the Moth until Allen had finished his chores, after which they went to the hotel together. Next day, after refuelling at Sirte, they reached Tripoli from where, when leaving next morning, they were escorted by two RAF 'planes. 'A most unexpected honour,' the Duchess wrote, 'they were flying so close when I last saw them, I hoped they did not collide.' At Tunis they stayed at the Hotel Magnifique where the food left much to be desired. 'Began dinner with *very* thick mutton broth evidently collection of kitchen scraps of some days. This followed by toughest steaks, and poor Flight Lieut. Allen laid down his knife and fork in despair though he must have been hungry as last meal at 8.30 am. We finished with caramel pudding, the only thing not needing machinery to cut it, and standby at home for every hostess who has to provide guest with 'early luncheon before leaving'. Coffee also defeated us though Flight Lieut. Allen had been known to swallow most things of that name. Left Tunis without regret.'

After a night in Algiers they continued via Oran to Grenada where they had more hotel trouble. 'Hotel delightful,' the Duchess wrote, 'but service of the worst; had greatest difficulty getting any breakfast indeed coffee never came. Whilst Flight Lieut. Allen complained to manager, two other parties came up on same errand. Manager blamed the Republic for not allowing waiters to work more than eight hours a day, but I think he must have come under the same regulation.' On leaving Grenada the Duchess was presented with an enormous bouquet of flowers from the garden of the officer's quarters. 'If one were given a posy on these occasions it would be very welcome, but a huge bouquet leaves one with no alternative but to scatter it out of the window as soon as one is safely away from the aerodrome. We flew up to top of Sierra Nevada to take photos. As Flight Lieut. Allen handed over control to me when we were close to the top so that he could take photos, he apparently has confidence in his pupil.'

On the way home, they landed for fuel at Barcelona where no sooner had they landed than an agitated British pilot with an Avro Avian, rushed up to them and introduced himself as Bill Lancaster. He was he said on a record flight to the Cape, hoping to break Amy Mollison's England to Cape Town record of four days, six hours and fifty-four minutes, which she set six months earlier. He had planned on this his first leg to make Oran, but headwinds had forced him to land at Barcelona to refuel. When Allen and the Duchess arrived he had been waiting two hours for petrol and, as he could not speak a word of Spanish, had been unable to find out why - hence his delight at seeing them. Allen did what he could to help him and shortly afterwards, Lancaster got his petrol. The delay meant that he would now reach Oran after dark. When Allen asked him whether Oran had been warned of his late arrival, Lancaster said that he had no idea - however he took the hint and went off to telephone. When he returned, Allen offered to swing his propeller for him and when the engine didn't fire, carried out the usual procedure for an overprimed engine, of asking Lancaster to turn off the ignition and open the throttle so that he could turn the propeller backwards. When ready to start up again, Lancaster switched on the ignition but forgot to close the throttle so that when the engine fired, Allen was lucky to get away with nothing worse than a grazed sleeve. Meanwhile the Duchess, watching the goings-on, observed that seeing that Lancaster was only eight hours from home and was already a physical wreck and bundle of nerves, she was certain he would not get far. As was so often the case, she was quite right in her prognostications.

By the time Lancaster landed at Oran at nine o'clock that evening, he was already four-and-a-half hours behind Amy's record and, by the time he left, he had lost another two hours. He left at three o'clock next morning, setting off south, hoping when it got light to pick up the Trans-Sahara motor track. Having no cockpit lighting he had to light matches to see the compass. After five hours without picking up any landmarks, he came across an aerodrome and landed. The aerodrome, some 500 miles south of Oran was Adrar, which it so happened, was on the motor track so after refuelling, he took off again aiming to follow the track to Reggan, a further hundred or so miles south. Shortly after Adrar the track divides and as Lancaster ended up at Aoulef, he almost certainly followed the wrong branch. Aouflet although well east of course, was within fifty miles or so of Reggan; so once more he set off, and again got lost, ending up back at Adrar. By now he was at least ten hours behind schedule and still had to refuel at Reggan before starting on the 700-mile leg to Gao.

It was well into the afternoon when he reached Reggan and with a strong wind blowing, he was strongly advised not to continue. But although physically exhausted, frustrated, and with all chance of the record gone, he would not listen. He left Reggan at four o'clock in the afternoon and in failing daylight, it would soon have become impossible to follow the track - and that was the last that was heard of him. When he didn't arrive at Gao, an air search instigated by the French authorities, was concentrated on the area round Gao where it was thought he had probably run out of petrol. The story ends twenty-nine years later. In 1962 his Avian *Southern Cross Minor*, was found by a French Army patrol forty miles off track, and only 170 miles south of Reggan. The aeroplane contained his skeleton and also a perfectly preserved diary that told how he had survived for eight days before succumbing to the heat of the desert by day, the cold by night, hunger and thirst. But more about crossing the Sahara later. In 1935 the Duchess and her pilot were to travel the same route in her Puss Moth, many restrictions imposed on them a direct result of the long and expensive search the French had laid on for Lancaster.

From Barcelona the Duchess and Allen flew to Marseilles where they spent the night, continuing to Cannes next morning. In the afternoon while being driven to Monte Carlo, their driver was involved in an accident for which the Duchess claimed, the other car was wholly to blame. *'We have flown hundreds of miles over mountains, deserts and seas only to have two narrow escapes of being smashed up when motoring and yet there are*

(Top) At the Guild of Air Pilots rally at Brooklands in May 1933, the Duchess's Puss Moth G-ABOC won the Concours d'Elegance for the second year running and was awarded the Tatler Cup. Judges included (l to r) Col H W Outram, Frederick (later Sir Frederick) Handley-Page and Mrs Nigel Norman. J B Allen is seen second from right.

(Above left) The Duchess receives the Tatler Cup from Mrs Shelmerdine, wife of the Director of Civil Aviation. She flew solo to Brooklands in her Gipsy Moth G-ABXR and was awarded a special prize for the smartest Lady's turn-out. Her Puss Moth was flown in by Allen

(Both photos Richard Riding Collection)

still people who consider flying a greater risk than motoring.' she commented. They reached home next day refuelling at Lyons and Lympne, the latter a leg of four hours and forty minutes, after probably the happiest tour the Duchess was ever to make.

May 1933 was a turning point in the life of the 'flying' Duchess. During the first two weeks of the month she put in several solo flights and on 2nd May, passing Hendon en route to *Whispers*, noted that she saw the wreck of Lord Knebworth's machine that had crashed the day before. On 16th May she again appeared before the Air Ministry Medical Board and this time they passed her. 'They refused it two years ago,' she wrote, 'ostensibly because of deafness; actually I believe on account of age, and now they have passed me two years later, when I am no less deaf and two years older (67). I had done fifty-three hours solo.' The Duchess, who had already passed the flying and technical tests required for a licence, lost no time in taking to the air in her own right.

She had entered as last year, both her Puss and her Gipsy Moths for the *Concours d'Elegance* competition organised by the Guild of Air Pilots at Brooklands. As proud possessor of a pilot's licence she could now fly there on her own so this year, she flew herself to Brooklands in the Gipsy Moth while Allen followed in the Puss. This, her first appearance in public as a pilot after all the months of waiting, must have been an extremely satisfying experience. The Puss Moth again won the Tatler Cup but a Special *Concours d'Elegance* Cup was awarded to the Duchess for the smartest aeroplane owned *and flown in* by a lady. *The Aeroplane* reported the occasion thus:

"The *Concours d'Elegance* was won for the second year in succession by Her Grace the Duchess of Bedford's Puss Moth. The Duchess also won a special prize for the smartest Lady's Turnout with her Moth, which she flew in singlehanded to the Meeting. We hope the Duchess will excuse us betraying the fact that she is 68 years of age. Her exploit on a day when the air was certain to be full of assorted craft at her destination was as courageous as it was creditably performed. When sought out at the request of the Prince (of Wales), she was found helping Flight Lieut. Allen her pilot, to put a final polish on the two aeroplanes."

Of the awards the Duchess wrote, 'my pilot certainly earned them with W Todd to help, for though they have both done over 200 hours flying, they looked like new.'

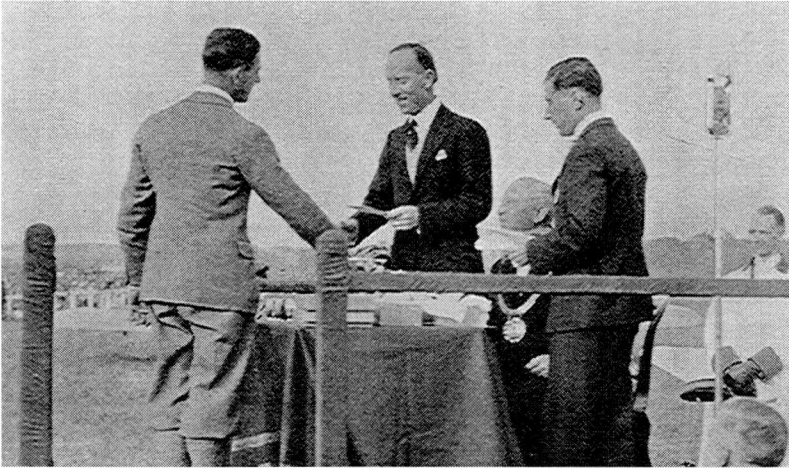

The Secretary of State for Air, Lord Londonderry, opening Liverpool
(Speke) airport on 1st July 1933. The Duchess, flying Gipsy Moth
G-ABXR, took part in an 'Arrival' competition associated with this
event. Allen, flying the Puss Moth, arrived thirteen seconds late and
won third prize. (Airman Friday)

Three weeks later the Duchess entered her Moths for
competitions at Eastbourne, where a Jubilee Rally was being
held to celebrate the town's fifty years as a Borough. This, an
altogether grander affair than the meeting at Brooklands,
included a large lunch at the Grand Hotel, with many
excessively long speeches, from which the Duchess escaped. She
recorded afterwards that she thought that *very* few people in
the world should be allowed to speak for more than twenty
minutes, then only if they could keep their listeners intensely
interested or amused. It was another successful outing for them
both, coming away as they did with two 'firsts' and one 'second'
prize.

Between June and September 1933 hardly a day passed
without the Duchess and Bernard Allen flying somewhere
together. They made excursions to Frinton, to Rugby and to
Liverpool and, on 26th June, the Duchess flew herself to
Ratcliffe for the annual luncheon given by Lindsay Everard for
flying members of the Houses of Parliament. Allen followed in
the Puss Moth. 'A rather wet and stormy day,' the Duchess
wrote, 'but cleared up after tent luncheon.' On 30th June she

positioned the Gipsy Moth at Lympne for the start next day of an 'Arrival' competition at Liverpool, which was being run in association with the opening of the airport by Lord London-derry. She returned to Woburn for the night in the back of the Puss Moth. The description in her diary shows exactly what was entailed in these competitions, which in the 1930s were commonly run by flying clubs.

'July 1st. - Left Woburn at seven am for Lympne in Puss. For Arrival competition we had to telephone from Lympne time we expected to arrive Liverpool calculated on correct speed of various machines and wind. we also had to take sealed envelope signed by responsible officer at the aerodrome from which we started, giving time left. I left at 8.31 am and arrived Liverpool at 11.37, two minutes thirty-seven seconds later than my time, which for first effort and such a long run was I think not bad. Flight Lieut. Allen won 3rd prize with thirteen seconds late, which we have reason to think was only four seconds as our watches had been set very accurately and both were same at end of day. He also won 3rd prize for Puss in *Concours d'Elegance*. We flew our respective machines back and arrived Woburn at 9.15 pm.'

The following day they were off again in the Gipsy Moth to Aldergrove, where the Duchess had been invited to watch an air display. They landed at Liverpool to refuel before setting off across the Irish Sea, where in deteriorating visibility they became unsure of their whereabouts. 'When we sighted land,' the Duchess wrote, 'my pilot did not know where he had got to. He suggested Mull of Galloway, but I knew that too well. We dipped to see the name of a station and saw 'Ballaugh', which we thought would do for Ireland, but could not find it on the map nor the railway running along the coast. Finally we had to land in a field and found we were in the Isle of Man! For many years I have wanted very much to visit it, but the present moment was not quite the right one and, as it was then 3.15 pm, there was nothing for it but to return to Liverpool.' However it was all for the best as here they found Barnard and Alliott with *The Spider*, in the area for a spot of joyriding. It was the first time the three had met up since parting company in Karachi at the end of the abortive flight to India in 1929, from which the Duchess had returned by sea. One can be sure, therefore, although nothing is recorded, that a happy and convivial evening was spent recalling old times.

On the afternoon of 5th July they flew to south Wales in the Puss Moth, en route to the Isle of Man. 'A lovely flight and to me all over new ground,' the Duchess wrote. 'It looked delightful birdwatching country on the southwest coast. The thousands of holiday-makers on the beaches with their bare pink limbs and light-coloured clothing looked from the air liked the sweets known as hundreds and thousands.' They spent the night at Port Erin, which the Duchess described as a 'rather nice little town.' 'I was pleasantly surprised,' she continued, 'to find what an attractive place the Isle of Man would be for birdwatching, with its nice sandy bays and cliffs. I had always pictured it overrun by the trippers and bungalows.' The following day they drove to Douglas to watch the motor racing which, she wrote, 'took place right through and round the town, a formidable proposition for the organizers. There were three crashes due to skidding, but only one where one or two of the crowd were injured and that, I gather, because they had pressed in where they should not have been.'

In the three weeks between 19th June and 8th July there was only one day on which the Duchess did not fly, either on her own or with Allen. On the 19th they took the Puss Moth to Amsterdam to see Mr Blaaw, who had not been well enough that year to visit them at Woburn. While there, the Duchess took the opportunity to take up a long-standing invitation to visit the Fokker works, where they were shown round by the firm's founder, Anthony Fokker. 'I was glad to meet this interesting little person,' the Duchess wrote, 'an entirely self-made man against parental and all other opposition. I had read his autobiography, which he told us he did not write himself. He is anxious to get a footing in England and thinks competition would do us a lot of good. Probably it would, but with the present opposition to foreigners and their imports it is not likely he will get it. He got permission for us to see the famous Aascher Diamond Cutting Works and came with us as he had not seen the process himself. We saw the whole of the operations from the diamond embedded in the rock to the finished gem. Cutting the Cullinan Diamond was entrusted to this firm.

'As service at Amstel Hotel abominable and the mattress of mechanically compressed straw quite the hardest I have ever attempted to sleep on for years, decided to spend second night in Brussels, where we fared better. We visited two galleries in Brussels in the morning and then flew back to Woburn. Had cup of tea then Flight Lieut. Allen and I flew the two Moths over to Reading, where the 'Puss' has to undergo its annual overhaul. *I returned in time to walk out with Herbrand, which completed a varied and well-filled day.*'

Shortly afterwards, another milestone was passed when the Duchess made a flight from the Park without her pilot around to see her off. Since gaining her pilot's licence, her confidence had grown steadily, with flying taking on a new dimension. The event was recorded in her diary thus:

'July 23rd - As Flight Lieut. Allen was away for the weekend and the weather is very hot, I decided to go out on a spree of my own in the Gipsy Moth. Though I have now done over 75 hours 'solo', this is my first venture from the Park entirely on my own. A trianguler (route) round Reading to Oxford was accomplished with success.'

At the beginning of August the two Moths were again entered for an 'Arrival' competition, this time at Scarborough. As before they elected to start from Lympne, where the Gipsy Moth was positioned overnight. This time, owing to bad visibility, the Duchess failed to make it. She wrote:

'August 7th. Flew down in Puss Moth with Flight Lieut. Allen to Lympne and left there in the 'Gipsy' for Scarborough at 8.35 am. Though a little misty and thick over the Thames and Blackwater, I was well up to time and getting on very nicely till I was near Halstead, when I flew into thick fog and had to rise above it. As there was clear blue sky above, I hoped it was only early-morning fog and that it would clear. But I flew on for fifty minutes and as it was getting higher and thicker, and as Scarborough is on the east coast and the aerodrome nine miles from it and not easy to find in bad weather, I felt compelled to turn at the Wash, or what by that time must have been the Wash, for of course I could not see it. I set my course SSW and when at last the fog began to get thinner, I went down through it and found myself close to Cardington Aerodrome. Not a bad shot for my first 'solo' navigation over fog. Flight Lieut. Allen, who in the faster machine had started an hour later than I did, found clear weather just over the Wash. It was a sad disappointment as I knew the route so well and was so well up to time that I had a good chance of winning a prize. Flight Lieut. Allen came back the richer by a beautiful silver cup, and silver flask and £30.'

On 8th September the Duchess left for *Cairnsmore* a week ahead of the Duke, to get in some local flying before the household arrived. Last year there were doubts because of the financial climate as to whether they could continue renting the house. As has been mentioned, Sir Keith Stewart, owner of *Cairnsmore* and other houses in the district, was having difficulty letting or selling and had made a special request to the Duke to continue renting *Cairnsmore*, if only for one year. 'It would have been a calamity to Sir Keith Stewart to have the place on his hands,' the Duchess wrote, 'so Herbrand has consented to take it by the year only, and by reducing expense hopes to keep it a little longer. *Dallash* has been sold to the Forestry Department, no great loss as there should be no building on it and a forest will in no way detract from the beauty of the valley.'

The day after arriving, the Duchess and Allen flew to Machrihanish, where they now found an official landing ground, laid out by Scottish Air Ferries, who were running a twice-daily service between Glasgow, Renfrew, Kintyre, Islay and Belfast. This was of great benefit to them as it meant that the Moth could now be left without worries as to its safety. Next day they flew to Oban, some two hundred miles north, to look for a field where they could land when, a few days later, they planned to attend the Oban games. 'Flight over lochs and mountains *most* lovely,' the Duchess wrote, 'and we found an excellent field for landing, just over the bridge which spans Loch Etive and *Mirabile Dictu*, not a soul came to visit the Moth apparently the whole time we left it there. Lunched at station hotel in Oban. Place does not seem an atom changed since I was here with *Sapphire* (her yacht, requisitioned at the outbreak of World War

157

One) except that there are a few small yachts. Despatched postcards to my old Captain and one or two who had been with me in the old days.'

Their next enterprise was to fly to Northern Ireland. 'Went with intention of seeing Giant's Causeway,' the Duchess recalled, 'but whatever it may be from land, we were not at all impressed from the air.' They were, however, much impressed by nearby Dunluce Castle and decided if possible to land and visit it. They managed to land safely in a not entirely suitable field, within a mile or so of the castle, from where they walked 'to the beautiful and romantically situated ruin, which with Whitby Abbey and Corfe Castle are three of the most impressive ruins I have ever seen in these islands, though looking down on them from above. Tintern Abbey, Melrose Abbey, Fountains and one I saw in the Yorkshire Dales must be equally beautiful. Flew home (to *Cairnsmore*) via Rathlin Island, which I last visited in *Sapphire*.'

Next day while out in the Duchess's old Rolls-Royce the axle casing broke - the first time, she said, it had let her down in twenty years. This no doubt put an end to any plans they might have had that day for flying. The following day they returned to Oban to watch the Oban Games. The Duchess was particularly impressed with the caber tossing and the fact that it took *four* men to carry the caber back after each throw. They spent two nights in Oban and of the return journey the Duchess wrote:

'I returned to *Cairnsmore* flying via Inverarary and Loch Lomond and I can safely say that in all my travels I have never seen anything more beautiful than that flight over lochs and mountains. I have seen mountains on a much larger scale, snow scenery, which is wholly different, and weird and wonderful deserts and mountains, but none excelled this flight in actual beauty, as I saw it all in glorious weather. We had a few uneasy moments between Inverarary and Loch Lomond. I started over this part at 4,000 feet, but finding I was losing height opened more throttle - this had no effect whatever and we lost 1,000 feet in a few minutes. Fortunately we were nearing Loch Lomond, where things soon righted themselves. But we were being sucked down by a down-draught owing to the precipitous mountains and very narrow valleys. However, it was worth the

The Duchess hired Monospar G-ACKT from the General Aircraft Company to compete in the 'Tour of the Oases' competition in December 1933. It is seen here in the hangar at Croydon.
(A J Jackson Collection)

short-lived anxiety, though I shall give it another 1,000 feet next time!'

Shortly after they got back the family party arrived and the following day Allen returned south with the Moth. 'So no more flying for the next two months probably,' wrote the Duchess, 'I have done 332 hours since March 19th and over 100 hours solo.'

Herbrand and the household returned to Woburn on 11th November; the Duchess flew back a day later. She had entered the 'Tour of the Oases' Air Rally, which was to be held in Cairo in December and for which the General Aircraft Company had lent her one of their Monospars, a twin-engined monoplane fitted with Pobjoy engines. For this event the aeroplane had been painted in her colours and registered in her name and on 15th November they flew down to Croydon to see it. 'It looks awfully nice in my green,' the Duchess wrote, 'Much more attractive to my mind than any other Monospar I have seen. I do not think we will have a chance of winning such a big competition but it will be fun competing.' Sadly, this was not to be.

On 6th December Allen flew the Monospar up to the Pobjoy factory at Hooton Park on the south bank of the Mersey for a final engine check before leaving for Egypt. Allen, looking forward very much to the trip, would have been in high spirits when he left Hooton on his return down south. Leaving later than was planned, he arrived at Woburn after dark, without warning them of his impending late arrival. Weather in the south that evening was not of the best; it had been a day of east wind and clear sky and, as the sun went down, ground mist followed. Charles Gardner, King's Cup winner in 1936 and 1937, left Hooton for Croydon at much the same time, also in a Monospar. As he approached London he ran into bad visibility, low cloud and even experienced carburettor icing. When Allen appeared over Woburn with navigation and landing lights flashing, action was immediately taken to light a flare, but before this was done Allen had disappeared to the east. He crashed nose-down in a field at Thrupps End Farm, near Lidlington, only three miles from the Park. One theory was that, flying low to establish his position, he stalled when suddenly confronted with some unlit power lines. Had his seat-belt been fastened he might, it was thought, have survived with broken legs, but as it was he was thrown forward and fatally injured, dying shortly afterwards in Bedford Hospital. 'As a pilot,' C G Grey wrote in *The Aeroplane*, 'Bernard Allen was certainly one of the best and most careful in the country. The pity is all the greater that he should have been killed in an accident that might have been avoided if only he had not been intent on getting back to Bedford that particular night. And even so, the accident might not have happened if only he had reached the point at which high-tension cables are properly marked at night. Without playing up for popularity, Bernard Allen was liked wherever he went, and he made numbers of friends wherever he worked. By his death aviation has lost a most valuable worker and many of us have lost a very good friend.'

The Duchess noted in her diary that, but for an appointment, she would have been with him and if she had been, one feels, the accident might well never have occurred. 'He is a terrible loss,' she wrote, 'as we have had such *lovely* flights together, and all his work for me has been all that could be wished for and I have lost not only a skilled pilot but a loyal and trusted friend. He has had a very sad life for many years and I think enjoyed his flying times with me, but for him I try to feel that it is best that he is now at rest. I have now flown 1,819 hours, most of which have been with him.

Monospar G-ACKT after the crash at Lidlington, Bedfordshire on 5th December 1933 and in which Flight Lieutenant J B Allen, returning to Woburn from Hooton Park, was killed.

(A J Jackson Collection)

'So ends a chapter of my flying times which I think we both enjoyed equally. For him it has been the best of deaths for an airman to die, and suffering for the tragedy is only for those who knew him.'

The story of 'JB', as he was known to the Woburn staff, has a somewhat curious ending, remembered clearly by Todd's then schoolgirl daughter Audrey. Allen's marriage had not been a happy one and at the time of the accident his wife was not living with him. His house, Froxfield, was being run by a Mr and Mrs Prestwood. On the morning of the crash a Gipsy woman called at the house and asked to see 'the Master'. The Prestwoods fobbed her off and she went away, only to return three times. 'It's absolutely imperative,' she told them, 'that I see the Master to stop him going on a journey.' One must however doubt whether, even if he had met the Gipsy, Allen would have changed his plans. Sadly, such warnings tend to be recognised only after the event.

Chapter Ten

1934: Bathurst and Grand Canary

For the Duchess, life was never quite the same. In Bernard Allen she had found a kindred spirit and where ever they went and whatever they did, they enjoyed it equally; it was a truly happy relationship. But flying had become both her means of transport and her main recreation, a part of her life from which there could be no going back. So while deeply mourning the loss of Allen, she lost little time in seeking a replacement and within a month, had engaged as her Flight Manager, Flight Lieutenant Raphael Chevallier Preston.

Preston, an Ulsterman, had served in the Army until 1917 when he learnt to fly and transferred to the Royal Flying Corps. After the war he remained in the Royal Air Force, serving in Palestine and later as a flying instructor, at Cranwell and with No.502 Squadron at Aldergrove, Northern Ireland. On leaving the RAF he became personal pilot to the Honourable 'Freddie' Guest, former Secretary of State for Air, with whom he flew round East and South Africa. Someone who knew him recalls that he possessed the Irish characteristics of being quite unpredictable, liking his own way, able to turn on the charm when he wanted and equally capable of sulking when he didn't get what he wanted. A public school boy, Preston was by both background and experience a very different character from either Barnard or Allen. He was older - 41 years of age - much travelled and above all accustomed to organising, none of which really suited the Duchess. She was not endowed by nature with an excess of patience and was anxious to get the matter settled. His flying qualifications could not be questioned and she allowed herself to be swayed, in the absence of other suitable candidates, by the fact that through the Monospar, he had become friendly with Allen. Nevertheless, an excellent judge of character, she took him on largely against her better judgement, as will be seen from the following correspondence in which many doubts expressed, proved in the fullness of time to be all too well founded. In the meantime as there could never be another Allen, she was perhaps wise not to spend too much time looking for one.

At the time of Allen's death Preston, somewhat at a loose end, was working at Croydon as test pilot for General Aircraft, the company that had leased the Monospar for the 'Tour of the Oases' rally. As well as knowing Allen therefore he had also met the Duchess and, as a matter of courtesy, attended Allen's funeral. He also sent a note of sympathy to the Duchess offering to return her Puss Moth that Allen had left at Croydon on the morning of the crash, at the same time applying for Allen's job. The somewhat unseemly speed with which he did this can be judged by the fact that the Duchess's reply is dated only six days after Allen's death. It read as follows:-

"December 12th, 1933 - Dear Mr Preston; I wonder if you quite realise how very much tied my Pilot is? I am a radiographer for this district and a pretty wide area, and also Assistant to my two London surgeons at all operations in the hospital. I am frequently at work there most of the day and look upon flying as my almost daily recreation. The hours for it are entirely irregular and depend on the work of the day, and though I always let Flt. Lt. Allen know as early as possible it was only a day by day arrangement. Then owing to my deafness, I am very dependent on my Pilot when I travel, and he was always in very close attendance and did everything for me. I have difficulty in hearing my own language and a foreign one is impossible. Of course he had a good long holiday when I was in Scotland."

On 1st January she wrote again still expressing reservations;

"Woburn Abbey, January 1st, 1934. I am really sorry to be so long in making up my mind about my Pilot but every time I try to fix up an interview and a flight, we have this fog and owing to other engagements there are so few days on which I can fly just now. There is a lot of shooting to get through and we have already lost three days through fog over that. I can only ask you not to forgo trying to get another appointment on my account. I only ask to be given first refusal if it is a choice between being my Pilot or some post you care less for. Your own personality and abilities give me no qualms and if I select any other pilot it will not be on that account."

Three days later the Duchess wrote in her diary that she had tried another pilot but had not liked him at all. Though still in the Royal Air Force and at the end of twenty years flying, he had been unable to taxi the Moth straight and on take-off, had treated it 'like a high-powered RAF machine'. Later that day she wrote again to Preston whose application, despite her doubts, she had not yet ruled out.

"Woburn Abbey, January 4th, 1934. - I think I must tell you why I am hovering over your application to be my pilot. First of all I am sure that your family could not get into Flt. Lt. Allen's house, and we have no other to offer now. The only other which in time might be made possible would need bathrooms made and other alterations and when done, would be far less convenient for me. If there was any question about weather or plans I could run down in my motor, blow my horn at his garden gate and we could discuss it so much better than on the telephone. Then he could at any time run down to the hangar in five minutes. For me this was a great blessing as it meant no loss of time to speak of when going to or from my Hospital as I do almost daily.

"Perhaps you will feel that if it were you, you would be just as well if you were a little farther off! But I have not taken this into account when hovering over your election. Secondly, I derive two-thirds of my pleasure when flying abroad from going somewhere which gives my pilot pleasure also. If I felt he were going only where I wanted because he was paid for it, I would not enjoy myself a bit. Flight Lieut. Allen had been very little abroad (only in the War) before he came to me. Being pretty deaf also, he never cared about going amongst strangers socially. I can only get away for quite short holidays and then it is a relief to get away from radiography, theatre work, a big household and the eternal struggle to listen to people I cannot hear. Therefore when I go away I like to fly most of the time unless there are expeditions to make or places to see and mountains and deserts meet the case! This suited him down to the ground, but I have a feeling that you have travelled so much that you would probably far rather go and see a little more of your fellow creatures. I should feel that you were bored though I know you would try not to show it."

Having by now interviewed a number of even less suitable applicants, although clearly foreseeing the problems likely to arise between them, she wrote again to Preston as follows:-

"Woburn Abbey, January 6th, 1934 - I have had a feeling at the back of my mind all along that it had to be you and so I have decided that it must be! It may amuse you to hear that my mechanic (Todd) decided for you some time ago. After witnessing some rather painful episodes with trial Pilots he said 'If your Grace will pardon my saying so, I should have thought Flt. Lieut. Preston was the Pilot for you. He is more like Flt. Lieut. Allen!'

"You received quite the wrong impression about the shooting and fishing. The Duke used to be a very good shot but is now quite blind in one eye and sees very little with either. He is also very decidedly getting on in years. Still, when he can see birds well against the sky he still shoots well. He does not like inviting outside guests to help with our big shoots, partly because it almost compels one to go out whatever the weather, and partly because he is naturally rather sensitive about his shooting. It therefore all devolves on me and it is a pretty hard job at times especially as I can so seldom go out. I taught Captain Barnard to shoot and at times when we really needed a 3rd gun, he used to come as he loved doing it, but Flt. Lt. Allen was one of those who never cared to take the life of anything, so I never pressed his learning to.

"The fishing was only referred to because at times you might be spending a day or two in Devon or Scotland with us and you would probably be intensely bored. For many years I have been too deaf to do any calling or entertaining and the Duke has never been socially inclined and is moreover shy. Therefore our establishment is a very dull one for an unfortunate compulsory guest unless he can amuse himself.

"Doubtless you and Mrs Preston would like to see the house and if so would you give us the pleasure of coming to luncheon on Thursday 11th at 1.45 pm?"

Would that today a prospective employee could find himself thus addressed!

When Ralph Preston, his wife and children moved into Froxfield House on 30th January, he had already made a couple of flights with the Duchess. After twenty-five years, flying for him had become little more than a business and as a flying instructor, he was used to flying by the rules. Climbing above clouds to see a sunset or flying low for the sheer joy of it was no longer his form and this deprived the Duchess of much that with her previous pilots, she had especially enjoyed. Also, as she had foreseen, he was more gregarious than suited her, meeting old colleagues wherever he went and involving her with people whom she had little interest in meeting, when she would have preferred to be on her own. His lack of interest in country pursuits and his preference for sitting and sketching rather than sightseeing, meant that on the ground he was no companion for her. However, because of his undisputed qualifications as a pilot, she accepted him as he was. It is of some significance that until now, the Duchess had filled in times and places in her pilot's log book; from now on, however, Preston kept, and filled in, this very personal document for her.

Nevertheless the Duchess's pattern of flying during the Spring of 1934 remained much as before. In February she resumed her solo flying and by the end of March, had accumulated 105 solo hours. Meanwhile, Preston felt it to be part of his duty to organise trips for her. Thus on 21st March, he arranged a flight to Bircham Newton near Kings Lynn, to visit a British Industries Fair. On the strength of her name, he obtained invitations to a large business lunch at which the Duchess was the only women present among 300 to 400 heads of business firms. 'I was afterwards presented to a very affable Lord Mayor and taken to the Lady Mayoress's parlour,' she wrote, 'a very pleasant, unassuming lady. I was subsequently photographed many times which no doubt will result in some awful mementos of the occasion.'

On 7th April they set out on an ambitious tour down the West Coast of Africa. There can have been few private aircraft that at the time had flown a route that took them through Spanish Rio de Oro (or the 'Rio de Orror' as Preston preferred to call it), the

The Duchess with her aircraft on the tarmac at le Bourget.
(DH Gazette)

French provinces of Mauritania and Senegal and finally Bathurst (Banjul), in the small British colony of Gambia. The Duchess wrote:-

'April 7th, 1934 - After the usual harrowing time of preparation for a long flight, consequent on trying to combine a clearing up of X-ray work with dress fittings, etc. etc. in London, I left with my new pilot for Orleans. The landing at Orleans was somewhat bumpy but I think it must have been a bad bit of the aerodrome as we never found it so before. The man in charge immediately produced a very good photo of J B Allen and myself taken two years ago. It is rather wonderful how these men immediately recognise an aeroplane.'

Their next night-stops were at Barcelona, which Preston thought very dull, and Grenada, places with which the Duchess was by now familiar. At Alicante. where they stopped to refuel, the manager of a small café which had recently opened produced a photograph of the Duchess and Barnard in their Moth at Malaga, taken during her memorable first flight abroad in 1927. Preston was more interested in a Lufthansa Heinkel mail plane that arrived while they were there, en route from Malaga to Marseilles. 'With flaps down she landed well,' he wrote, 'but when she went off and returned over the aerodrome downwind with undercarriage retracted, she fairly shook the local inhabitants who had evidently seen nothing like it. She is something to be proud of though - and they say she is making a new record on this trip.'

At Grenada they stayed in the Hotel Alhambra and Preston as was his wont at most places they stopped, sat down and sketched. The Duchess, ever mindful of her pilot's enjoyment, regretted that for Preston's first visit to Grenada, the weather was so cloudy and wet; nevertheless they managed a tour of the Alhambra. At Tangier, their next refuelling point, it was bucketing with rain and sheets of spray were put up by the aeroplane as it hit puddles on the muddy surface. To the Duchess's 'chagrin', Preston had failed to order petrol in advance so as there was no waiting room or restaurant, they had a long, wet wait until it arrived from the town. 'I wonder that Tangier is not better served,' the Duchess wrote, 'as it is the crossing place for North and Western Africa. Probably the reason is that it is everyone's land and therefore nobody does anything. Very uninteresting flight to Casablanca. R.C.P. and I walked out in the evening and sat in an outdoor restaurant to watch passers-by.'

They spent two nights in Casablanca. On the first morning, while Preston carried out a routine inspection of the Puss, the Duchess sat in the hotel garden 'surrounded by tortoises.' For the rest of the day they were entertained, as became routine with her new pilot, by the local Shell Company representatives. They left early the following morning for Agadier and Cape Juby in the Rio De Oro.

The Duchess described her experiences at the Spanish military outposts of Cape Juby and Port Etienne, and at French controlled Dakar in considerable detail that still makes interesting reading:

'April 12th - Left for Capo Juby (alias Cape Juby). Very flat and uninteresting country at first then mountains along the coast, but somewhat thick so couldn't see much. Passed Mogador lighthouse and landed Agadier for petrol. A good aerodrome. After leaving Agadier we were instructed to keep near to the coast in case of a forced landing as natives not disposed to be friendly inland. Cape Juby nothing but a Fort and barracks set in the desert and I believe, a convict settlement. Lodged in grubby rooms in barracks but invited to dine in Fort. CO spoke no French or English so had to get No.2 to interpret into French except when I aired my best Spanish! R.C.P. and I walked along the shore before dinner and saw some strange jellyfish with Zeppelin shaped iridescent blue bags which exploded with a loud report when trodden on. There were gulls and waders, *but with a companion who is devoid of ornithologocal interest it is impossible to watch birds.* Our dinner with the Officers was peculiar but they must have to live very largely on tinned food in these desert stations. Our first dish was some species of tinned cabbage, then we had fresh fried fish, then what Flight Lieut. Preston suggested were hunks of camel, and finally tinned peas.

'I breakfasted off some very awful coffee with tinned milk of the consistency of thickened oil which was quite too much for me, and what appeared to be dog biscuits, but I was relieved to find that they did not require a hammer and chisel and were soft enough for me to eat the corner of one. One is fortunate to find any accommodation in these desert stations and were it not for the hospitality shown one, one could not at present fly this way. Therefore if I describe things in this diary as I found them it is not through any feeling of ingratitude or desire to criticize, but only to show what others must expect who follow in our footsteps, and what the life is that the officers and their wives have to lead. The life must be particularly hard for the women as there is nothing but desert around them, and they cannot walk; they have no outdoor games and no cars. Some of these have spent several years here and none to whom I spoke expected less than two. It is noticeable however that the French do themselves better under the circumstances than the Spaniards - or is it that their ideas of comfort coincide more with my own?

'The bedrooms we occupied in the barracks had stone-flagged floors which may at times have seen a broom but rarely water I should say; for water in these places may be very strictly rationed and brought from a great distance. The one window usually does not open and air is admitted through the open door only. There is a bedstead with what, to a pampered mortal like

169

myself, seems an incredibly hard mattress and my *Bete Noire*, a bolster. This by the way is popular in most European hotels and I try to fathom why? A second pillow would not cost more and the well-filled bolster is about the most uncomfortable fitting imaginable. A wash-basin is provided, one or two small chairs, a table and sometimes a small cupboard and an allowance of water for minor ablutions. The sanitary arrangements are the weak point and it is preferable when they are external and conspicuous, rather than in the greater privacy of the building one occupies. But as a rule, this is not in accordance with the architect's design. The above description does not of course apply to the officers own quarters, which may be furnished with as much comfort as the situation permits or their tastes decree, but there is no luxury even here.

'April 13th - I rose at 3.20 am as I thought the outside air would be more wholesome. We had a very desolate flight along the shore to Villa Cisneros, absolutely flat desert all the way, and we flew too high to see anything but Flamingos. Warned to speak Spanish and not French if we had a forced landing. The Fort is on a thin peninsular, and there is nothing but the Fort and hangar and a large settlement of tented natives. I was persuaded to go into one of their tents and though it was so dark I could see little, it was more orderly than I expected from its external appearance. I will not say - clean. The Commandant invited us to luncheon with his wife and four children. The luncheon was quite good. The language question was again a difficulty as the Commandant's French was rendered more difficult to understand through an absence of teeth on one side of his mouth. *But he was not shy and neither is R.C.P.* and they got along quite cheerfully and without too much embarrassment. On arrival at Port Etienne we were very kindly received by French ladies and given really good coffee, fruit and chocolates. We were lodged in the Commandant's quarters and dined with him and another officer. He was rather a stiff young man and gave me the idea of being impressed by his authority. He commanded 100 Senalgese troops. The Fort was surrounded by barbed wire. There was big native encampment, the occupants of which seemed to live largely by fishing. We were driven down to the shore before dinner, and it seemed to be a rather unheard-of proceeding that we were anxious to walk back for the sake of exercise.

'Flight Lieut. Preston brought a backgammon board with him which has been a great solace on these occasions, and we filled up the time with it till dinner. We had a very good dinner though I should be puzzled to say what constituted some of it, and we taught our host the English method of playing backgammon.'

Preston for his part wrote, 'Port Etienne is no place to linger and I propose on return, to try out the domesticated Governor of Villa Cisneros instead; however we shall see.' So after lunch they took off for Thiers, a big military aviation camp and the outpost for Dakar; the flight took three and a half hours. But back to the Duchess's diary:

'April 14th - Left Port Etienne shortly after nine am and pursued our way south along the coast. Desert on one side and very blue sea on the other, a combination which for all its lack of variety, never bores me as do the miles and miles of hedgeless, treeless, flat, cultivated country one meets with in many parts of Europe. The sky is a shade deeper blue than the sea and the horizon disappears in mist, where the shore shelves gradually into the sea; the colours are often very beautiful below water. I again saw large flocks of Flamingoes and they are not likely to become extinct for a very long time, seeing that these desolate regions suffice them for livelihood. The marvel is that they should ever survive at home out of doors, as some of ours did for some years. In parts for miles there is not even camel-thorn growing.

'We landed at Thiers where we had a long wait for permission to go on to Dakar. The French guard this neighbourhood very carefully and one is only allowed to fly up one side of the peninsular. R.C.P.'s camera was sealed up. My own was not discovered but needless to say I did not take advantage of the fact; I was however offered the use of one whilst waiting there by the Consul. Whilst waiting for our permission we were given cool drinks and then invited to lunch-tea at the local Governor's house. It was a very pretty drive to it down avenues of Baobab trees and the streets were gay and picturesque with crowds of natives in their many-coloured garments.'

'The Governor's house was delightful,' the Duchess wrote, 'and his wife a most charming little lady, who gave us an excellent meal. On returning to the aerodrome we were told that we had been invited to stay at Government House, Dakar and we soon started off once more.'

At Dakar, forewarned of their coming, they were met, much to the Duchess's discomfort, by the Governor's ADC, the Consul General and agents from Shell, Air France and the local paper. She would, she said, have much preferred to stay in a quiet hotel, but they were committed to the Residency. She wrote later, 'We were given delightful quarters in a separate building from the Palace, and it was indeed a contrast to our accommodation of the last few days, the large bath being especially appreciated. Our hosts, the Governor-General of Afrique Occidentale Francaise and his wife Mme Bremie, were charming people but unfortunately spoke no English, so I had to make myself as civil and appreciative as I could in French.' The first evening they had a quiet dinner with the Governor-General and his wife, a lady-in-waiting and the ADC.

Next morning the Duchess accompanied Preston to the aerodrome from where after attending to the Moth, they returned to the Palace for a lunch party where they were introduced to the Algerian dish *cous-cous*. 'Very good,' the Duchess wrote, 'but from the quantity of its ingredients calculated to stem the appetite of most people; but much more followed of which after our recent frugal meals, it was somewhat difficult to take even a civil quantity.' Preston too recorded their stay at the Palace by writing, 'It was a beautiful dinner and the table decorations were quite lovely. The centrepiece was a four-inch slab of green glass which looked like ice, with three diagonal thick glass vases or troughs overflowing with roses. Wines of all varieties were poured into ones glass by dextrous Senegalese servants and we finished with champagne. What we ate I cannot say but it was superb cuisine. Similarly at lunch today which was taken at twelve noon with several other guests, glorious cooking. One dish, Cous-cous, a native concoction was a feast in itself. His Excellency is an engaging personality, long beard and perfect manners. It is sad that Her

Grace has to miss so much of what goes on but they made all possible efforts to ensure her entertainment.'

After lunch the Consul General drove them round Dakar, which the Duchess described as a thriving town with College, hospital and other institutions. 'Except for the heat of the sun at midday,' she wrote, 'it is difficult to realise that we are nearing tropical Africa. But nights positively cold and woolly garment needed after sundown.'

That evening, a dinner was laid on for them by the Consul General; this was also attended by their hosts from the Palace. At the dinner much to her embarrassment, the Duchess found herself on the right hand of the Governor-General, giving her precedence over his wife who was sitting on his left. Preston later wrote of the tricky situation that arose as a consequence. After dinner, the Governor assuming that the Duchess had precedence, waited for her to move first. The Duchess however was waiting for His Excellency to move so that at the end of the meal, they sat on and on and on. Eventually Preston, realising that the Duchess would never move before the Governor, had words with the Vice Consul's wife who had words with the Consul General. He in turn had words with Mrs Bremie, after which the Governor-General rose. The Duchess wrote:

'April 16th - We went up to the Palace at nine am to say 'Good-bye' to our host and hostess, and the Governor-General gave me a book about this part of Africa. We left Dakar at 10.30 am arriving at Cape St. Mary Aerodrome, Bathurst after only one hours flight. Here for the first time one felt really conscious of being in tropical Africa, palm forest, swamps, gorgeous birds, monkeys and glorious gardens of tropical flowers and a sun which makes itself felt in spite of the wind which never abates, at all events at this season. Two Officers here in charge of 150 men of West African Defence Force. Only about 750 sq. miles of the Island of Gambia but our Protectorate goes some 250 miles up river. Only bad month October at other times, heat tempered by wind. Delightful Mess and 'Garden of Eden' close at hand. Below low sandy cliff and a very deep blue sea and deeper sky. Parrots and other gorgeously plumaged birds and beautiful butterflies flit around. Gambia a protected area for birds and beasts. Long drive to Government House, where we have been invited to stay, through palm forests, swamps and over a river. Our hosts Mr and Mrs Richards (later Lord and Lady Milverton), have only just been transferred from Borneo and arrived here only two days before us. Mrs Richards even displayed an uncertainty as to the way up to my room, I fear we must have been *very* inconvenient visitors, though we were most emphatically not made conscious of it. Here again we were of course lodged 'in the purple', and all our surroundings English, the whole place indoors and out made me feel very much that I was back in my girlhood days in India, but with the inevitable sadness that the 'girlhood' was the one thing lacking. One misses the picturesque native turban, replaced by sun helmet ie. Solar Topee. Even woolly-heads who further down south wear nothing, adopt this. In afternoon R.C.P. played tennis and I wandered round trying to identify birds. Found a flying fox in my bedroom on arrival. At Government House Dakar and here, quinine handed round at dinner but residents didn't seem to take it, so probably not needed at this time of year.'

Preston wrote of their stay in Bathurst as a peaceful two days:

'Yesterday, I went off to Cape St. Mary where the aerodrome is, and spent the morning on the machine (more beer in delightful Mess) then in the evening we played some tennis - the first evening on an asphalt court and the second on a grass one - neither particularly good but good fun and exercise. Mrs R. is a very strong player and I fancy HE will get the courts in good order as they are keen. The weather for the time of year is cool, certainly at the moment I would call it ideal, but the old residents shake their heads. Apparently about October it is a miserable country. The birds make up for the interest lacking in big game; colours and the noises they make are quite in excess of any one sees in East Africa. Incidentally, birds protected here; no shooting allowed. Also there are dozens of little flying foxes which hang head downwards by a prehensile tail from palm trees. There are many strange trees and lovely flowers and even the natives are more colourful than the Eastern gentlemen, the ladies especially dolling themselves up in all manner of bandana of gorgeous hues. The Duchess is in seventh heaven with it all and it is a pity we cannot stay a little longer as there is so much of interest to her.'

In the West African Defence Force Mess adjacent to the aerodrome, Preston would have been in his element. 'R.C.P. spent the morning at the Mess overhauling the Moth.,' the Duchess wrote of the morning after their arrival. 'I had lovely time watching birds but no books to identify. So wonderful being in a tropical forest and should have loved to spend a month in Bathurst.'

Six months earlier, Bathurst had received two other flying visitors. Charles Lindberg and his wife Anne Morrow Lindberg had paid an unscheduled visit in their single-engined Lockheed Sirius float-plane. Unscheduled because they were planning to cross the South Atlantic by the shortest possible route, from the Cape Verde islands to Natal on the east coast of Brazil. In the Cape Verde Isles however, rollers and trade winds made problems enough for landing on the sea, but after three highly uncomfortable days and nights during which they had been forced to sleep on their aircraft, it had become clear that conditions were such that in no way were they going to be able to take off with the fuel load necessary for the Atlantic crossing. There was no alternative for them therefore but to return to mainland Africa. A radio message to Dakar seeking permission to land elicited a negative response as they had a yellow fever epidemic. Thus Bathurst, a British Colony completely unknown to them became the next possibility and in reply to a request to land there, the Morse operator in Porto Praia received the very British reply, '. .*Pleased to grant authorisation . . . kindly advise time arrival.*' After the nightmare of the past few days they could hardly believe their luck.

Even before they had tied up to a buoy in the Gambia, a motor boat had appeared to bring them ashore to where a car waited to take them to Government House. 'Here we are again,' Anne Lindberg, who was also a flying diarist, wrote, 'with the English taking care of us. How they love to take care of people. I suppose that is why their colonies are so well run. . . We were driving down well-paved streets lined by freshly whitewashed houses with tin roofs and green shutters. Cement posts marked off the lots. Trees evenly spaced shaded the sidewalks. Carts

175

and cars and people on bicycles filled the road keeping well to the left. Negro women in wide calico skirts, children strapped to their backs and baskets on their heads; Negro men with their European shirts hanging outside like tunics; men in sun-helmets, in fezes, in large straw basket-hats; women with only cloth skirts around their hips and bandannas on their heads - all jostling and hurrying along the sidewalks as if they had some work to finish or some place to go. Life was going on here; it meant something. Policemen in white uniforms and sun-helmets stood on the corners. Here was a fenced off cricket ground, a grandstand, a British flag. It all breathed of peace and security. I remarked on this fact. It certainly feels good to be on British territory my husband agreed.' And before World War II, that was the way it was in this and many another British colony.'

After two nights they left again for St. Louis. 'I should have loved to stay longer,' the Duchess wrote, 'and seen more of the forest and swamps, but as my hosts had so recently arrived I did not like to suggest staying longer than one whole day, though they were both so charming that I think they would gladly have kept us. A trip up the Gambia in a boat would be wildly interesting. So we leave the flesh-pots and return for a brief space to the hospitality of those whose lives have not fallen in such pleasant places. It was sad to be leaving tropical Africa when we seemed only just to have found it, but on the West Coast there is such a vast area of desert to fly over, devoid even of camel-thorn for much of the way (i.e. it appears to be so from the height at which we fly), that one gets little but the arid side of tropical Africa and little or nothing of its beauty till one comes to Dakar. *I think a short cut over the Sahara to Sierra Leone would be a better way even if attended by more risk.'*

It took them two hours against a strong headwind to reach St. Louis, a one-time busy port at the mouth of the Senegal river. Flying at 4,000 feet above the dust haze the Duchess said she had never felt hotter in the air before. Having been told that the only available hotel was far too dirty for them to stay in, they accepted hospitality from the local Shell Agent.

Before dinner Preston and the Duchess walked by the deserted harbour on their way to send a telegram and there met a superior-looking youth who turned out to be the Governor's ADC. He told them that the Governor, who had intended asking them to stay at Government House, was not expecting them until next day and was out of town. 'So,' the Duchess wrote, 'we returned to our quarters and had a dinner of good soup and a weird omelette with crusts of fried bread in it. I fear the Diary treats largely of food but travelling as we were for some 1,500 miles over the desert, there is not much to write about in the day except food and accommodation, and the strong contrasts we experienced both in quality and quantity provoke one to lay rather more stress on it than in fact we really did. Except when living *en Prince*, we rarely had more than a biscuit or dry roll for breakfast and some almost if not quite undrinkable tea or coffee; no luncheon, and perhaps a cup of tea. We were therefore not otherwise than ready for dinner.'

They left St. Louis for Port Etienne early next morning after a restless night in which they were kept awake by barking dogs. They had been flying for about an hour when the engine spluttered and then stopped altogether. They were at the time at some 6,000 feet so while descending, Preston tried various ways of clearing what appeared an obvious fuel stoppage - but to no avail. He had no option therefore but to land which he did successfully in a large salt pan. It took him some 45 minutes to clear the jets watched throughout by a distant group of Arabs, they then took off again for Port Etienne, where they landed in half a gale. After a quick lunch with the aerodrome manager - which the Duchess commented must be very difficult to provide as everything they eat is tinned - they continued to Villa Cisneros. Here while Preston was given a room in the barracks, the Duchess was invited by the Spanish Commandant to stay in his quarters where they allocated her the room of his two daughters. On reaching the quarters, however, she found the whole place so basic and unsanitary that she hastily excused herself saying that she would *hate* to disturb the girls, and that if there was room, she would be *quite* happy to stay in the barracks. Never, the Duchess said, had she been more thankful for primitive barrack quarters! 'What a state of filth for a sophisticated person like the Spanish Commandant to live in.' was Preston's comment. 'The whole place smelt of an unclean lavatory and the pigsty in which this family lives had to be seen to be believed. Two days growth, a few yellow decayed teeth and filthy white overalls don't somehow fit in with ones idea of Governors. I swear I will send the Governor a toothbrush and a razor as a thank-you offering! Never mind,' he continued, 'Her Grace and I have had some good laughs over it all and as nobody had any English, it was possible to get some quiet asides without offending anyone's feelings.'

During the night, banging doors and creaking shutters made them fear that they might be stuck there for a couple of days. The wind proved to be less bad than it sounded and by eight am they were off with few regrets to Cape Juby, where they planned to refuel and get a weather report, before setting off for Grand Canary. At Cape Juby, fuel was available but no weather report but having by now had their fill of Spanish hospitality, they decided to press on without even stopping for a meal.

Another two and a half hours flying saw them at Gando in Grand Canary where, as the radio station had broken down, they were not expected. The Duchess wrote:-

'We flew over banks of cloud as we approached the Canaries, but the actual landing was clear. It was dreadfully windy and there was no hangar for a landplane, so the Moth had to be tethered and covered up with folded wings, all of which required some care in the high wind. Nobody had heard of our coming so there was no one in charge of the landing-ground and no car. However, in my best Spanish I prevailed upon a man to go and telephone for one. It is a long drive to the town (Las Palmas) fully an hour, and not a particularly pretty one. The Hotel Metropole where we stayed was good.'

It was while they were at Gando that Preston discovered two holes in the fabric of both upper and lower sides of the right wing. They were later assumed to be bullet holes that luckily had missed the fuel tank. As they had been flying at 6,000 feet they were somewhat puzzled about how the holes had got there, but were told later that the rifles used by the Moors could easily reach this height.

Private aeroplanes at that time were something of a novelty in the Canaries, so that the residents who had little else to do, paid Preston and the Duchess almost embarrassing attention.

Bathurst, 1934

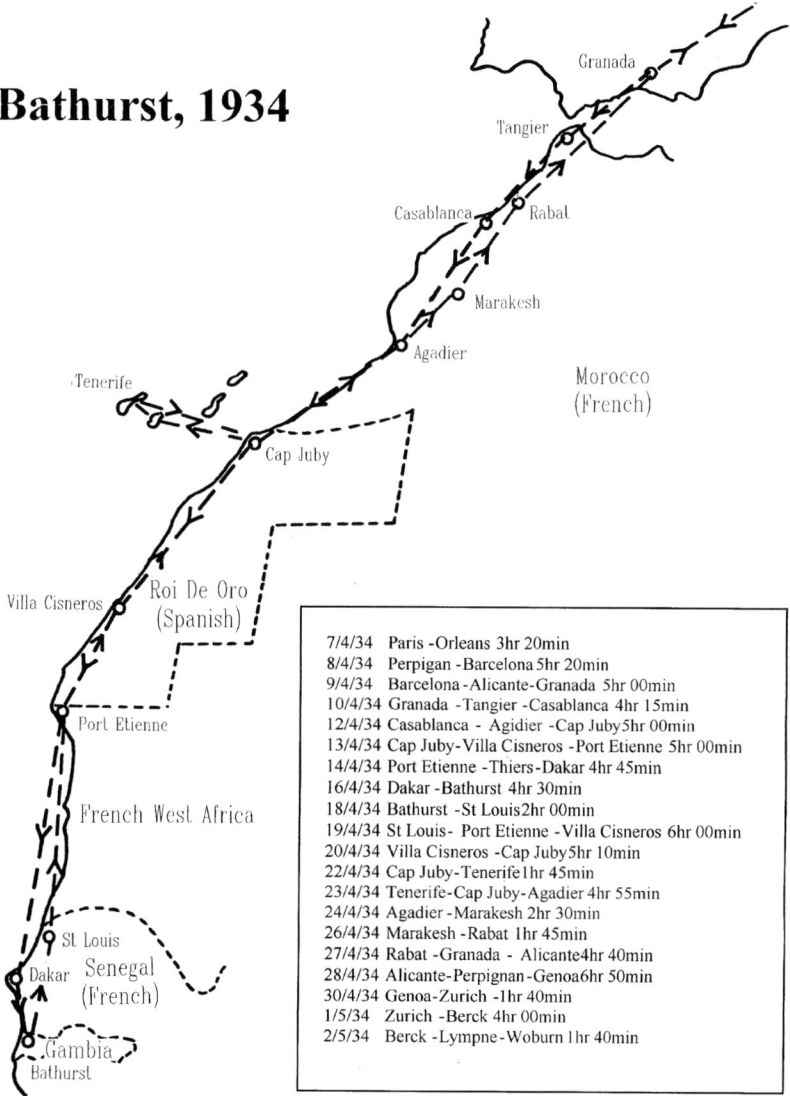

7/4/34	Paris -Orleans 3hr 20min
8/4/34	Perpigan -Barcelona 5hr 20min
9/4/34	Barcelona -Alicante-Granada 5hr 00min
10/4/34	Granada -Tangier -Casablanca 4hr 15min
12/4/34	Casablanca - Agidier -Cap Juby5hr 00min
13/4/34	Cap Juby-Villa Cisneros -Port Etienne 5hr 00min
14/4/34	Port Etienne -Thiers-Dakar 4hr 45min
16/4/34	Dakar -Bathurst 4hr 30min
18/4/34	Bathurst -St Louis2hr 00min
19/4/34	St Louis- Port Etienne -Villa Cisneros 6hr 00min
20/4/34	Villa Cisneros -Cap Juby5hr 10min
22/4/34	Cap Juby-Tenerife1hr 45min
23/4/34	Tenerife-Cap Juby-Agadier 4hr 55min
24/4/34	Agadier -Marakesh 2hr 30min
26/4/34	Marakesh -Rabat 1hr 45min
27/4/34	Rabat -Granada - Alicante4hr 40min
28/4/34	Alicante-Perpignan-Genoa6hr 50min
30/4/34	Genoa-Zurich -1hr 40min
1/5/34	Zurich -Berck 4hr 00min
2/5/34	Berck -Lympne-Woburn 1hr 40min

Preston was in his element socalising with locals and Mr McKellar, the head Shell agent; the Duchess, however, drawn unwillingly into the social round, was less impressed. At one point she managed to escape to visit the Cathedral and church where she wrote, Christopher Colombus 'went to invoke heavenly blessings that were lavishly granted later when he tumbled by mistake on to America, and handed his name down to posterity as a great discoverer instead of an indifferent navigator. (N.B. He thought he had reached India!).' But on the whole, she found the Canaries windy and cold and only the mountain areas beautiful. 'I asked the wife of a retired judge who had spent three months in a hotel in Las Palmas, what there was to do there,' she wrote, 'She replied somewhat emphatically 'Nothing' and I wondered how they could waste life by remaining three months. Certainly they had intended she told me to go round the world but she had broken her arm on arrival, which put an end to that though this had long healed. I think I should have taken the next steamer home and had another bid at circling the world; but three months in an hotel in Las Palmas no, thank you!' During their three days in Las Palmas they took a flight round the 12,000 foot crater on Tenerife, an experience Preston wrote that he fancied few had enjoyed and next to Kilamanjaro, the finest and grandest sight he had seen from the air.

They left the Canaries on 23rd April for Marrakech and were about half way between Grand Canary and Cabo Juby when the engine again started popping and banging, bringing visions of another forced landing. But this time they were over a rough sea, the nearest land the then practically uninhabited, lava-strewn island of Fuerteventura. Until he was sure that he could make land Preston, hesitating to take any action that might cause the engine to stop altogether, turned towards the island and flew on, loosing height steadily. After about ten minutes which to the occupants of the Puss Moth must have seemed a lifetime, Preston reckoned he could just about reach land so in the hope of clearing what he assumed to be another petrol blockage, he started to dive alternatively shutting and opening the throttle. This seems to have worked as at 3,000 feet, the engine more or less righted itself and the decision had then to be made, whether to land and wreck the aircraft and possibly themselves, or to continue over the remaining sixty miles of sea trusting that the engine would keep going. Having managed to climb to 7,000 feet Preston decided to continue and in due course, they arrived safely at Cabo Juby.

The Duchess in her diary described the episode thus:

'When some twelve miles off Fuerteventura the engine showed very decided signs of going on strike again. Flight Lieut. Preston by various mishandlings of the throttles and dives, tried to rouse it to a sense of its duties but without success, and for quite a times we had the interesting experience of feeling quite certain that our flying career was about to end in a very rough sea. However, the engine did not as we expected entirely fail and Flight Lieut. Preston turned round and said 'I think we may reach land.' With a prospect of wild mountains and rocks and an irregular sandy spit on which there was a lighthouse, I told him I thought the sea was preferable and apparently he thought so too when he saw it closer, and he turned out to sea again. By this time the engine had picked up more or less and we were able to regain height. It gave us another threat of collapse when Flight Lieut. Preston turned off a tank to try and locate the trouble, and thereafter behaved itself for the remaining hour, which enabled us to reach Cabo Juby. *I am persuaded that when faced with apparently certain death in this way, one does not experience terror which those who do not live to tell the tale are supposed to feel. Flight Lieut. Preston was engaged in trying various devices to restart the engine but I, who had nothing to do but consider the situation, felt a little disappointed that our flight would be wasted and that they would hear nothing about it at home; but I thought it a good way of finishing up compared with most ends which are the lot of man, and certainly the one I had most desired; for with not a boat in sight and a very rough sea, the process could not have lasted long. At all events I should have gone down knitting a prosaic sock and the reporters would have pictured me clinging round Flight Lieut. Preston's neck and imploring him to save me. Only our height, 6,000 feet, saved us as we dropped to 4,000 feet. I write this with other similar experiences in the past to confirm my opinion.'*

181

At Cabo Juby, Preston could find nothing wrong with the engine. Later he learnt that the problem was almost certainly caused by a vapour lock in the fuel lines, something he had never previously experienced. It was by now too late to make Marrakech but not wishing to spend the night in Cape Juby, they pressed on to Agadir, the port in Morocco famous for an episode in 1911 when a German gunboat sent to assist the natives against the French, nearly precipitated a European war. Here the wind was so strong that blowing sand made the dunes look as if they were smoking. 'Just before landing,' the Duchess wrote, 'the wind was blowing up the sand almost vertically off the dunes; I have never seen anything like it before. Flight Lieut. Preston could hardly put the Puss down and it bounded along like a rubber ball. The man in charge of the aerodrome said that if we had come an hour earlier, we could not have landed. All the same, he and his companions made no effort to help us by holding on to a wing, so I had to get out and do it.'

They had a very rough ride again next day along the base of the snow-covered Atlas mountains to Marrakech; Preston taking no chances with the engine, climbed to 12,000 feet where the Duchess's fingers were too numbed and cold to knit - her usual pastime when Preston was flying. They stayed two nights in the luxury Mamounia Hotel where after World War II, Churchill stayed and where to this day, the suite he used is preserved with its leather chairs, desk and in his bedroom with a giant canopied bed, overlooking the Atlas mountains. On the afternoon of their arrival they motored out to the tombs of the Sultans; they then visited the gardens of the Aquedal where huge tanks of water reflected the greenery and legendary colours of the old Palace for in those parts, there was no shortage of water. 'At last one is amongst tropical birds again,' the Duchess wrote of the gardens, 'and as it is a Sanctuary they swarm and are very tame.'

Next morning Preston overhauled the Puss Moth and drained both fuel tanks. Whether this had any effect on the stoppages is open to question but at least thereafter, they had no more trouble. The Duchess meanwhile, returned to the Aquedal Gardens for some bird-watching but without reference books, it was an unrewarding pastime. After lunch they motored to Asni, a beauty spot in the foothills where Preston described the colour of the soil as changing in different lights, from an amazing vermillion to light red, golden rose or a mixture of the lot. 'R.C.P. sat down to sketch as usual,' the Duchess wrote, 'whilst I prowled around, bought an amethyst in the rough and watched some domesticated Barbary sheep.' Preston wrote of Marrakech, 'There can be few cities sited quite so happily and no one has seen Morocco who does not come to Marrakech - wish it were British -what a lot of Africa the French do own! Never have I heard the muezzins to better advantage than here; the air at dawn resounds with the weird chants and they quite take the place of cock crowing.' The Duchess also wrote that she was very sorry to leave Marrakech and would gladly have spent a week there - but time for her was short.

As the north wind would have made a one-day flight to Alicante exceedingly tedious, they broke the journey at Rabat where, after lunch, they took a taxi to the cork forests. On their way back they called at a very beautiful garden in the Kasbah des Oudyahs where Preston, once again, sat down and sketched.

En route to Alicante they refuelled at Granada where according to the Duchess they 'had an amusing luncheon of horrible viands with the man in charge of the aerodrome, and the Air France man who had known me for some years. 'R.C.P.,' she continued, 'managed to consume what was provided with relish but it was beyond me, being soaked in oil and underdone at that. Unfortunately my lack of appetite aroused comment and they wanted to know if I was ill. *Difficult to explain that I was not but should have been if I had eaten the lunch!* The Air France man acted as interpreter to our host and when R.C.Ps Anglo-French and his Hispano-French failed to come to a mutual understanding, I aired a little of my Spanish to bridge the gap.'

The aerodrome at Alicante had changed a great deal since the Duchess came there with Barnard in 1927. 'Stayed at Palace Hotel,' she wrote, 'good rooms but indifferent food and still more indifferent drink and coffee.'

On the way home they spent two nights in Geneva where they had been invited to visit the International Aero Exhibition as guests of the Swiss Aero Club. On the evening of their arrival they attended a large Exhibition dinner where inevitably, Preston ran into many of his aviation friends and aquaintances, including John Grierson and his new wife, and Bradbrooke of *The Aeroplane*. The Duchess soon had enough of the Exhibition which didn't impress her unduly and the following day, took a long drive in the mountains with her maid Bailey who had flown out from England to meet her. Hotels in the mountains were not yet open so for lunch, they returned to the Lake and Lausanne. Meanwhile Preston, never one for exerting himself, spent a more leisurely and social day with some of his friends, taking a Lake steamer to Nyon and back. After a night in Zurich where the Duchess deplored new developments which now extended practically all round the Lake, they had planned to fly home, but fog in the Channel forced them to land at Berck. '*L'homme propose et Dieu dispose*,' she wrote, and later, 'Drove over to Le Touquet for the night, *Of all dismal things that can happen to an aviator in this world, to be fog bound in what at times is a very large, gay seaside resort out of season, is surely one of the most depressing. It is a city of the dead and unfortunately, fog is wont to last more than a day.*' The only bright spot for the Duchess was a meeting with John Grierson, also returning from Geneva and similarly fogbound. The Duchess was much intriqued with his Gipsy I Moth, G-AAJP -suitably named *Rouge et Noir* as it was painted red on one side and black on the other - the fuselage and wings of which were inscribed with records of his many travels. These included a flight to India and back in 1931 when as a Pilot Officer in the RAF, he had flown out to join his Squadron, returning in a record time for a light aircraft of four days, ten hours and fifty minutes. A 9,000 mile flight to Samarkand in southern Russia in 1932 and, in February 1933, a flight to Iceland testing a Marconi homing device, in all of which the Duchess was greatly interested. Later that year in Fox Moth G-ACRK he was to make the first east-west crossing of the Atlantic by the Northern Route.

Next morning fog presisted until lunchtime, when things started to look a little better. They were just about to take off when a bad leak in the exhaust manifold was discovered which had to be rectified. When at last they got away it was only to be forced back again by fog. Later in the afternoon, Lympne reported sunshine so they set off again, this time climbing above the fog. Lympne and Woburn were in due course reached without further problems, but Preston recorded the Channel crossing as one of the most unpleasant he had experienced.

'It is interesting to record,' the Duchess wrote, 'that all our friends with the exception of Mrs Preston, are greatly thrilled by the bullet holes in the wing of which we knew nothing until we landed, and entirely ignored the airlock over the sea when we both thought death was inevitable in a few minutes.

'Both events had been recorded together in the newspapers. By letter some expressed the hope that I did not suffer from shock on seeing the bullet holes, others that it, 'will not destroy my nerve for flying!' However it is just as well, for the engine may stop anywhere at home at an inconvenient moment, whereas target practice in an aeroplane is not likely to occur in peace-time, except where there are sporting Senegalese and their kind. It is certain however that with the combination of incessant high wind and sand which obtains on the west coast of Africa, ultra precautions have to be taken if one is not to suffer from a choked jet.' On arriving back to an English spring, everything at Woburn looked so lovely that Preston was left wondering why anyone wanted to leave it, even for three weeks!

So ended another of the Duchess's spring holidays. Although the companionship and flying which had been so much a part of her trips with Allen had been lacking, Preston had steered her though a remote and unfrequented part of Africa probably better than her previous pilot could have done, adding to her already long list of unconventional experiences.

The week following their return the Duchess put in some solo flying before on 11th May 1934, going to London to take her medical for the renewal of her private pilot's licence. Before the war, and for some time after in the case of professional licences, all medicals were carried out by the RAF's Central Medical Board, 'A detestable proceeding,' wrote the Duchess, 'but they had the grace to pass me.' She was now in her 69th year. On 17th May she flew with Preston down to *Endsleigh*. When coming to collect her ten days later, Preston collided with a car at Plymouth (Roborough) and damaged the Moth's wing. The

Duchess, who was waiting for him, immediately went to Provinicial Airways and booked a seat to London. However before their 'plane left, Preston had managed to patch the Moth's wing thus in the event, she returned in her own aeroplane. One must assume that once back, more comprehensive repairs had to be made as two days later, the Duchess returned to Plymouth in a DH Dragon of Provincial Airways, noting that it was a comfortable machine but very draughty and adding, 'I think it must be designed to revive those who are fainting from fright or air-sickness as I observe that fresh air is recommended on their time-table cards, for those suffering from this disability. Flight one hour and fifty minutes calling at Southampton, then along the coast.'

The years had passed and the uninhibited flying of Barnard and to a lesser extent Allen, that the Duchess had so enjoyed, was now less acceptable. For the Duchess, her Moth was now little more than a means of transport used to travel to events that she would not otherwise have attended. Thus on 9th June she flew to Nottingham to watch a Test Match against the Australians. 'A dull affair as our team doing badly but glad to have seen a Test Match for the first time.' she wrote. She flew to Bradfield College to watch a Greek play acted by the boys and to Heston, en route to the Aldershot Tattoo, afterwards spending the night at Great Fosters. On another occasion she flew to Hanworth to attend the Richmond Horse Show. 'Crawley and Horsham hounds one of the attractions,' she wrote, 'but day hot and hounds discovered the water jump and left huntsman and whips to take salute to Royal Box alone - to amusement of crowd. Streets had just been painted with white bars where pedestrians in future will be compelled to cross. Well known horsewoman riding her pony to show stopped by policeman for pedestrians to cross. Pony took lines to be a gate and jumped the lot knocking down policeman.'

On 24th June she flew herself, as in previous years, to Ratcliffe for the luncheon given by Lindsay Everard, this year for the Parliamentary Air Committee. Three days later she flew to Heston en route to the first post-war horse show at Olympia. On 5th July as a Liveryman and Honorary Warden of the Guild of Air Pilots, she attended a dinner at Shelley's restaurant, stayed the night in London and returned next day for a mornings work in her hospital. On the same afternoon she flew with Preston in the Puss Moth to Brussels where they spent the night, en route to Munich. From there they motored to Oberammergau to see the 31st ten-yearly Passion Play - the first having been held in 1634 as a thanksgiving for the abatement of the plague. Here she stayed with Anton Lang, who at one time took the part of Christ but now related the prologue.

'Play began at eight am.' she wrote; 'Had seats in eighth row which gave perfect view. Of the play I can only say I was enthralled from beginning to end. *The music and singing are lovely and have a character all of their own.* The colouring and groupings are beautiful and one sees all the Bible scenes of ones childhood's picture books brought to life without any sense of play acting. It all seems so entirely real and natural. . . After the Play we walked up in the hills till dinner time. After dinner we again walked out and did some shopping as, in spite of being Sunday, shops open until ten pm.' There is no record of what Preston did in the meantime!

Returning home via Switzerland, they landed at Berne, and took the train to Zermatt, which Preston had not previously visited. Next day they took another train to Gornergrat - 'View from top wonderful,' the Duchess wrote, 'but very touristy so glad to escape and walk down alone to Zermatt. Left R.C.P. to sketch with strict instructions that if he did not find me at Riffel Berg at lunchtime, he was not to bother about me. *I had no intention of being there but wished no argument.* Just before dinner porter came to tell me that R.C.P. was waiting for me at Riffel Alp and had missed last train down. *As I did not feel responsible I proceeded to eat my dinner and it did not disagree with me.* He appeared about an hour later having walked down and rubbed his toes.' Returning home, the train to Berne was late and with a strong headwind, they just managed to make Heston where the car sent from Woburn to collect them did not arrive until 11.30 pm. 'Reached home 12.45,' the Duchess wrote, 'dined and went to bed two am. A fairly long day seeing that I had taken an early morning walk at Zermatt at seven am.' Never still for a moment, the Duchess must have been hard to keep up with!

On other flights during July the Duchess visited Liverpool to see the new Cathedral that, she wrote, 'Should be worthy of the old cathedrals if it is ever finished.' and while there she took a drive through the newly opened Mersey Tunnel, commenting that the lighting was pleasant and the ventilation excellent. On the 27th they had 'a very boisterous flight' to Burnham-on-Crouch where the Duchess opened a new flying ground for the Royal Corinthian Yacht Club and afterwards, went for an equally boisterous sail with Commodore Mitchell. All these trips were made in the open Gipsy Moth, which the Duchess greatly preferred to the back seat of the Puss Moth. On most of these flights, while Preston made the necessary administrative arrangements and looked after the aeroplane on the ground, the Duchess did the flying and the navigation and would have been entitled to list as such in her log book - but as we have seen, her log book was now written up by Preston. During the month she also put in some twenty hours solo cross-country flying bringing her logged solo to 132 hours.

Amongst her travels in August was one to Durham Cathedral of which she commented, 'For situation and its simple grandeur I think it still reigns supreme but for actual beauty, I would still give the palm to Lincoln.' They landed at RAF Usworth and before visiting the Cathedral, lunched with the Commanding Officer, Squadron Leader the Hon. W L Runciman[3] and afterwards took tea with Dean Alington, late headmaster of Eton. On another outing they flew to Norwich, visited the Cathedral then flew on to Norfolk and had tea at Cley Mill.

In 1934 the Duchess again entered the Liverpool 'Arrival' competition at Speke, starting this time from Hornchurch. Unfortunately, she wrote, she forgot her chronometer and had to use the aeroplane watch that was four minutes fast, 'exactly the time by which I was too early. A foolish mistake but it was foggy at first and very bumpy all the way and as I had not done many of these long flights I had plenty of time to think about *experientia docet*.' Preston, who had hired a Moth for the day as

---

3. Commanding Officer No.607 County of Durham, Auxiliary Air Force; Director General of BOAC 1940; Viscount Runciman of Droxford 1949.

the Puss was having its annual overhaul, won second prize. This flight is not recorded in her log book.

On the 25th Anniversary of Bleriot's flight across the Channel on 25th July 1909, the Guild of Air Pilots and Air Navigators laid on a luncheon at the Savoy Hotel to commemorate the event, at which Bleriot himself was the chief guest. 'Saw his machine when it was exhibited at Selfridges after the flight,' the Duchess wrote, 'and bought two postcards recording that he flew 31 miles in 43 minutes and attained a speed of 40 miles per hour. He volunteered to sign them which now greatly adds to their interest. Ela Russell (Herbrand's sister) at the time predicted that he would be the last man to do it. Today I hear that Mr Tyson is to try and fly the Channel upside down. (Later he did it in a Tiger Moth in sixteen minutes).'

The Londonderry's had arranged a large house-party at Mount Stewart, their Northern Ireland home, to celebrate the opening of Newtonards aerodrome on 30th August. After a mornings work at the hospital, the Duchess, with Preston in the front seat, flew up to Creetown, spending the night at *Bargaly* - a house on the *Cairnsmore* estate rented by the Duke for use by the Duchess's hospital staff - before continuing to Ireland. Among the guests was the Duke of Abercorn who was to open the new aerodrome. '*R.C.P. being Irish and having been quartered there for a time some five years ago, met a host of friends.*' the Duchess wrote. She also recorded that she had a long talk with Herr Kronfield 'the great Austrian glider' who she found pleasant and interesting and who promised to send her a copy of his book.

Dinner was scheduled for eight o'clock and as there was a house party of some thirty people, the Duchess made a special point of being changed and ready at least ten minutes beforehand. She was waiting to go down when a maid arrived with a note saying that after dinner, the garden was going to be floodlit, and not to 'dress', so the Duchess hastily divested herself of her evening clothes and changed back into a day dress. She had barely finished changing when Preston and a daughter of the house, called at her room to see what had become of her. Not liking to blame her hostess the Duchess followed them down, leaving her room in chaos. Later Lady

189

Shelmerdine told her that because this trick had been played on her before, she had delayed changing until she was sure of the form! The following day they motored to Belfast to watch the Tourist Trophy races where the Duchess had an excellent view, as she was invited to join the Londonderrys in the Governor's box. After this they returned to *Cairnsmore* for the night and next day, flew to Machrihanish where the Duchess hoped to do some birdwatching - only to find that the birds had been disturbed by busloads of trippers. On returning to the airstrip she found a depressed and displeased Preston who had found it too cold to sketch and also, as the Duchess put it, 'suffering from reaction after joviality of his Irish friends and sumptuous meals.' It was therefore with relief all round that they returned to Creetown.

With the return south delayed by gales and rain, the Duchess drove instead to Glen Trool to visit her son Hastings, only to find him out - presumably telephones had not yet reached those parts. However, before leaving, she had tea with an Admiral and Mrs Mitchell, who were staying in the house. In September the Duchess flew to Leuchars for more birdwatching, piloting herself the whole way. 'St. Andrews is still filled entirely with respectable, unpainted and somewhat elderly golfing crowd and its pre-war atmosphere is most refreshing.' she wrote. Next day they flew to nearby Kinnard Castle, landing in a field near the house and spending the night as guests of Lord and Lady Southesk. She spent three days at St. Andrews before returning to Creetown and *Cairnsmore*, by which time the Duke and household had arrived. There was one more flight before Preston took the Moth south. This was to Renfrew to watch the launch of the Queen Mary, at which function the Duchess had been invited to lunch with the Directors. 'Long wait before King and Queen arrived but met a good many friends from all parts of the country.' she wrote. 'The little bottle on the destruction of which so much depended, hung suspended from the roof of our shelter decked with flags and red, white and blue ribbons. At last suspense ended and after a speech from the King, it dashed itself to pieces douching reporters and press below with champagne. Hitherto the ship had been known as No.539, the name kept secret. Her builders Messrs Brown had also built my beautiful *Sapphire* which the war deprived me of.'

During her time in Scotland the Duchess drove up to Glen Trool, and brought her younger grandson Hugh, aged eleven, back to *Cairnsmore* to meet his grandfather for the first time. Her interest in aviation and especially in any aeroplane built by de Havillands was such that she recorded in her diary the result of the 1934 England - Australia air race. 'C W A Scott and T C Black in de Havilland Comet, two 225 h.p special engines, reached Melbourne at 05.34 GMT,' she wrote, 'and won £10,000 gold trophy offered by Sir Macpherson Robertson for fastest flight from England. Left Mildenhall 06.35 on 20th October thus covered 11,300 miles in 70 hours 59 minutes. They spent 63 hours 55 minutes in air and seven hours four minutes on ground. They landed six times.' She then went on to list the six landing places. She could have also recorded that another Comet flown by Cathart-Jones and Ken Waller was only 80 minutes behind. She would also no doubt have been interested to read later, that a Puss Moth flown by Australian C J Melrose, arrived safely at Melbourne - after gliding into Darwin with an empty fuel tank - in the very creditable time of nine days and nineteen hours, to be placed third in the handicap race.

The Duchess left Scotland for Woburn on 12th November in lovely weather that made her regret leaving. The last entry in her diary for 1934 dated 18th December records that during the last sixteen years she had radiographed between 200 and 409 cases *per annum*.

Chapter Eleven
1934-1935: Problems With Puss Moths

Towards the end of 1934 the structural integrity of the Puss Moth, which had been used for so many long-distance and record-breaking flights past years, came into question because of some unexplained crashes. The designers at Hatfield, assisted by scientists from the Royal Aircraft Establisment at Farnborough and even the National Physical Laboratory did everything they could to find the cause. Instability of the centre-section structure above the pilot's head, the large cutout in the fuselage to provide doors and tail-flutter were among the many areas subjected to intensive scrutiny and test. Precautionary modifications were incorporated but no specific reason for the crashes was ever determined. Richard Clarkson, later Head of Aerodynamics for the de Havilland Aircraft Company at Hatfield, was involved in the structure tests. He said that the answer eventually came from 'Captain DH' himself when he said, 'We'll start again from scratch' - the result, the Leopard Moth. Meanwhile although Puss Moths were never 'grounded', Preston took it upon himself to suggest to the Duchess that she should change her Puss Moth for a more modern type.

Although nothing is shown of this in the Duchess's diaries, the acrimonious correspondence that followed, which all but ended in Preston's dismissal, shows that discussions on this subject broadened into other matters that had become a source of irritation to the Duchess - for as we have seen, they were of very different and in many ways incompatible temperaments. Preston, used to leading, was often too direct in his approach for the Duchess, tending to take decisions for her on matters she preferred to decide for herself. In this case, she would have been well aware of what was going on in respect of the Puss Moth crashes, and was sufficiently experienced - and intelligent - to decide for herself what to do about it.

In fact, the Duchess had good reasons for not wishing to change her aircraft at this juncture. First, by January 1935, she was already planning to use the Puss Moth for her annual flying holiday that normally started around March. Secondly, it was an inconvenient moment financially as Mrs Allen, widow of her late pilot, had in her words, deprived her in various ways of all and more than she had put aside for a new machine, 'probably to her great satisfaction if she knew it.' Thus, having decided that she would keep the Puss for another year, she wanted it re-covered and wrote to Preston thus:

"Dear Flt Lt.Preston,

I have decided to have a new bag for the Puss Moth for I do not relish the idea of its looking below par for a whole year, and then having to provide it when there is more chance of my having to sell the machine. I am quite sure that out in the sunshine it will very soon look a very dull affair, even if it does not do so now, and I DO care about the appearance of my Moth as well as the internal, for all you may sniff at the folly of it. . ."

For Preston, a family man, would not, like Allen, have given time to cleaning and polishing. If Preston did not want to risk foreign travel in the Puss she continued, she would not ask him do so but since she owned it, she wished it to be kept in the condition worthy of the reputation it had won.

Preston in his reply explained that he had expressed his views concerning the Puss Moth at a time when considerable sums were about to be spent on it. He did not want her to incur this expense without being fully aware of what he termed 'the general consensus of opinion' about Puss Moths. This further irritated the Duchess as it implied that she was not aware of what was going on. Regarding the continued use of her Puss Moth he wrote:

"Having done quite a considerable amount of foreign travel with different Puss Moths, I have no hesitation in taking yours again to any part of the globe you wish me to. But Your Grace, it does not alter ones opinion that the machine has weak structural points and one can only hope that one will never meet with circumstances that provide the straw that breaks the camel's back. If one did then the aviation world from Lord Londonderry downwards would probably say, Flight Lieut. Preston ought never to have let the duchess go about in a Puss Moth, or words to that effect. The fact that yours is old and well tried does not altogether clear it because metal had been known to suffer fatigue and 'crystallisation' due to vibration etc. However I know your point of view and what is good enough for Your Grace is good enough for me. Your position in the world of aviation is such that you must pardon a justifiable wish on my part, to see you always in possession of the best."

The inference that it was for Preston to permit or forbid the Duchess to fly her Puss infuriated her still further and in her reply, she asked his permission to show his letter to de Havillands. Her letter continued:

"It is of course a very serious matter for me, as I cannot ask you to fly the Puss Moth again."

She then changed to another tack:

"Why did you once say to me 'I wonder when Your Grace will get tired of the Gipsy' if you do not hate it as I have many reasons for thinking you do? I am not at all surprised at this for it must be a cheerless, boring business for you who have flown so much, to sit doing nothing except seeing that I did nothing specially foolish. but it is because I love flying in the open that I do it and there are even some foolish pilots who love it too. Heaven knows I gave you enough of it in the summer but I do hesitate to do it, if I think you have some pleasanter occupation or that the weather conditions are not attractive . . .

"But short uninteresting flights are all I can do when I am tied to my work on the one hand and not to leave the Duke too much on the other. I again repeat that you have laid yourself out to please me on many occasions and given me the chance of seeing things under pleasanter auspices than I should probably have done with any other pilot, and certainly the late one who had not quite the social standing of yourself. But I have a strong feeling that you are not happy with either of my machines and that makes me unhappy."

Preston's reply to this was that he too liked flying in the open.

He continued:

"but surely we all hate draughts, and it seems impossible to keep draughts out of the front seat of the Gipsy I Moth. Whether all open machines are subject to the same fault I do not know but fancy that with inverted engines they suffer less. I love the Gipsy Moth under reasonable conditions but then, some six years have elapsed since they were designed and many improvements have materialised in that time so that now one can get better comfort and performance and still be in the open. But as again this is largely a question of outlay, one is perfectly prepared to take what comes ones way. . . . I can only end by assuring you that I am happy with both your machines as I am shall I say with my own car. I should love to own a Straight 8 Lagonda but cannot the same time as keeping a family. Probably your hospital corresponds to my family?"

This remark did little to mollify the Duchess who replied thus:

"Dear Flt. Lt. Preston,

I wish I were not obliged to write this letter in answer to yours but it had to come. *I am very unhappy about the Puss Moth.* I cannot ask you to fly me abroad in it again. There have been one or two other minor difficulties but I have always realised that you stepped into a very difficult pair of shoes and I cannot ever again expect such mutual understanding as I had with my late pilot.

"I have been putting off saying anything day after day because I hate to think that it may temporarily do some harm to your family, but I am old and it is a serious matter contemplating losing this years flying holiday for I may never get the chance again. By the time the three months I owe you are up, it will already be late to contemplate any trip to the South, and perhaps a little off the beaten track.

"I hope you will not think that am forgetful of all you have done for me. You have given me a lot of pleasure in the past year which I would not otherwise have had and I am really grateful for it. As to going to see new developments, I like going to see them very much and am always glad when there is some expedition of mutual interest to us both. That in all probability they will never be for me makes no difference to the interest.

"I see again that there is some urgent modification called for with the Dragon engines, and it seems to take years before they are properly tried out and then, as with the Puss Moth, may be condemned.

"I did not see you last night because I feared you were almost certain to refer to your letter. I did not want to spoil your enjoyment with your family today and I thought for our mutual sakes it was better written.

"With many regrets if it causes any unhappiness."

To this letter Preston replied:

"Your Grace.

Am I to take you Grace's letter of 9th inst as definite notice that my appointment is to be terminate three months from now, or does it offer me any opportunity of expressing the assurance that such differences as appear to exist, exist only in Your Grace's mind? If the whole crux of the matter is one of 'no confidence' I can then only apologise for the 290 odd hours of anxiety I must have given you in the past year."

The next letter dated 19th January, 1935 shows that further discussions had taken place about a replacement pilot, it reads:

"Dear Flt. Lt. Preston,

You told me this evening that I might find difficulty in getting another pilot who might fit in as well as yourself and implied that the job was not a sinecure.

"As this is rather an unkind thing to have said, to say the least of it, I should like to have your assurance that it has not been worse than I led you to expect. I told you before you came to me that you would be very much tied and that I went for short flights just when I had time and opportunity, because it is the pleasantest form of recreation I have. Evidently I did give this information to all applicants for the post or I should not have received the answer I did from one of them in a less courteous form that you gave it: 'I'm paid for it.'

"I warned you that Woburn was a dull place, but I have done what I could to interfere as little as possible with your making the best of it. If I have not seemed content of late it is because you have assumed the attitude of Dictator rather than Adviser, and obviously disliked both my machines. For the rest there have been one or two small ways in which I have been ruffled and I think a good many would agree, not without reason; indeed one or two of my friends have noticed them without my saying anything, but as they affected my *amour propre* (*not* as a Duchess!) as much as anything, I have said little or nothing. There had to be some 'flies in the ointment.'

"You knew a good deal about me before you engaged to come, and therefore were not wholly in the dark. It was but a few days ago you told me that it had been a very happy year, so it was disappointing to learn that it had been a difficult one."

The following letter from Preston shows, however, that for him and his family, well established in a comfortable home and no doubt with a good salary, it was not a convenient time to move on; he wrote:

"Jan 20th, 1935

Your Grace,

In reply to your note of yesterday, I must apologise if I made any remarks in the course of our conversation which appeared to you unkind. Such was not my intention - but in referring to my job as 'not too easy' I meant really that try as I will to do all I can to please you and carry out my duties within the written and unwritten meaning of our Agreement - I seem to bring about misunderstandings and reproaches - as witness a rapidly growing correspondence. Nobody is more sorry than I am - and as you ask for assurance, I sincerely reassure you that this last year has been a completely happy one for myself and my family, and we were looking forward to many repetitions.

"You refer to me as Dictator - again I am sorry - it is not a role I have ever been accused of adopting or have any desire to adopt. You are my employer and such remarks as I have addressed to you apropos machines, instruments, etc., have been bona fide expressions of opinions and advice which, whether called for or not, Your Grace is in no case bound to take. As regards other matters I am sorry again that I offend and sorry that you cannot find it possible to tell me where the fault lies.

197

"I hoped I understood my position and my job fairly well but if it is not so - I am still willing to learn, and things might be easier."

While all this was going on the Duchess made some flights with other pilots and in particular, flew down to Littlestone near Folkestone for some bird watching with Herbert Travers, an experienced flying instructor whose account of the flight survives.[5.] The Duchess had written to him on 1st February as follows:

"Dear Mr Travers.

Your address was given to me as 'Major' and the telephone calls you 'Mr' so I am giving you some of each until I know better.

"I am afraid the weather is not at all promising for the particular purpose for which I wanted to go to Littlestone viz. a little sea bird watching, but I had also done very little flying lately and the birds were really an excuse for the flight.

"I must ring you up in the morning - also if we go, learn whether you would like us to send for you or whether you would prefer to motor yourself over.

Yours sincerely, M.Bedford."

Travers records in his log. book:

"2/2/35. Gipsy Moth 90 h.p engine. Woburn - Littlestone. 50 minutes. Self for take-offs. Her Grace flew most of the way. Littlestone - Woburn. 1 hour 55 minutes. Self and landings. Very strong NW wind."

The wind had cleared away the sea birds, his daughter writes, but the flight had been a success and he would have been delighted to fly with her again, but it never happened. Four days later the Duchess wrote asking how much she owed Travers for flying with her. No payment had been discussed so after much heart-searching and bearing in mind that they had used the Duchess's own aircraft, fuel etc., Travers finally decided on what he thought was a fair sum. This elicited the response,

---

5. *Cross Country* By E Travers; published by Hothersall and Travers, 1990.

'. . In view of what I have been asked for similar services in the past, I really cannot accept the estimated value of your own and have ventured to double the amount of the cheque . .' 'She is a brick.' was Travers's response; her thoughtful action touched him deeply. In the autumn his daughter writes, the Duchess telephoned several times but Travers by now had got a job as a supernumerary Captain with Imperial Airways giving in-flight navigational training, and could not get away.

Meanwhile, Preston had retired to Brighton to get over a bout of 'flu. By the time he returned the rift between them must have been healed as plans were afoot for the most ambitious of all the Duchess's tours, a flight across the Sahara. The idea had come from an article in *Shell Aviation News* telling how a Mr Knight had recently flown across the Sahara in a Blackburn Bluebird

Chapter Twelve

1935: Across The Sahara

It was particularly important for the Duchess that she got away in March this year as she had to be back by May, to take part with the Duke in the King and Queen's Silver Jubilee celebrations. This left barely sufficient time to make the necessary preparations although compared to today, it was a relatively easy matter as the Aviation Department of the Automobile Association (AA) arranged for maps and permits, and Shell for supplies of fuel. Thus on 20th March, with Preston in the front seat of the Puss Moth and the Duchess plus some 180 lb of luggage in the rear, they were waved off from Woburn on a glorious Spring day, by a large gathering of friends and relations.

After landing at Lympne and Le Bourget for customs, they continued to Tours where they spent the first night. Next day after refuelling at Toulouse, they planned to take a short cut over the Pyrenees directly to Barcelona, but rain and cloud forced them to retreat to the low ground to the east, and to land in pouring rain at Perpignan. Next morning, with grey skies and drizzle prevailing, they remained in the hotel till midday when, in Preston's words, they 'transferred their inactivities to the aerodrome only to continue peering into the cloud-obscured Pyrenees.' By three pm the forecast for Barcelona was suffi-ciently good for them to continue, so they loaded up the Puss and taxied out. They were about to take off when 'meteo' rushed out with a report of fog and as at the same moment, rain again descended, there was nothing for it but to taxi back, unload and return to Perpignan for another dreary night.

The following day was worth waiting for and with a following wind, they made Barcelona within the hour; Valencia, where, because Shell didn't operate, the Puss was refuelled with an unknown brand of Spanish 'gasolina' in two hours fifteen minutes, and Oran after a 130-mile sea crossing in a further two hours thirty minutes. 'We had a lovely flight over the Pyrenees above clouds in bright sunshine,' the Duchess wrote, 'It is a long time since I have done this which to me is one of the greatest joys of flying, but Flight Lieut. Preston does not encourage it at home as his predecessors did.' In Oran they stayed at the Grand Hotel and, to pass the evening, went to the local cinema. Apart from the Pathé news that showed Malcolm Campbell at Daytona and a recent rail crash at Kings Langley, the French film proved too soporific for them. So with many 'pardonnez moi' they squeezed their way out, much to the annoyance of the audience who filled both seats and gangway.

At Oran they encountered the first of a series of setbacks. The AA had told them that no special authorisation would be needed for the flight to Columb Bechar but on arrival at Oran, they were told that they could go no further without a permit from the Governor General. But it was Sunday, his office was closed and everywhere they were met with *'Dimanche, peut-etre demain.'*. On the following morning the permits duly arrived and after an early lunch, they set off for Columb Bechar. 'We crossed the Atlas Mountains,' the Duchess wrote, 'where they appear to be only about 3,000 to 4,000 feet high. There was a curious low fog hanging over us and at 5,000 feet my fingers were numb with cold when I had control. The general colour of the desert is red and the shadows purple and blue but the atmosphere is so thick that were it not for the railway, it might be difficult to find the way. It took my fingers a long time to recover after landing.'

At Columb Bechar, a French military encampment on the northern edge of the mountains, they encountered further delays. Shortly after landing Preston was sent for by the Commandant to be told that the regular mail plane that was to be their compulsory escort from Reggan to Gao, would not be leaving for ten days. 'This for me,' the Duchess wrote later, 'meant going home as I could not spare the time and I doubt many people being able to stand for ten days, the Columb Bechar hotel where baths are unknown, food very indifferent, and the sanitary arrangements are of the worst.'

After much consultation the Commandant was persuaded to telegraph Paris headquarters of the Compagnie Generale

Trans-Saharienne for authority for the 'plane based at Reggan to be used as their escort. This arrived next day with the condition that they paid seven francs per kilometre to defray costs. As the distance from Reggan to Gao was roughly 800 miles, this, allowing for the plane's return flight, amounted to £265. £150 had been paid in advance in London leaving £114 still outstanding. 'This', wrote the Duchess, 'rather naturally gave me pretty serious cause for reflection before taking the plunge, but it would have been too ignominious to return home when we had gone this far, and probably it would be the last chance I would ever have of doing this flight. I think Flight Lieut. Preston would have been dreadfully disappointed also. So I risked bankruptcy and wrote my cheque. On top of this they required another 10,000 francs (approximately £100) to be given to our escort in case we lost him and ourselves. The cheque was to be returned to us in full by our escort if we clung to him as far as Gao.' The insistence by the French government on the *control depannage* resulted in the main from Bill Lancaster's ill-fated attempt on the Cape record two years earlier.

So on Wednesday, 27th March, already behind schedule, they set course for Reggan, a staging-post in the desert approximately half way between Oran and Gao. The railway ended at Columb Bechar so for this leg as they had no radio, they were enjoined to 'suivez la piste' and on no account try to fly by compass. At first the track was reasonably easy to follow and in just over an hour they passed Beni Abbes. They were then in the Grand Erg, a region of rocks and curiously shaped sandhills. The strong easterly wind was lifting sand from the dunes and depositing it on the track, making it hard to see and further reducing visibility, which invariably worsened as the sun rose in the sky. The Duchess suggested that they might see better if they flew lower - they were flying at 3,000 to 4,000 feet on top of haze - but Preston thought not. Later the Duchess wrote, 'I did not question the wisdom of my pilot but my own very definite opinion was that it would have been better to have flown much lower because he would have seen the track far more easily and for a far greater distance ahead. If one crosses the Sahara,' she continued, 'one must be prepared to take risks, and I think the risk of a forced landing in our case was infinitely less than that of losing the track.'

They had been flying for three hours or so when Preston started to circle; the track had finally disappeared from view giving him, he recorded, a very unpleasant feeling! Over the 'phones the Duchess heard a woeful voice saying 'I'm afraid I'm lost,' and as she was afraid so too, she did not, she said later, 'offer any other opinion.' Meanwhile, Preston handed over control to her while he took a bearing on the sun. To continue on a compass course in hope of regaining the track was out of the question, so he flew west until he was sure of being west of the track then turned north, on a course that must at some point cross it. 'I did not,' the Duchess wrote, 'in the least expect to see it and the ground below us looked pretty impossible for a forced landing, but as before on similar occasions, I looked on the situation with tolerable equanimity. I was sure the warning to start early was a necessary one and 'early' should mean as soon as there is enough light to take off. Flight Lieut. Preston's practice of waiting for weather reports and starting at what we call an early hour in England, I believe to be attended by much risk.'

It was forty-five minutes before the track again hove into view some fifty miles south of Beni Abbes, which was where in due course they landed. They had taken four and three quarter hours to cover 100 miles. The authorities at Reggan were already worrying about them and to forestall any stories the press might concoct, the Duchess telegraphed home saying they had landed at Beni Abbes due to bad visibility. The family she heard later were quite unmoved! In the event, they were both delighted to have seen Beni Abbes, an oasis with the reputation of being one of the prettiest in the Sahara. The town, surrounded by multicoloured dunes, stood on a plateau over-looking a river thickly planted with palms. There was a delightful small Trans-Atlantique hotel where a telegram arrived from the Duke, forwarded from Reggan.

By next morning the wind had dropped and with visibility 10 miles or more, the track was easy to follow. At the point where they got lost they now saw that the track took an almost right-angled turn through a *djebel* and for a short distance, was covered with sand. With good visibility however there was no problem seeing where it emerged. They reached Reggan, a distance of some 300 miles in three hours thirty minutes without further incident. This turned out to be a small, desolate oasis consisting of mud buildings, some palm trees and a Cié Trans-Saharienne hotel or rest-house situated near the landing ground that was some distance from the town. The menfolk in the hotel in their voluminous cotton trousers, shirts and sandals looked for all the world as if they had come out of the Arabian Nights. There were also some highly painted females and after supper, dancing took place to the blare of a gramophone. A party of motorists apparently tired of driving, asked the Duchess if they could get a lift in the escort plane to Bidon Cinque, the next refuelling point. This she said they could do if they made a contribution to costs, but this 'they did not smile on' - which was just as well she reflected as if anything had gone wrong, they might have needed the seats themselves!

The following morning Preston was not in the best of shape after a disturbed night, a result of the local diet, and only a pill from the Duchess enabled him to start. The pilot of the escort plane, which from now on they must follow, invited the Duchess to fly with him but she preferred, she said, to stick with her own Moth. It was now flat desert from horizon to horizon. The track was marked at some ten-kilometre intervals with white *balises*, which looked from the air to be the size and shape of a small hut. Although they appeared solid, some had been blown over giving the appearance of wrecked aeroplanes. Occasionally they passed a car - the Duchess did not envy their occupants! Soon after eleven o'clock they landed at Bidon Cinque, which she described as the acme of desolation. Water could only be obtained if really necessary at five francs a bottle, and motorists spending the night had to sleep in a most unwholesome tent. It was also prodigiously hot. Other than the native in charge of the station there was, they were told, no human, animal or vegetable life within 500 kilometres - with the exception of flies. Visibility up till then had been quite good but after Bidon Cinque the air became dust-laden and it was again difficult even with the *balises*, to see the track. Preston later admitted to doubting whether, without the escort, he could have managed

Across The Sahara, 1935

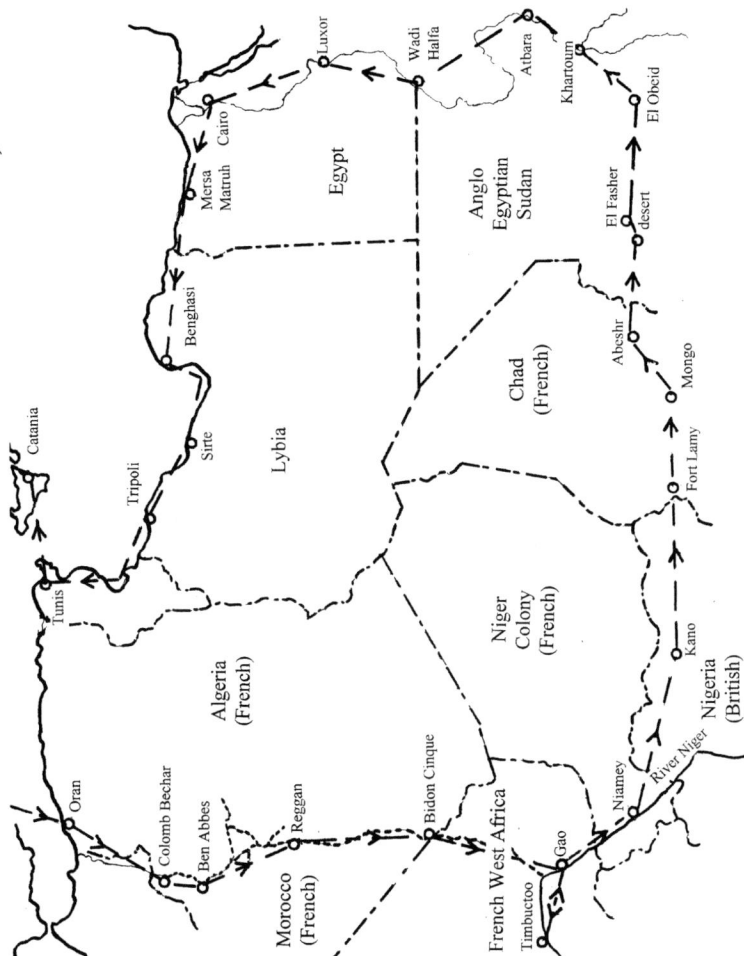

Date	Destination	Time
20/3/35	Woburn	1.00
	Lympne	1.40
	Paris	1.20
	Tours	3.10
	Toulouse	
21/3/35	Perpignan	1.30
23/3/35	Barcelona	1.00
	Valencia	2.15
	Oran	2.30
25/3/35	Colomb Bechar	4.45
27/3/35	Ben Abbes	3.30
28/3/35	Reggan	3.30
29/3/35	Bidon Cinque	4.45
	Gao	
30/3/35	Timbuctoo	3.10
31/3/35	Gao	2.30
1/4/35	Niamey	4.15
3/4/35	Kano	6.00
4/4/35	Fort Lamy	
	Mongo	
	Abeshr, desert	
5/4/35	El Fasher	.20
	El Obeid	3.20
	Khartoum	2.40
8/4/35	Atbara	2.00
	Wadi Halfa	3.45
9/4/35	Luxor	4.15
	Cairo	3.10
13/4/35	Mersa Matruh	5.15
14/4/35	Benghasi	3.20
15/4/35	Sirte	2.30
	Tripoli	4.20
16/4/35	Tunis	2.30
18/4/35	Catania	3.30
19/4/35	Naples	1.20
	Rome	3.20
20/4/35	Nice	2.15
	Lyons	2.30
22/4/35	Paris	1.20
	Lympne	1.00
	Woburn	

this leg. After some four hours some scant vegetation started appearing against which the escort was even more difficult to see. Eventually they reached Gao without losing him, their total flying time from Reggan, eight and a quarter hours.

The Duchess wrote thus of the Sahara crossing:

'Having now crossed the Sahara by air, I have quite made up my mind that I have no desire to motor across it under present conditions, though doubtless in the course of time, there will be a well-defined road across it as far as blown sand permits. The heat must be unpleasantly great and the scenery over a great deal of the route, especially round Bidon Cinque, inexpressibly dreary and monotonous. Some of the intermediate stopping places, I was told, are very horrible.'

Gao was a large French Air Force aerodrome with a good Trans-Saharienne hotel where for the first time since Oran there were baths, and it was a joy, the Duchess wrote, to feel really clean. Before leaving England they had agreed that they would visit Timbuktu, a place that before the advent of aeroplanes and cars, had been regarded as the 'end of the earth.' There was no hotel and no cars other than those owned by the French Commandant, so authorisation for the visit had to be obtained. Moreover the aerodrome was a fair distance from the town so the day after arriving in Gao, they telephoned the Commandant to ask if one of his cars could meet them. The aerodrome at Timbuktu proved to be a good one with a hangar, but the car was a longish walk away on the other side of a river over which they were carried pick-a-back. The Colonel's ADC met them and after cool drinks with Colonel Chaplus and his wife, they toured the town, which with its red-brown mud walls and narrow streets the Duchess found very peaceful and picturesque. A meeting had also been arranged for them with the legendary 'White Monk', a one-time French missionary who had turned native and among his many contributions to the colony, had founded a local college. The Duchess had brought with her Seagrave's *The White Monk of Timbuktu* and was obviously delighted at the chance to meet him. 'In appearance,' she wrote, 'he was about as typical a Patriach as one could wish to see, a benevolent face, long white hair and beard, and long flowing garments. We were introduced to his thick-lipped, jet-black native wife (Selima). She too must be rather a wonderful and very intelligent person. We were taken up to the White Monk's study where he talked French to us and made us do the same though I have little doubt that he, being a great linguist, could have conversed very much better in English than we in French. Pere Yakouba, as he was called locally told us of his schools and work and though it was not my usual practice to ask for autographs, I begged for his as proof that I had really been to Timbuktu. Afterwards we went to see his school which was as neat and orderly as any school of little European boys. It seemed strange that these thick-lipped fuzzy-headed black masters were scholars of considerable achievement, having themselves received a College education.' Preston also obtained his autograph - on his Shell carnet - and in return, they gave him a copy of Seagrave's book about him, which he had never before seen!'

After lunch with Colonel and Madame Chaplus they returned to the Moth, the Duchess, who had rubbed her heel, using an opportune donkey to convey her from the river to the hangar. The Niger, over which they flew for most of the way, teemed with birds but they were too high for the Duchess to identify anything other than the larger ones such as Storks, Flamingoes, Ibis and Egrets. Preston's landing at Gao ended in a ground-loop that broke the tail wheel. Luckily full repair facilities were available at Gao and the military *Chef de Usines* obligingly got up early on Sunday morning to do the job so that by mid afternoon, they were able to leave for Niamey.

Visibility was still poor and navigation, over the featureless scrub between Gao and Naimey, was almost as difficult as over the desert. Although this was only a two and a half hour flight, the delay caused by the broken tail-wheel meant that they now must stop the night. Temperatures at Naimey were sweltering and, as the Trans-Saharienne hotel did not run to baths, the Duchess had to make do with a basin of water to wash in. Preston, in another building, did slightly better with a 'shower' in the form of a bucket swung aloft, operated by a string. The French Governer General of Niger Colony sent his respects, saying that he had expected them the previous day and was unable to meet them. This was a matter of considerable relief to both the Duchess and Preston, who were by now struggling to socialise in French. It was with particular pleasure and relief therefore, that next day they arrived in Kano, in British controlled Nigeria, where they were welcomed by the Resident and his wife, Colonel and Mrs Lindsell, who invited them to stay at the Residency, where with comfortable beds, baths with unlimited water and English-type meals, the discomforts of the previous ten days were quickly forgotten.

At the Residency, after the inevitable 'sundowner' drinks, a dinner party was given to celebrate their arrival. Among the guests was one R H W Knight, whose article in *Shell News*, on his crossing of the Sahara, had inspired the Duchess to make this flight. An agent for the United Africa Company in Agades, Knight had flown his two-seater Blackburn Bluebird from Oran to Kano with his wife as passenger. Unable to get clearance for the route via Reggan and Gao, he had followed the more easterly 'Hoggar' route via In Salah, Tamanrasset and the Ahaggar region, which was said to be the worst area in the Sahara for heat and sandstorms. This, in such a small aircraft, was a truly amazing feat. Thus it was with great sadness that, on reaching Cairo some ten days later, the Duchesss read of his death. He had crashed shortly after they left Kano, leaving his wife stranded. 'What a waste!' Preston wrote. 'His firm ought to have got him something decent; a more unsuitable kite for that country I can't imagine.'

During their two thoroughly enjoyable days in Kano, the Duchess visited Native and European hospitals, a school, a printing works and the barracks where Preston met a school friend he had not seen seen for thirty years. The highlight of the tour was, however, a visit to the Emir of Kano in his mud-walled palace, which was described by the Duchess thus:

'Wearing a high turban and stately flowing black robes and preceded by a retainer carrying some sort of mace, he conducted us with stately swaying gait through labyrinthine passages, into the inner recesses of his home. Last year he visited London and, I regret to say, was so much impressed by English furniture that he resolved to furnish his palace with it even to the baths and cooking arrangements. The baths, drains etc. are no doubt of great advantage, but Maple's furniture does not go well with rooms, and their crude african decoration in black and gold on mud walls. However, when we go to Africa we bring things back to decorate our rooms which may appear equally incongruous to the Emir. After a little, Mrs Lindsell and I were taken off to see the Emir's six wives.

'This indeed was a change of scene after the Emir's Europeanised apartments. Led by an eunuch we went through a maze of high mud walls, courtyards and small dark rooms, bare of all furniture but swarming with women and innumerable black brats, all looking very grubby. Finally we were shown into the presence of the chief wife and her rivals (?).

'We were told that we were not to shake hands, so confined our greetings to smiles and, when they gave out, relapsed into mutual stares. The chief wife was sitting on the ground at the end of a long, wide sloping shelf on which was placed a marvellous collection of china of European origin. Teapots, plates, bowls, vases, jugs etc. etc. all huddled in confusion and said to be her hobby. Anything more awful to the English mind than the method of life of these well-to-do women can hardly be conceived. In almost airless squalor, shut up with the concubines and eunuchs, they very rarely leave the palace and then only closely veiled - and yet I have read, and was told, that they are happy.'

On 3rd April they left much refreshed for Fort Lamy in French Chad, the Duchess remarking that with the prospect of no baths for some days, she had taken all she could. After take-off Preston, as was his wont, immediately climbed to 5,000 feet where the Duchess in the back became cold and bored. There had been no hangar at Kano and, standing in the sun, the Puss Moth windows had blistered, making visibility from the rear even worse than usual. She was not sorry therefore when heavy rain compelled her pilot to descend to a few hundred feet, in order to keep the road in sight. After Maiduguri the road petered out altogether and, with some 150 miles still to go, they pressed on over the vast sun-scorched prairie without any landmarks to guide them. Five and a half hours passed and with only half an hours fuel left Preston, uncertain of his whereabouts, started looking for somewhere to land. Finding an area clear of scrub near a village he managed, with the aid of a

Smith's wind indicator, to pull off a safe landing. The inevitable bunch of natives quickly surrounded them led by a genial and intelligent old man, who pointed them in the direction of Fort Lamy but was unable to impart distance. By getting him to name villages in the opposite direction Preston was able from his map to get some idea of his position. Setting off in what they hoped was the direction of Fort Lamy it was with considerable relief that, just as another forced landing seemed imminent, a junction of rivers signalled the approach of Fort Lamy. Here they landed after six hours flying, with petrol gauge floats out of sight and less than ten minutes fuel left. 'A pretty narrow squeak,' the Duchess termed it.

A small resthouse at Fort Lamy provided basic accommodation and large basins with petrol cans of water for washing. A cafe alongside the resthouse run by a Shell agent, provided indifferent food on tables swarming with ants and on which a cheetah, which was periodically let loose, bounded. Nevertheless the Duchess described Fort Lamy as a pretty little station with avenues of trees along the river, and in such light as remained, she went out birdwatching while Preston, as was his wont, sat and sketched.

Due to what the locals termed *brume seche*, a condition resulting from the proximity of Lake Tchad, visibility next morning was little improved. Told that this could last for several days and not drawn to a long stay in these surroundings, they decided to take off on a flight which, after another long days flying, was to end with a night in the desert. The plan had been to refuel at Abeshr some 400 odd miles from Fort Lamy, and then continue to El Geneina in British controlled Sudan - or if time permitted, to El Fasher. Taking off in thick haze Preston set course for Lake Fittri, the only readily identifiable landmark in a land of scrub, villages barely distinguishable from the earth, tracks leading nowhere and dried up river beds. There was still no sign of the lake when after four and a half hours and now over hills and thick bush, an unexpected landing ground appeared. A downwind landing ended in a ground loop to avoid some donkeys and it said much for the repairs made at Gao, that the tail-wheel was not again damaged. The aerodrome, some thirty miles south of course and not shown on the map, proved to be Mongo and after they had landed, some French non-commissioned officers lit a belated fire to show wind direction. After checking their position they immediately took off again for Abeshr.

At Abeshr, still in French Chad, the Commandant and a bodyguard of very tall men met them with some very welcome iced water, and a less welcome telegram from Fort Lamy recommending that because of the *brume seche*, they should go no further; they would, it said, telephone again with more information on Saturday. But it was only Thursday and the idea of waiting till then did not appeal. So in spite of this advice, after refuelling, they took off again for El Geneina, some hundred miles further east in the Anglo Egyptian Sudan.

By the time they reached El Geneina it was already late afternoon and why Preston decided to continue to El Fasher instead of landing, we shall never know. They were now over mountainous country but still flying in thick haze and, with both daylight and petrol running out and no sign of El Fasher, Preston was again looking round for somewhere to land. To quote his own words, he chose a good-looking wadi, dropped his last smoke bomb and landed 'with no small relief.'

They immediately set to filling bags with stones with which to anchor the Moth, by which time darkness had fallen. Supper consisted of fruit salad, a meat lozenge, a piece of barley sugar and biscuits all washed down with the iced water supplied to them at Abeshr. They were just finishing their meal when they heard voices and three or four natives appeared with a donkey. 'They halted a little way off,' the Duchess recorded, 'and Preston advanced to meet them to try and get some information about our whereabouts. By giving the names of various places to which they pointed he gathered we were very near El Fasher.'

When the men had departed they set about preparing places to sleep. This was a simple matter as all they had was one Moth cushion apiece. For a pillow the Duchess wrapped a pair of shoes in a jumper, after which they settled down to play backgammon by torchlight. Hardly had they begun when they again heard voices and the natives reappeared with a load of firewood, a huge bowl of milk, a chicken, eggs and some water. They lit a fire, borrowed the tin which had contained the smoke-bomb to boil the eggs, poured the water over the chicken and after holding it over the flames, plucked it. They then speared the bird with a stick and held it over the fire to cook. As cooking promised to be a slow business the Duchess at this point retired to 'bed'.

The ground was hard and stony and at first the Duchess lay on her flying coat but during the night, a cold wind got up and she put it on, using her suitcase as a windbreak. Some time during the night the natives, deeming the chicken to be cooked, offered it to Preston who managed to dissuade them from 'disturbing' the Duchess; although they had already had an adequate supper, Preston felt bound to participate and, after ten hours flying and an additional meal of four eggs and stringy fowl, he fell deeply asleep. They woke at four in the morning went for a short walk to unstiffen, then slept again till six. *'It was all great fun,'* the Duchess wrote later, *'and glorious to sleep out in the open desert with all the romance that accompanied the situation. Secretly I had rather longed for this to happen. We had been so near it once or twice and a night out in the desert, with our aeroplane safe and sound and sufficient petrol to get to our destination was an experience not to be missed.'*

The self-appointed guardians stayed all night and provided them with breakfast of milk and hard-boiled eggs, for which they would take no reward. 'We took leave of our guardian at 7.10 am,' the Duchess wrote, 'The headsman's name was Sheik Omda Hassabullah al Bulbecher and I hope he received the food which I paid to be sent to him later from El Fasher.' Preston, who was celebrating his birthday, was determined not to arrive at the British garrison town looking as if he had spent the night out and somehow managed to shave. El Fasher was indeed nearby. Thus at 7.30 in the morning after only a fifteen minute flight, they landed on the polo ground to be met by three Officers who, as there were no landing grounds within miles, were puzzled as to how they could have arrived so early! While Preston relaxed in the Mess, the Duchess was hustled off to Government House to stay with Mr Dupuis who, it so happened, had for a short time been tutor to her son Hastings. 'I slept on the roof for the first time since Persia,' the Duchess wrote, 'I have been longing for this as it is a great joy to lie and look at

Paintings from the sketchbook of R.C.Preston.
(Upper) Agadir, before it was devasted by an earthquake on 25th
February 1960.
(Lower) The Market Square at Coulomb Bechar, 26th March 1935

213

the stars and I often wish I could do it at home; it is not the cold that deters me.'

The British Army Post at El Fasher, run on the same lines as others throughout the Empire, bought back for the Duchess, nostalgic memories of the India she had known and loved before she married. The Officers with their polo ponies and syces, the bungalows and the loyal native servants, all reminded her of the pre-Ghandi India to which the years no doubt lent enchantment. 'As I look back upon it,' she wrote, 'I see what a gloriously happy time it was for those last six years of my unwedded life. The girl of today with her cocktails, smoking and motors may be happy, but cannot have as good a time as we had. . . Only in the matter of dress has the modern girl the advantage. What would I have not given for a ride-astride habit, the short skirt or even the absence of it. But even in those days I rode astride with my father when there were no Europeans looking on. We shared a pony on some of our trips and also his saddle. Later I was the first woman to ask Busvine, the London tailor, to make me a ride-astride habit though not of course the first woman to ride that way in London. I shocked my relations by what were then regarded as very short skirts for shooting, and I now marvel that I could ever have walked the moors in them, seeing that they were down to my ankles. Short hair is another boon of today which we were denied, and certainly the girl of today with her slim figure and loose, scanty clothing, is an infinitely more graceful being.'

They left for Khartoum early next morning, refuelling and stopping for breakfast en route at El Obeid. After El Obeid they were back over desert and as they neared Khartoum, could see the new White Nile Dam and the native village of Omdurman. The Duchess spent her first morning in Khartoum replenishing her wardrobe and in particular her shoes, which she described as being in the last stages of dilapidation. Preston, who had passed through Khartoum before, inevitably found many acquaintances. 'Flight Lieut. Preston,' the Duchess wrote, 'who comes across friends or relations in most places that he visits on the earth's surface, has come across a nest of them here.' This resulted in her spending the afternoon in a launch on the Nile with his friends from which, defying danger from crocodiles and disease, they swam. After two nights in Khartoum they left for Wadi Halfa following the Nile to Atbara where they refuelled, and then the railway to Wadi Halfa where they night-stopped. Next day they continued to Luxor where the Duchess was tempted to stay the night and revisit Karnak, which she had so enjoyed when two years earlier, she had been there with Bernard Allen. However, as time was running short, they pressed on after refuelling to Cairo, a flight which, against a strong headwind, took them over four hours.

In Cairo they were met by Tom Russel, who dropped them off at Shepherd's - a place of more memories for the Duchess as it was here that she had stayed with Herbrand when returning from India after their marriage. It was here too that she read 'with great sadness' of the death of Knight who they had met so recently in Kano.

After three nights in Cairo they left for home. The first night of the homeward journey was spent at Mersa Matruh and the next at Benghazi where after a flight of over five hours, they landed very short of petrol. *'Benghazi,'* the Duchess wrote, *'has become very military, especially at the moment when large numbers of troops are being sent to Abyssinia.'* From Benghazi, after refuelling at Sirte, they continued to Tripoli and next day, flew on to Tunis. In the four days since leaving Cairo they had put in eighteen and a half hours in the air, nevertheless the inexhaustible Duchess on the afternoon of their arrival, hired a car and drove out to Carthage, took tea at a village in the hills and on her return visited the Tunis Souk. 'Dined at a restaurant where Flight Lieut. Preston said we should get a super excellent French dinner, but I think we would have done as well or better in the hotel.' she wrote, affinity between them as ever lacking. Next day they took their baggage to the aerodrome and while Preston checked over the aeroplane, a Shell representative drove the Duchess to a place where she could watch birds. By lunchtime Sicily was reporting gales of over 100 mph, which put any thought of leaving out of the question. They therefore returned to Tunis, took a further drive and after tea, returned to the Souk, which the Duchess described as not so crowded as many and with more interesting goods for sale. 'They apparently extend for miles,' she wrote, 'and Flight Lieut.

Preston, who affected to be able to find his way about them, was very soon lost. The fat old Tunisians in fez and voluminous pants sit cross-legged in their tiny shops, and those who preside over perfume shops for which Tunis is famous, surrounded by decorative scent bottles and lit from above, look for all the world as if they had jumped out of the *Arabian Nights* or *Haji Baba*. It is difficult to believe they are the real thing. Others preside over their famous carpets, shoes and clogs, pottery and brasses, and it is the making of these on the spot that makes these bazaars so much more attractive than many I have visited. They are only rivalled I think by the beautiful lofty bazaars of Isfahan, though even there I do not think the work displayed was so thoroughly native. May it be long before they are ruined like Constantinople! I was longing to buy one of those beautiful brass trays but Flight Lieut. Preston would give me no encouragement, and as I could not have taken it in the Moth I submitted to his cold douche and have regretted it ever since.'

By the following morning the winds had modified and at 8.30 am they left for Catania with the wind behind them, registering a ground speed of 118 mph. Here they suffered the fuss and delays that they had come to expect from Italian Customs. The Duchess was made to empty her cases and her dresses, in a depressing state after crossing the Sahara in a small suitcase, were given a long, hard look while officials decided whether they were being imported new! Her camera was sealed up to prevent photographs being taken presumably from the air, as tourists coming by car or train could use cameras freely. For some reason they stayed in Taorimina, some thirty-five miles from the aerodrome and where the hotel, as elsewhere in Sicily, was crowded with Germans.

In the morning, the car ordered to take them back to the aerodrome failed to turn up so they made a late start. 'We flew across the bay,' the Duchess wrote, 'where Miss Winifred Spooner had to swim for it when her fellow aviator landed her in the sea on their would-be record-making flight to the Cape (in 1930 with Flg. Off. E C T Edwards in a Desoutter II). Landed Naples for petrol then flew on to Rome. Vesuvius belching forth good deal of pinky sulpher smoke from centre cone. Stayed at Excelsior hotel.'

It was now Easter Saturday, and next morning before leaving Rome, they went to St. Peter's to see the Pope holding High Mass. Then, short of time as ever, they tore through the Vatican galleries and Sistine Chapel. 'The remainder of our time,' the Duchess wrote, 'was filled by driving round and seeing the exterior of many of the places of chief interest. Flight Lieut. Preston thought this an excellent way of seeing Rome but I cannot say I do, and it is the second time I have been hustled through in this way as Herbrand and I saw it thus on our return from India.' In Rome, her thoughts inevitably turned back again to Allen, the friend and companion with whom she had shared so many happy times. 'I came two years ago with Flight Lieut. Allen,' she wrote, 'and thought of him with great regret as we stood looking down at the Forum where he and I had studied it all so carefully together. He would have loved to have done all our flight this time if only Fate had not been too hard on him.'

Of their departure from Rome the Duchess wrote, 'Flight Lieut. Preston was much 'wound up' by the dilatoriness of the officials at the aerodrome who kept us one and a quarter hours making up the log books etc. - but this is Italy. Eventually we took off and he cooled down in the air. We did not stop at Pisa this time. I had spent one night at a Pisa hotel and wanted no more.' They arrived at the 'wretched little Nice aerodrome' to find a *Concours Hippique* (or horse-show) in progress on it. 'Nice is very full of fashionable folk for Easter and I felt very like Cinderella in my crushed and drab outfit,' the Duchess wrote, 'There was a big dance given by the Members of the *Concours Hippique* at the hotel in the evening and I could not but reflect on the contrasts in our days experiences, beginning with High Mass in St. Peter's and ending with the Cabaret in Nice.'

Easter Sunday was a day of very high wind and Preston decided against leaving so, instead, they drove via the Grande Corniche to Monte Carlo. In the *Salles Privees* of the Casino the tables were full but not overcrowded, and the people more pleasant-looking, the Duchess thought, than in the old days, though less smart. 'One used to see a host of bejewelled women with rings up to the joint of every finger, including thumbs, clearly living for gambling,' she wrote, 'but formerly there was a smart world of another sort, the absence of which may be partly attributed to the change in climate. We never *dreamt* of bringing anything other than gay summer clothes at Easter when we came to stay with the Malets at *Chateau Malet.* All we suffered from was dust. An old riddle of those days was:

'Why are the Monte Carlo roads like a cat's back? Because they are covered with Poussiere! (dust).

'The pink geraniums which then hung in masses are now showing barely any blossom and there are cold winds and rain every time I come. Of those whom we used to meet at Chateau Malet which Sir Edward built, so many are gone: the Malets themselves, the Salisbury's, the Empress Eugenie and many more.' It was late April so they could certainly have expected better things!

They left for home early on Easter Monday, refuelled at Lyons and lunched in Paris at the Ritz, where the Duchess had her mail directed. Then after clearing customs at Lympne, they continued to Woburn - the end of a day that included seven hours of flying. *'It had been a wonderfully interesting flight,'* the Duchess wrote later, *'and somewhat of an adventure for the Sahara was first flown in 1932. There has probably been a good deal of flying done in connection with planning the route, but private aviators are rare. There were none at Kano and only one besides us this year.* Our return came very near King and Queen's Jubilee celebrations. Had seat in front row at St. Pauls and saw all there was to be seen in that most beautiful setting. Attended Court Ball and met for the first time some of my sister Duchesses. Prince of Wales evening party at St. James.' For these occasions the Duchess would fly to Heston on the day of the event, stay one night in London and return to Woburn in her aeroplane next day. Thus she escaped from much of the social round that, as her deafness grew, became more and more of an effort for her.

The family party left for *Endsleigh* this year on 18th May and while they were there, Preston came to collect the Duchess for the 1935 Empire Air Day tour. This was organised as previously as a publicity event in aid of the Royal Air Force Benevolent Fund. During five hours flying they visited Bristol, Dorchester, Bournemouth, Portsmouth and Hanworth ending the day at

In 1937 the Duchess flew to Fen Ditton, then drove to Mildenhall for the Silver Jubilee Year Review of the Royal Air Force. This was attended by three Kings: King George V (seated in leading Rolls-Royce), future King George VI to the left of the second Rolls-Royce and future King Edward VIII on his left. (Author's Collection)

Woburn where they spent the night, returning to Plymouth next day.

Although the Duchess made several flights in June, there is only one entry in her diary for the month. This tells of a flight to Trent Park to see Sir Phillip Sassoon's collection of water fowl, an invitation not unconnected, the Duchess wrote, with the fact that the latter wanted two of Woburn's rare Red Breasted Geese. There is no record of whether he got them! Flights shown in her log book include a solo flight to Old Warden - probably to visit the Shuttleworths - one to Heston to attend the Horse of the Year show at Olympia and two days later, to Heston for a visit to Wimbledon where she had been given seats in the Royal Box. She also flew to Aldenham (Elstree) to watch the RAF

219

display, which she had been invited to watch from Sir Philip Sassoon's box at Hendon.

In July, the Duchess flew on 22 out of the 31 days. On the 6th she flew to Fen Ditton from where she motored to Martlesham for the Review of the Royal Air Force by King George V. Photographs of this event include three Kings; George V and with him the Royal Princes who were to become Edward VIII and George VI. On the 10th she attended Sir Philip Sassoon's garden party at Trent Park and on the 13th flew to the opening of the new Leicester (Braunstone) Municipal Aerodrome by Sir Phillip Cunliffe Lister, Secretary of State for Air. Only three miles from the city centre, the aerodrome was at the time seen as an ambitious and farsighted project that it was envisaged, with air liners 'radiating to the four corners of the Kingdom and the nations overseas', would greatly benefit the commercial city. Events laid on for visitors included aerobatic displays by a Gauntlet, three Furys and an 'Arrival' competition that the Duchess won in her Gipsy Moth and for which she was presented with a cheque for £10! On 16th July the Duchess flew to Southampton where she joined a party who were motoring to Plymouth for the Review of the Fleet. 'Having hitherto only witnessed from my own big yacht found it a dull affair.' she wrote, 'Long way down line, King's yacht never came near. Not allowed back into harbour till midnight, everybody horribly bored and sleepy. Stayed at Botley for the night.'

On the 27th, the Duchess flew herself to Ratcliffe for Lindsay Everard's annual lunch for flying members of the Houses of Parliament, attended this year by a hundred or so guests. Lunch served in the hangar was followed by a Church service after which guests repaired to the swimming pool for a bathing party. The Duchess records that Lord Londonderry, principal guest at the function, got lost on his way up and arrived an hour late!

During August the Duchess put in some fifteen hours solo, making the most of her Gipsy Moth I G-AXBR, whose days were now numbered. In June that year, de Havillands had announced that, after ten years in which over 4,000 Gipsy Moths has been produced, they were stopping production to concentrate on Tiger Moths, which had been adopted for training by the RAF and sixteen foreign Governments. Any remaining wooden Moth

Major fuselages were to be converted to 'Queen Bees', the radio controlled version of the Tiger.

Thus in late August, the Duchess took delivery of Moth Major G-ACUR, the last of the DH.60 Moths to be produced. This was fitted with a 120 h.p. Gipsy III, the first inverted version of the Gipsy engine and for flying, was judged by some - but my no means all - to be the best of all Moths including the Tiger. The 130 h.p. Gipsy Major fitted in the Tiger Moth was an improved version of this engine. The Duchess had her first flight in the new Moth on 5th September when, with Preston, she flew to Newtonards to stay with the Londonderrys for the Kings Cup elimination race, for which Belfast was a turning point, and to watch the Tourist Trophy races. The elimination race consisting of a 1,300-mile race round Britain, included for the first time an over-water leg on which Alex Henshaw in a Miles Hawk Major, came down and was picked up by a passing steamer! It was a sign of the rate of development of the British light aircraft that 34 out of the 36 entrants were now monoplanes. These included Captain E W Percival's Mew Gull, seven other Gulls entered by various pilots and F G Miles's Sparrowhawk, which was one of thirteen Miles aircraft entered. De Havilland, who for so many years had led the field had only four entries, a Dragonfly entered jointly by John and Geoffrey de Havilland, the T.K.2 by Hubert Broad and two Leopard Moths. The race was won by Tommy Rose in a Hawk Speed Six at 176 mph, the aircraft in which five months later he was to reach Cape Town in three days seventeen and a half hours and would return in four days, breaking both existing records.

After her visit to Northern Ireland the Duchess spent a couple of nights at Bargaly, the property owned by the Duke on the *Cairnsmore* estate. There she took the opportunity to revisit Machrihanish and Oban, passing en route over Ordmaddy Castle 'to greet Miss Mackinnon'. She returned to Woburn on September 9th and on the 18th, attended the opening of Southend aerodrome by Under Secretary of State for Air, Sir Philip Sassoon.

'September 26th - My seventieth birthday. I had to go to London in the morning and, though rather thick and threatening, celebrated the occasion by half an hours solo flight on my return.

'September 27th - Did a much longer flight today all around London, flying to Gravesend to see the new Percival Gull plane which will be ready shortly. There I met young Melrose who did the unofficial record flight from Australia. He also had bought Percival Gull with which he hopes to return there.

'Very murky to the east of London so we (Flight Lieut. Preston in the new Moth) flew back to Hatfield via Croydon and Heston. *Here I had to leave my beloved G-ABXR, the last relic of my flights with Flight Lieut. Allen. I did not at all want to get rid of it but de Havillands are making no more open Moths so I was obliged to buy the last available.* Its letters are G-ACUR and at present it has behaved like it. Oil leaks etc. It has a Gipsy III engine, but I do not think the plane is a bit faster than the old one and is not so comfortable.'

The Duchess flew to Scotland for the annual visit on 28th September, forced down temporarily en route at Liverpool for bad weather. The following day Herbrand arrived and the Duchess drove Preston to Stranraer to catch a boat 'to his beloved Ireland.' Her comments show that their relations were still ones of mutual tolerance and for the first time for many years, because 'Flight Lieut. Preston seems unlikely to face the weather for some days', she returned to Woburn on 9th November by train. A couple of days later they flew to Haldon, a very basic aerodrome even for those days, situated on top of a hill adjacent to Haldon Racecourse and the main (as it was then) Exeter-Torbay road. The object of the visit was to attend a wedding in Exeter Cathedral and one cannot but wonder how in an open Moth and in pouring rain, she managed to arrive attired for a society wedding! 'If I were the owner of Haldon Aerodrome,' the Duchess wrote, 'and could afford it, I should plant all the steep slope on one side of the narrow landing ground with the thickest and softest low bushes I could find. There is no room for overshooting; it would be 'good-bye' to one's aeroplane when the wind is west and possibly to the world as well, if one overshot it ever so little.' It must have been an exceptionally wet autumn as the return journey was also made in pouring rain, the Duchess remarking that she had never seen the country so flooded.

'November 19th: Spent four nights at Sarratt Mill and on the last morning of my visit, motored myself round what was once lovely country. But I had not done this since the War and the change was enough to make the angels weep. Hideous bungalows and little villas by the hundred have been erected, the lovely beechwoods laid low, the winding lanes made straight, the hedges and roadside trees cut down to enable the motorist to tear through the country where there is no longer anything to linger for. In the place of lovely lanes we have wide roads and footpaths bounded by stiff-built-up white stone edge, three traffic lanes down the centre and hideous road signs every few yards. I suppose the railways were once looked upon with equal horror, but the change came far more gradually, and it was possible to get away from them. But now it will not be long before the National Reserves will be the only beautiful places, and by that time I hope not bestrewn with newspapers, cigarette cartons and picnic paper, as most of them now are. *Above, cloudland may for yet a little longer remain unspoiled for those who love it. but this which to me was one of the greatest joys of flying in my late pilot's time, is now denied me. The present incumbent never goes anywhere unless compelled.'*

On Christmas Day the Duchess wrote, 'Christmas has dissolved into fog and rain. Compelled to leave Moth at Heston. Here endeth Jubilee year.'

223

Chapter Thirteen
1936: Death of the King

On 1st January 1936 the Duchess, an excellent shot, recorded in her diary that she had opened the New Year by shooting forty-one pheasants and two rabbits with forty-eight cartridges. The shoot however ended at lunchtime when rain and fog descended. That was the way it was for most of January. On 2nd January, en route to London, the Duchess flew to Heston and because of fog had to leave the Moth there. Next day Preston flew her back to collect it in her new Percival Gull G-ADSG, which she christened *Kittywake*. Suprisingly there are no comments in her diary about her new aeroplane, or how she found the side-by-side seating. However, she wrote later, 'before ordering my Gull, my only objection which I made several times to makers and R.C.P. was that if one landed on soft ground, its spats would be dangerous. Pointed out that if we had had spats when we landed at Budapest we should inevitably have turned over. Later Barnard came to grief in Africa for this reason. Both my pilot and the maker pooh-poohed my objection and though perfectly certain I was right, had to take machine spats and all. They give less wind resistance but I care more for safety than speed,' - a view that would be heavily supported today.

In all, January proved a somewhat depressing month apart from the weather. On 18th January news arrived of the death in Holland of Mr Blaauw, the Duke and Duchess's friend of many years standing and two days later, King George V died, bringing with it a train of official engagements for both the Duke and Duchess. 'He has done his duty to the limit of his strength,' the Duchess wrote, 'and probably in the last few years since his illness, beyond it and he deserved the happy death he died. A few days of probably almost painless illness, decreasing strength lapsing into unconsciousness only in the last few hours, and a peaceful passing to the Great Beyond. What better, happier end could one wish for him?'

In January 1936 the Duchess took delivery of a new Percival Gull G-ADSG, which she named Kittywake. It is pictured at Gravesend before she took delivery. (A J Jackson Collection)

Ten days later the Duchess received an invitation to the funeral service in St. George's Chapel, Windsor. For this, special trains were laid on from London and but for a very long wait until the procession arrived the Duchess wrote, it was all made very easy. The ceremony is recorded in her diary thus:

'Five Kings were present and most of those would have been considered minor Royalties in King Edward's time; the Emperor of Germany, the Czar, the King of Spain, the King of Portugal, the Emperor of Austria are all gone, and with the King of Italy, owing to the Abyssinian War, we are on strained terms. The glass precincts of the Chapel were covered with wreaths - one could not but reflect how often beauty is sacrificed to size. I had a seat in the Choir Stalls, probably almost where Herbrand, as a Knight of the Garter, has his stall as I saw his banner was not in the opposite side. Unfortunately owing to our thick, long veils which were 'regulation' and the dark panelled walls of the Chapel, we could see practically nothing when the procession came in, but I was almost in line with the King and Queen Mary, who stood behind the coffin, with the Prime Minister on my right.'

A week later the Duchess, wearied by official duties wrote:

'February 3rd: Being very deaf and pining for a little rest from struggling to listen to people I could not hear, I accepted

Sister Rachel's invitation to come to Cley Mill for a few days. It is indeed a peaceful spot at this time of year and she has made it most comfortable. Flew down in *Curlew* (Moth G-ACUR) and found a good landing field at Langham; rather a cold and misty flight but shortly after my arrival a very heavy snowstorm came on. I was driving myself along the coast route, and periodically the snow, which caked above where the windscreen wiper worked, slid down *en masse* and completely obscured my view. I was thankful to get back to the Mill and to hear that Flight Lieut. Preston had reached home in safety.'

The day after arriving there the Duchess wrote to Preston thus:

"Dear Flight Lieut. Preston,

I am afraid I shall have to forgo the proposed flight to Africa. Owing to our having to postpone shooting so often and the King's death, I have been unable to do the necessary shopping and fitting, and now that I could do it (though too late), I have in the last ten days had a very bad turn of deafness and noise in the head and so cannot do London business even now.

"The luggage should be starting the day after tomorrow if it is to get to Cairo in time for our arrival as it takes three weeks by sea.

"We must try and fix up something later but the Fates have been against it this time."

Although the diary contains no indication of what had been planned, it seems likely that it was again for the Oasis Rally.

The Duchess remained at the Mill until 11th February when after a week of fine weather but bitterly cold north and east winds, she flew back to Woburn. 'I was very sorry to leave the Mill,' she wrote, 'I think my little household as well as myself have been happy there and enjoyed getting away from the formalities and discipline of Abbey life. Two of the chauffeurs are old Bird Club boys (W.B.O.C.) and keen bird-watchers. Bailey has busied herself turning housemaid temporarily. Young kitchen-maid presides over the kitchen pro.tem; Knight the first chauffeur we ever had turns I believe into a very efficient scullery-maid! And I bird-watch, and idle and read. All very nice!'

The Coat of Arms, designed by
the 11th Duke to depict the inter-
ests and achievements of his wife.
This was rejected by the Garter
King of Arms.
(Trustees of Woburn Estates)

Meanwhile, owing to the late King's death, the Duke, who had
been awarded the Zoological Society's Gold Medal, was presented with it by Edward VIII at a private audience. 'A medal
worth having,' the Duchess wrote, 'of large size, with a group of
well-designed birds in relief on one side and of beasts on the
other. He said the King had a very dark and indifferent little
office, quite as untidy as his own study! It was a nice informal
interview and entirely after the heart of the recipient of the
medal!' The Duke had just retired after 37 years as President of
the Zoological Society. His most notable achievements in this
time included the securing for Woburn, at the time of the Boxer
riots, the only surviving examples of Pére David's deer,
previously the property of the Emperor of China; preserving
from extinction the European Bison and most important of all,
the setting up in 1926 of the Zoological Park at Whipsnade.

Herbrand, who was extremely proud of his wife's many
achievements, had decided that she merited her own Coat of
Arms and in 1936, an article about this must have appeared in
the Press, as the Duchess included in her diary for 5th February
that the 'cutting' had been partly (where not wholly) inaccurate.
As early as 1931 the Duke had submitted a design for a coat of
arms to the Earl Marshal, the Duke of Norfolk. This portrayed
in the quarterings episodes in the Duchess's life: the Fokker in
which she and her crew had made record flights to India and
Cape Town; a common Tern representing her interests in birds;

227

the Banyan tree in the garden of the Viceroy's country house at Barrackpore near Calcutta, and the Wille glacier on Jan Mayen Island. The significance of the Banyan tree was that it was under this tree in 1888, that they had held their wedding breakfast; Jan Mayen because the Duchess, who visited the Island before World War I in her yacht *Sapphire*, was still the only woman to have landed there.

The submitted design proved unacceptable to Garter King of Arms because it was not 'heraldic'. 'True heraldry,' he wrote, 'like true art is imaginative and not realistic, symbolic not pictorial.' The Duke appealed to the Earl Marshal to have the decision reversed, but the Duke of Norfolk replied that he agreed with 'Garter', so that virtually put an end to it.

'I heard nothing of the matter.' the Duchess wrote, 'Except that Herbrand wanted me to have a coat of arms and asked me to choose a bird and give him a photograph of *Sapphire*. Had I been consulted I would have urged conforming with the dictum of Garter King of Arms, as if one is to have a Coat of Arms it is better to have a correct and patented one, *but in his great kindness of heart he had done all this for me and it was not for me to cavil at the result.'*

The damp, foggy and cheerless weather continued into March when on the 13th, Herbrand went down with a virulent form of 'flu. This spread to his nurses and to many of the household including by the end of the month, the Duchess herself. In a letter to Preston during this time she wrote: 'If people did not shut themselves up in airtight compartments with drawn blinds, which they have to do as soon as they send for a Doctor, I think they would get well more quickly. . . . Its no use holding theories if you do not put them into practice yourself, so with a temperature of 103 and over, I have sat out in my car in a sheltered spot; in the sun when available, in fog or rain when it was not. I invited the opinion of no medical man and have carried on doing things for myself, with the result that for the last four days the temperature has gradually been coming down and the cough for the first time today is really better.

'If things continue to go as I hope, I shall have no medical bills to contemplate! I have slept all along with my bed as close to the widely open window as the wall permits. I may not be out of the wood yet so perhaps it is early to crow, but I think it will only be some new evil spirit if I have to eat humble pie now.'

The Duchess's predilection for fresh air was not as eccentric as it sounds today. In an era when central heating hardly existed, rooms would be heated by large coal fires and windows kept tightly closed. There were some, however, who like the Duchess considered fresh air to the more healthy than the inevitable fug, and patients with chest infections such as Tuberculosis were sent to sanatoria where fresh air and open windows were the recognised treatment.

In spite of her 'flu and the bad weather, the Duchess managed during March and April to fit in a surprising amount of flying, the only gap of any significance being between 21st March and 8th April. One can only imagine that in an open machine, Preston would have hated these flights and certainly, the Duchess's log book is scantily filled in. On 21st April she wrote, 'Never, I should think, was there such an April. There has been an abundance of fog but little rain with the result that it has been a wonderful year for spring flowers, and the golden glory of the daffodils has been the one and only redeeming feature of a truly horrible winter and spring.' On arriving at Heston that morning she accepted an offer of a flight in an American Vultee 'fast' passenger 'plane. 'I flew it myself for a short time,' she wrote, 'and felt I was back in the old *Spider*.'

On 18th May the family moved down to *Endsleigh*, the Duchess following next day in a record flight-time of one hour thirty-five minutes. Three days later she flew back to London to attend a Royal Aeronautical Society Lecture and Soiree at the Imperial Institute. The lecture entitled *Slippery Surfaces* was she wrote, 'above the heads of all but the deeply scientific,' so she didn't reckon to have missed much by her bad hearing! Next day, after a mornings work at her hospital, she returned to *Endsleigh*.

23rd May was Empire Air Day and at the special request of Air Commodore Chamier, Secretary General of the Air League, they made a tour of seven aerodromes starting with Gatwick and ending with Barnstable and Plymouth. The aim of the tours was to make the public air-minded but on this occasion, the weather was so poor that no one turned out to see them! 'Very

Log book entries (top) in the Duchess's hand June/July 1933 and (Bottom) in Preston's handwriting, May 1935.
(Woburn Archives)

futile tour,' the Duchess wrote, 'as met none but the aerodrome officials who are sufficiently air-minded already. But we have done our duty.'

On the coldest Whit Monday for twenty-nine years, Hastings moved into *Endsleigh* with his younger son Hugh and it must have been with some sadness that on the same day, the Duchess, her sister Zöe and the Prestons left for the last time. It was still cold when on 3rd June she set off north for some bird-watching. Their first stop was at Filey where, after landing on Scarborough Racecourse, they spent two nights at the Royal Crescent Hotel. They then went on to Perth for an official luncheon marking the opening of the aerodrome. In a car delivered from *Cairnsmore*, the Duchess spent the next day visiting old haunts round Meikleour, spending the night at the Atholl Arms in Dunkeld. Back with her aeroplane she flew with Preston to Montrose, lunched with the Southesks at Kinnard Castle and from there, continued to Aberdeen where she had been specially invited by Gander Dower to see his new aerodrome, Dyce; after this they returned to Perth for the night. On the way home they landed at Newcastle from where the Duchess drove to Seahouses, but it was too early for the autumn migration and breeding birds had all dispersed - so she continued north and visited Holy Island. Two days later Preston brought the Moth up from Newcastle and collected her from a field near Seahouses. They then returned to Woburn.

Shoreham had been in use as an aerodrome since 1909 but on 13th June that year, it was officially opened by the three relevant Mayors as the Municipal Aerodrome for Brighton, Hove and Worthing. The Duchess with some 80 other owners attended the opening. A week later they flew in the Gull to Bekesbourne near Canterbury for an Aviation Service at which RAF and Civil Ensigns presented to the Cathedral, were dedicated by the Archbishop '*In remembrance of all those who in the service of the King and their fellow men, pursued their business in the highways of the air.*' 'Delightful ceremony,' the Duchess wrote, 'tea in the precincts; intended to fly solo but Todd had put Moth on nose when swinging prop.'

Their next major expedition was to the opening of the aerodrome at Le Touquet on 4th July. 'I had a desire to fly the

Channel myself,' the Duchess wrote, 'the landing at Lympne and in France included. As we have always flown over in a closed machine because we were going on a long flight, and one cannot land the machine from the rear seat, I resolved to do the short flight in my own Moth and take the Flight Lieut. there and back as passenger.' Even this is entered in her log book under her pilot's name! 'We were greeted as guests,' she continued, 'and our hotel expenses paid. There was a luncheon party at the Picardy Hotel the first day which was chiefly remarkable for the scarcity of waiters, and the time before we got anything to eat. In the evening we went to the Casino and I watched Flight Lieut. Preston losing all that I had given him to gamble with, only mentally staking myself. As far as I could tell I should have won nothing. There was a flying display in the afternoon of Sunday, but spoilt by low cloud and weather generally, but it ended up with a wonderful display of fireworks in which I always delight and subsequently found some lovely mosquitoes or equally unpleasant bugs, who had taken advantage of my evening dress. Gambled for half an hour in the Casino; wins retrieve losses on donations to R.C.P. and more also.'

On Monday, just as they were leaving, the Duchess was presented with a bouquet that this time she took with her. 'Learn a little later,' she wrote, 'that cut flowers liable to duty at Lympne, however Customs Officer let me off!' The day after they returned the Duchess flew to Heston en route to a private opening of the War Museum in its new quarters at Lambeth, late Bethlehem Hospital alias Bedlam.

The 1936 Kings Cup Air Race was run from Hatfield on 11th-12th July, the Ansty-Hatfield leg of the elimination race passing on a day of very low cloud, directly over the Abbey. 'Race won by Charles Gardner,' the Duchess wrote, '26 entrants and every machine had a Gipsy engine. Witnessed final race from Hatfield in generous supply of rain.'

Towards the end of July some eighty aeroplanes from fifteen or so countries arrived for a *'Weekend Aerien'* organised by the Royal Aero Club. The planned arrival point was Heston but the weather was such that many arrived by train, having abandoned their aeroplanes at various points en route. The *'weekend'* started on Thursday, entertainments laid on including a cocktail party at the Royal Aero Club, 119 Piccadilly on the night of arrival, and visits on Friday to a choice of either Oxford or Cambridge, lunch being provided by Magdalen and Trinity Colleges respectively. This was followed in the evening by a reception given by Lord Londonderry in his Park Lane Londonderry House. On the Saturday, visitors were escorted to Great Fosters, Windsor and Eton and the weekend ended with a grand banquet at Grosvenor House - cost for attending, £1.15s inclusive of cigars and wine. As a finale, Lindsay Everard invited guests to drop in at Ratcliffe on their way home for Sunday lunch and here, some three hundred guests were entertained in a large marquee. The Duchess took part in all the events and after lunch at Ratcliffe, flew on to Trent Park to see Sir Philip Sassoon's 'wonderful collection of waterfowl'.

In early July the Reading Aero Club at Woodley laid on a competition specifically for women pilots. Lord Northesk, who lived nearby had presented a cup that was intended for the winner of an all-women air race. But as insufficient women seemed willing to race their aeroplanes, the format was changed to a test for women pilots of 'air knowledge'. The test, a twenty minute flight either with their own or a club aircraft, included 360 degree turns, figures of eight turns round predetermined points and an engine-off forced landing from 2,000 feet ending in the aerodrome circle. All the entrants were 'judged' by the same instructor and given marks for various manoeuvres, the Cup being awarded to the competitor with the most marks. The fact that the Duchess entered the competition is a clear indication of her confidence now as a pilot. Ever modest she wrote in her diary, 'Had the temerity to enter the Northesk Cup, a test of efficiency in Aviation for women. Twelve entrants; three did not complete their tests. Winner wife of manager of Bournemouth aerodrome dressed in riding costume breeches, top boots and all. Scores were not revealed but I later learnt that I was awarded 76%.' This was indeed a creditable result as Mrs Fisher and Ruth Moore from Brooklands tied top only six points ahead. After a further spot landing test Mrs Fisher was declared the winner and awarded the cup. An 'open' landing competition held during the afternoon was won by Preston in the Duchess's Moth.

The Duchess presenting the Northesk Cup to Mrs Fisher at Woodley aerodrome near Reading in July 1936. The cup was donated by Lord Northesk for a competition between women pilots, in which the Duchess herself took part.
(A J Jackson Collection)

Later in July the Duchess again entered both her aeroplanes for Eastbourne Flying Club's *Concours d'Elegance* at Wilmington. 'R.C.P. and I also entered Arrival competition,' she wrote, 'neither of us won. Moth second in *Concours d'Elegance*, Gull would have been first, judge told R.C.P., if it had done more hours.' The Arrival competition was won by Prince Chirasakti of Siam, killed in 1942 while ferrying a Spitfire for the Air Transport Auxiliary.

On 21st August, the Duchess set out with Preston for a weekend in Belgium. 'Flew Gull to Chateau d'Ardennes as most anxious to know what this much advertised Hotel is like,' she wrote, 'Chateau d'Ardennes, old Royal Palace built by King Leopold; grounds now used as golf courses. Visitors like those at St. Andrews eminently respectable and somewhat elderly! Unfortunately landing field on small side; landed OK but did not think it fit for take-off at full load so I took luggage down to St, Hubert about an hours drive, and met R.C.P. there. Night Le Touquet.'

At the beginning of September they set out for St. Andrews, bad weather forcing them to spend the night at the L. & N.E. Railway Hotel at Newcastle. *'Being anxious to do my 200 hours solo before the winter, I put in another half-hour at Newcastle aerodrome,'* the Duchess wrote, *'But it was pretty thick for solo flying in strange land.'* Next morning with visibility still bad up north, after a flight in a B A Swallow with the Flying Club's Chief Instructor, she put in a further hours solo, bringing the total solo time shown in her log book to 197 hours and 25 minutes. Next day in better weather they continued to Creetown; 'field much improved by being ploughed up and re-sown.' the Duchess noted.

During their stay in Scotland the Duke and Duchess motored to Glen Trool to visit their son Hastings and children Daphne and Hugh. 'It was a glorious evening,' the Duchess wrote, 'and Glen Trool was quite lovely. Hastings and I scrambled up to a little promontory overlooking the Loch and I would willingly have stayed there till sunset had impatient folks not been waiting below, for surely there can be no more lovely view in Scotland than this.'

At the end of October Preston arrived in Scotland, 'bent on a visit to Ireland', on a day of gales and storms that, the Duchess commented, he certainly wouldn't have faced otherwise! Four days later they returned to Woburn in the record time of two hours five minutes. Shortly afterwards Peter Scott, son of the Antarctic explorer came to Woburn to study Geese and Wildfowl and spent the night. 'An artist of merit,' the Duchess wrote, 'and a charming youth; we hope to see him here again.' He would at the time have been 27 years old.

'The Crystal Palace, built in 1851, was burned to the ground last night with the exception of the two towers at either end,' the Duchess wrote on 1st December. 'I well remember the delight with which I first visited it with my Aunt and Uncle when I was six or seven years old. To the little girl from the country it was indeed a marvellous building. I am not sure whether it was on that occasion or a little later that I saw Blondin walk the tightrope across the Central Hall. Later I attended a Handel festival there, and once spoke to the audience myself in the Central Hall, but I have entirely forgotten the occasion but it must have been the opening of some show. Today I flew over it to say 'Good-bye' to its smoldering ruins.'

On 11th December King Edward VIII abdicated after less than a year in office. 'A good thing too,' the Duchess commented, 'he would have been for ever discredited even if he had given up the woman.' - adding later, 'I think abdication has done us more good than harm though it might have been otherwise had people not behaved with sense. The minority of five in the House of Commons has shown that we are solid for the Monarchy and we have shown the world that we do not tolerate immorality in high places.'

By the end of the year the Duchess's log book showed 197 hours and 50 minutes solo - she would, however, undoubtedly have qualified for a good many more hours.

Chapter Fourteen
1937: An Error of Navigation?

The winter and early spring of 1937, much like 1936, was mild but unpleasantly wet and foggy and during January and February, the Duchess only managed half a dozen short flights. What few entries there are in her diary for this period refer for the most part to the weather. On 5th January she wrote, 'First snowdrops at the hospital. This is very late seeing how mild the winter has been.'

At the end of the month she spent ten days at Sarratt Mill writing, 'Though the whole neighbourhood is being spoilt by buildings, a motor road, pylons etc., Sarratt Mill itself remains a peaceful spot, and I have made it very comfortable after my own heart. But motors now tear up and down the narrow neighbouring lanes, which doubtless will soon be widened to oblige them, as the big lorries which come rumbling down leave no room for the pedestrians between their banks. Herbrand who has continued to picture the Mill as the dreary spot with a table and four chairs as he knew it in his fishing days, came over to luncheon one day, and I think really felt that even he could spend a few hours here in comfort.'

It was still about the weather that the Duchess wrote on 24th February: 'Aconites are up and now their brief little day is over, but the first harbingers of spring were all very late this year, in spite of a mild and horrible winter. There has been ice on the ponds only for one day. Now and again the sun has put in an appearance for a few hours, but for the most part it had been a succession of fogs, gales, and rain up to date.'

It is hard in these days when all we ever get is a heavy mist, to envisage what winter was like before the Clean Air Act came into being. At a time when coal was the main fuel in home and factory, on a still evening, smoke from thousands of chimneys would descend to be cooled by the earth, creating a temperature inversion so stable that until the next depression came along, the gloom would grow denser by the day. In March, some late snow arrived the Duchess writing, 'there have never been two consecutive days when flying was possible since I came from Scotland; nothing but a series of fogs, rain, gales and now snow. 'Tis dreary work being reduced to the weather for a diary!'

By mid-March, much of the snow had melted and on 17th March, the Duchess flew with Preston to look at 'unprecedented' floods in the Fens. 'At Littleport, about a quarter of a mile of railway was quite under water,' she wrote, 'and we watched a train very slowly creeping through it. It all looked very chilly and miserable for the poor inhabitants, many of whose houses were under water.' - and this is the last entry in her diary.

They flew next day to see the floods again and on the 19th, made a cross-country flight to Rugby - all of which in the open Moth, one can only imagine Preston intensely disliked. On the 20th the Duchess made a solo flight of one hour and ten minutes to Bicester and according to Preston's calculations, this brought her solo up to 199 hours and 5 minutes. It was from her solo flight two days later on which she aimed to put in the 55 minutes required to take the total up to 200 hours, that she never returned.

The Duchess took off from Woburn in her Moth G-ACUR at 3.30 in the afternoon, on a triangular course that should have taken her from Woburn to Buntingford, Cambridge and back to Woburn, a total distance of some eighty miles. She was expected back within the hour. When she didn't return, the Duke rang the Chief Constable of Bedfordshire setting in train a search from ten RAF stations. There were rumours that a light 'plane had been seen heading out over the Wash but this was quickly discounted, meanwhile, no trace of the Duchess's Moth could be found. Thus on Wednesday 31st March, with all hope abandoned, a memorial service was held in Woburn parish church.

Two days later and ten days after her disappearance, an inter-plane strut was washed up at Yarmouth. Later the remaining three struts and an airscrew boss were washed up further down the east coast. Todd, who was responsible for the airworthiness of the Moth and had also been the last person to see the Duchess, was completely shattered by her disappearance and when the struts turned up, it was he who was called in to identify them. There was a rumour that much later, the engine turned up on a German beach.

Preston wrote in her flying log book against 22nd March 1937, the day of her disappearance, 'To the sea'. This has been taken, assuming it to have been written by the Duchess, to indicate that she never *intended* returning from this flight. There is, however, another possible explanation for her disappearance.

On the Type P.4 compass that was fitted in Moths at that time, there is a rotating grid ring some four inches in diameter, graduated round its circumference from 0 to 360 degrees. Across this grid a pair of parallel bars marks the north-south direction, 'north' being marked with a large red arrowhead. When steering by this compass, the course is set by first rotating the grid-ring until the desired course lines up with the aircraft heading, and then turning the aircraft until the compass needle lies parallel to the bars across the grid-ring. Now on this compass, the north end of the *compass needle* is differentiated only by a small cross bar and thus it was not an uncommon mistake, for pilots to align the compass needle with the grid-lines, *but with the needle pointing south instead of north.* This resulted in the pilot flying in the opposite direction to what was intended.

Meteorological Office records, still available for the day of the Duchess's disappearance, show that winds during the period were light and from the north or northwest. One station for which records are available is Mildenhall, an airfield some twenty miles northeast of Cambridge and at the time of writing, a large American air base. At 13.00 hours on 23rd March, 1937, Mildenhall was reporting rain and a cloud base of 800 feet and at 18.00 hours, a cloud base of 800 feet with drizzle. Now, Mildenhall lies on the *reciprocal* of the Duchess's course from Cambridge to Woburn. If, therefore, the Duchess had set 'black on red' as the expression goes, instead of flying southwest towards Woburn she would have headed northeast and quickly ended up in some pretty unpleasant weather. Moreover, if she had maintained this course expecting that on reaching the Woburn area, something would turn up that she could recognise, she would have eventually crossed the coast in the area in which the remains of her Moth were found. Such reports as are available from the east coast for that afternoon vary from cloudy

The final page from the Duchess's log book, with the annotation 'To the sea!'. People have surmised from this that she intended not to return, however it is clear that this entry was made by Preston.

(Woburn Archives)

to continuous rain; in these conditions it would not have been at all surprising if, lost and with little instrument flying experience, she had eventually lost control and crashed into the sea. The facts all seem to fit.

Nothing in her diary indicates that at the time the Duchess was unduly unhappy or depressed; she had for the past six months set her heart on completing 200 hours of solo. Furthermore, it would have been completely out of character for her to have deliberately caused her husband Herbrand any distress - a view taken by the vast majority of those who knew her. This then is the way I like to think the story ends.

Among the bequests in the Duchess's Will were books to St. Hugh's College, Oxford and, to her old school The Ladies College, Cheltenham, etchings and engravings. She left her 'aeroplanes and their accessories' to her Air Pilot Ralph Chevallier Preston of Froxfield House, Woburn *'or if he is not in my employ at the time of my death, then to the Air Pilot who is in my regular employ as such at my death or if there is no such air pilot then to my grandson Lord Howland.'* To Robert Parkyn of the firm of Knibbs and Parkyn Motor Manufacturers, Manchester and to N A Gass of the Anglo-Persian Oil Company she left the sum of £2,000, 'in recognition of their great kindness to me in 1928', when she had been stranded in Bushire. She left £5,000 to the Royal Society - to be used for research, to Our Dumb Friends League and to the Guild of Air Pilots and Air Navigators of which she was Liveryman and Honorary Warden. Other bequests included £20,000 to her sister Mrs Zöe Beaver, £10,000 to her brother John Campbell Tribe in Ceylon, £5,000 to their faithful housekeeper and ex-governess Miss Flora Green and £3,000 to Flight Lieutenant Ralph Chevallier Preston. To every employee at her Woburn Hospital, including the Matron and Nurses who had been in her service for 'upwards of ten years', and were 'not under notice whether given or received', she left the sum of £200.

One motor car, furs and 'all jewellery set with diamonds and rubies combined' were left to her sister Zöe; jewellery set with sapphires and diamonds combined was left to her niece Marjorie Beaver. Remaining cars together with small brooches, pendents, watches, rings and other jewellery were left to her husband 'hoping that he will give any he does not want to keep to those who have been my friends and to the servants who have been a long time in my service.'

The Duchess wrote in her Will that she 'desired to be cremated'. This, one feels sure, would have been because of her dislike of pomp and ceremony. She would have hated the idea of joining Russell forebears going back as far as the 14th century, in the grandiose Bedford Chapel at Chenies described by Pevsner as the richest single storehouse of funeral monuments in any parish church in England, and the memorial to the 1st Duke as 'the most swagger of all monuments in Buckinghamshire'. But as her body was never recovered the question never arose. The Duke, as a token of his appreciation for the extensive search carried out by the R.A.F., gave £1,000 to the Royal Air Force Benevolent Fund.

Of the Duchess's death, an anonymous correspondent to *The Times* wrote:

"If it had to be, the fading into the twilight of that courageous lady was sublime. We of the same generation following less adventurously in her footsteps, recognize in her pioneer flights the dispelling of the old-established belief that flying was for the very young alone. . ."

Epilogue

The following are among the many tributes that have been paid to Mary du Caurroy, wife of the 11th Duke of Bedford, her husband Herbrand writing of her thus:

'It is not easy to show wherein lay the magic charm of her personality. Perhaps charm is too elusive a gift to explain or define, but I think in her it sprang partly from a union of contrasting qualities. Her strength of will was softened by her gentleness of heart; her rather austere and severe manner was contradicted by her genial, humorous smile, and infectious laugh. No one would have suspected that one who seemed to be the embodiment of common sense and logic could, on occasion, startle her friends by a sudden act of pure impulsiveness. Yet so it was. Her wrath was highly disconcerting to its object; but it passed, leaving no sting behind. And, though I never heard of a formal apology coming from her lips, her friends were made aware by some special little act of kindliness that the crisis was over! I have heard her say that she did not 'suffer fools gladly'. and I think, in the main, this was true. Her own intelligence was too quick for her to have much patience with the slow-witted, especially if that slowness hampered or obstructed her plans. But again, as I myself can testify, the resentment and impatience was short-lived. Anyone as highly gifted as the Duchess could not but be aware of her fitness to lead and rule, but she was never self-assertive. Indeed, occasionally she was strangely diffident and distrustful of herself, a rather pathetic trait in one who was usually so self-reliant and independent.

'She was indeed nobly blessed in her gifts and circumstances. But she had one cross to carry which no affection could lift from her shoulders. For nearly fifty years she suffered from a very trying form of deafness, with constant noises in her head. It was a cruel handicap which, had she not faced it with unusual patience and fortitude, might easily have spoilt both her life and

243

The Marquess of Tavistock with the Duchess's restored Rolls-Royce and a DH Tiger Moth, in tribute to his courageous great-grandmother. (Marquess of Tavistock)

her life's work. Her religion was essentially a practical religion of duty and service, not of dogma and ritual; but if she did not profess orthodox Christianity in its entirety, she obeyed through life its golden rule of charity. One thing is certain, she never wished to be put on a pedestal; her sense of humour was too keen, and, for all her cleverness, she was too innately simple and unaffected for any pose.'

Shortly after his wife's death, the Duke commissioned John Gore to prepare a full length biography for private circulation. 'For this,' Gore wrote, 'he spared no pains or money to make it a worthy memorial of a wife he greatly admired.' Towards this end the Duke wrote personally to perhaps forty or fifty people with whom she worked and flew asking for contributions, the replies to which are sadly no longer available. One hundred and fifty copies of the book were ordered and presumably distributed, every word of which was checked and personally approved by the Duke. Understandably, however, there is little in this book about her flying.

Sir Geoffrey de Havilland in his biography *Sky Fever* wrote,

"Another elderly lady pilot who flew our Moths but, as befitted her rank, learnt to fly privately in the grounds of her ancestral home, was the Duchess of Bedford. This remarkable woman was no temporary or fair-weather pilot, but gave to flying the enthusiasm she devoted to all her activities so that she was soon both capable and reliable. Whilst she was being instructed she suffered the disappointment of being prevented from taking a certain test by her instructor because of bad weather. She took him to the cinema instead. It happened that a film of mine of the life history of the swallow-tail butterfly, which I made as a pastime but which had been bought by a film company, was being shown at the local cinema. A few days later I received a letter from her saying that her disappointment at not being able to take her test had quite been forgotten in the pleasure she had experienced in seeing this film. This is typical of the courtesy and thoughtfulness of this very kind woman. Many will remember that the Duchess of Bedford died flying, the activity she loved best in the world. She just flew over the East Coast in her Moth and was never seen again."

C.G.Grey, Grand Old Man of *The Aeroplane*, wrote,

"A great lady and a charming woman has passed from amongst us. Those of us who knew her are the better for having done so. And British Aviation is much poorer for losing her."

Miss Constance Leathart who, co-partner with Walter Runciman (Lord Runciman of Droxford) launched Cramlington Aircraft at Cramlington, Newcastle on Tyne, in 1929 writes:

"The Duchess was certainly a most remarkable lady. She had the friendliest smile to any who approached her, perhaps not many did once she was unable to carry on conversation."

And from Wing-Commander Preston OBE AFC JP.:

"She *was* a terrific character, and so innately generous under a formidable exterior brought about probably by her 'noises in the head'. In an aeroplane she heard almost better through the speaking-tube than some of normal hearing would. But at the same time she could be a little 'deaf-minded' and fail to hear things which she didn't want to hear. I have never known what she thought of me. She seldom threw any bouquets, but her critics were nearly always flavoured with a touch of 'leg-pull'. She evidently thought I flew too high on these African trips, so that she couldn't see anything - though on more than one occasion it was lucky that we did. And she clearly thought that I was a bad starter in the mornings, though the difficulty here was to get *other* people to get going early - breakfasts and that sort of thing."

Eva Travers in her book *Cross Country* writes that although the family never met the Duchess, when she was lost they felt that someone 'rather remarkable' had 'gone for good'. Her father Herbert Travers, although he only flew with her once, was genuinely sad at her loss and very angry at suggestions in the press that she had taken her own life, *as he was quite sure that*

(Opposite Page) The Memorial Window, dedicated to the Duchess, in Woburn Church. The dedication speaks for itself.

(Woburn Abbey Collection).

WHOSE WORK WAS IN THE HOSPITALS

SAINT FRANCIS OF ASSISI

IN MEMORY OF
MARY DUCHESS OF BEDFORD
1865 — 1937

WHOSE DELIGHT WAS IN THE BIRDS

she would never have done such a thing. Audrey Todd, now Mrs Taylor, a teenager at the time, has many recollections of the Duchess's thoughtfulness for those around her. She recalls how because in those days X-Rays were dangerous, she would never allow the nurses to take them and how a bunch of local boys she called her 'bird boys', were given binoculars and notebooks for bird-watching. She has particular memories of how, when she had to have an operation, the Duchess brought her books and jigsaws and as she went under the anaesthetic, held her hand. After the operation the Duchess went straight down to the hangar to tell her father that all was well; there would be no scaring, she told him, as the finest materials had been used for the stitches and she had threaded the needle herself! Whenever the Duchess's aeroplanes won an award - often in *Concours d'Elegance* competitions - she would give it to Allen, but she always had a memento made up for Todd in recognition of the work he had put in preparing the aeroplanes. After Allen died, a magnificent cup, still in the possession of his family, was given to Todd.

The Duchess, painted by Preston, sitting beneath the Union Flag at the Officer's Mess, Bathurst.

Appendix I

My Air Experiences

by

The Duchess of Bedford

Some time in the early 'seventies, as a small child, I was taken
to see a wreck of a 'flying machine', as it was then called, on the
South Downs near Amberley. The designer was vaguely said to
have flown 'the height of a house' and then crashed and,
overcome with disappointment, taken his own life. I cannot
claim that my interest in aviation dates from the spectacle of
this sad little glider lying wrecked on the hillside, but neither
did it act as a warning. Many years were to pass however before
I saw another flying machine, and then it was the aeroplane in
which Bleriot flew over the channel. A few wiseacres said that,
like Webb, he would be the last to do it. The War brought many
aeroplanes and even an occasional *Zeppelin* over our quiet
corner of the Midlands, and it was always considered to be the
correct thing for friends to rush and tell me when they were
within hearing. A very definite longing did then arise to try
what flying would be like for myself. But it was not to be
supposed that those most interested in my remaining on earth
would welcome this entirely new departure. The way had to be
carefully paved with constant reiteration of my aspirations,
gradually growing into definite expressions of a determination
to try it. But how to try it I had no idea until a friend suggested
'Imperial Airways'. So in 1926 to Imperial Airways I went with
a request that they provide me with a machine in which to fly
from Croydon to my home. Their first suggestion of an enclosed
machine not being at all in accordance with my idea of
emulating the birds, we finally came down to the Moth.
Imperial Airways moreover, kindly volunteered to send sombody
down to report on the landing ground, but said that a Moth
could land almost anywhere. But when that 'somebody' reported
later that the best landing place seemed to be in the garden

immediately in front of the house, adding that in the event of the ground being wet, the tail-skid might mark the lawn, I was a little puzzled at the accommodating ways of even a Moth, for in no part of the garden is there a space of 50 yards clear of trees, ponds, fountains, bushes and flower-pots. However, the only place I had quite definitely made up my mind that my pilot should *not* land me in was a large open paddock of many acres wherein roams a herd of American bison. So to Croydon I went on a stormy afternoon, and was duly strapped into my Moth. A long run all round the aerodrome to please my pilot, who preferred to rise up-wind, and then my dream of years was realised and for the first time I flew! Now, those who do not want to fly generally have three very definite objections to it; they have no 'head for heights', they do not want to be air-sick, they fear the feeling of coming down that one gets in a lift. To these I invariably reply that on earth I have no head for heights. I greatly dislike a narrow footpath on a steep hillside the involuntary passage down which leads to broken bones. I cannot look over towers and precipices with any comfort, and do not greatly relish a ladder; but for some reason I cannot explain, unless it be by the security of one's position (I do not allude to the strapping in, for I have only been strapped in on two occasions since), one feels nothing of this in an aeroplane. As to air-sickness, I have only been in an enclosed machine for very short flights and though in the Moth, my pilot has on one or two occasions remarked 'A little more of that and we should both have been ill', we have had that 'little' and more also later, and I was not air-sick. If he was, he was safely behind me and I was not aware of it. The motion of flying is so different from the endless monotonous rocking of an ocean wave that at present I have a clean bill of health. '*Qui Vivra Verra*'. Of the feeling as of descending a lift there is none, and I think that would only happen in involuntary descents. *What have I gained?* And now for what I have gained from flying. Before the war I had a yacht but the war took her and, fond as I am of seeing the world, journeys by train are anathema to me. Therefore, but for restricted travels by ocean liner and motor-car, I thought my travelling days were over. My first long venture was to Scotland. Starting at my own time (no, my pilot's, for pilots are not punctual people having too many irrefutable excuses to draw upon when in need), I arrived in a field close to my Scottish home in three and a half hours, less time than the train would have brought me. Visions of travel abroad once more seemed possible, and the spring of 1927 saw the little Moth starting on a trip of three weeks unadulterated enjoyment to Tangiers, via Paris, Bordeau, Biarritz, over the Pyrenees to Burgos, Madrid, Seville, Jerez and home by Malaga, Grenada, Barcelona, Lyons and Paris. The next flight of interest was to see the eclipse of the sun, and we really did see it! There was no necessity to go to the area of crowded hotels, for by rising a little earlier, we could fly into the zone of the eclipse from a less frequented neighbourhood. Nothing could have been more unpromising than our start in a fog that almost precluded the idea of flying at all, but in a short space of time we were wafted above the clouds to a height of 10,000 feet. There in an absolutely clear sky, with a panorama of clouds below us, which did but add to the beauty of the scene, we had an uninterrupted view of the eclipse. Incidentally, it is fortunate that there is not to be another for 200 years for the sun was obviously very cross about it as he has hardly been seen in England since. Once more in the summer a short flight was taken to Naples via Paris, Lyons, Turin, Verona, the Lido and Rome, the return journey being made by the Riviera. We crossed the Alps at just under 14,000 feet, basked in the sun on the Lido, peeped down into the Coliseum, the Baths at Caracalla and the Crater of Vesuvius, revelled in a glorious view of the Bay of Naples at sunset, looked down on the terrible forest fires then raging on the Riviera and met the Mistral, which tossed us about like a feather. And all this in an eight days flight of some 3,500 miles. At home the little Moth has taken me many short flights for business and pleasure. 'But is not the scenery from an aeroplane terribly dull?' I have been asked by friends. If it is then I am afraid I have one of the 'little minds' which is 'pleased by little things' for I never have a dull moment in the Moth from the time I leave the ground; no, not even over the coal fields and manufacturing districts of England; and as to the scenery, in many of our longer flights, it has been wonderful beyond description. But why do I write all this for readers of *Flight*, who need no inducement to fly? I am reminded of an episode that occured in one of my tours abroad. Seated in the hall of an hotel waiting for a car to take my pilot and myself to the aerodrome, an enthusiastic lady came up an introduced herself to me, saying that she must congratulate me on my flight because it was 'so brave and wonderful' of me to venture on it. I was just beginning to feel a little elated at the torrent of flattery which, out of the kindness of her heart, flowed down on me, but I had an uncomfortable feeling that it was not making quite the desired impression upon the rather matter-of-fact and very experienced companion at my elbow. The suspicion was justified a moment later when, as she turned to leave, he remarked - 'What an *extraordinary* idea! One would think you are the first woman to fly!' In the language of aviation, I 'flattened out.' So it is with all diffidence that I submit the record of my first year as owner of a Moth, my only excuse being that I do it at the Editor's request.

Appendix II
The Duchess's Aircraft

Aircraft	Registration	First Flight	Last Flight	Remarks
Fokker VIIa	G-EBTS	2.6.28		Re-registered to Barnard, 1930
Cirrus Moth	G-EBRI	13.7.27	24.9.28	
Gipsy I Moth	G-AAA0	16.10.28	16.7.32	
Gipsy I Moth	G-AXBR	19.7.32	27.9.35	
Moth Major	G-ACUR	27.9.35	22.3.37	
Puss Moth	G-ABOC	28.7.31	22.4.35	
Percival Gull	G-ADSG	4.1.36		Re-registered to Preston, 1937

Record Attempt

June 1928	G-EBTS	To India, forced landing Bushire

Record Flights

August 1929	G-EBTS	India and back in seven and a half days
April 1930	G-EBTS	Cape Town and back in twenty days.

Summary of Overseas Tours

			Days	Hours flown
April 1927	G-EBPM	France, Spain, Tangier	22	47
August 1927	G-EBRI	France, Italy	10	37
April 1931	G-AAAO	Switzerland, Italy, France	16	41
August 1931	G-ABOC	Berlin, Vienna, Venice, Switzerland	18	--
May 1932	G-ABOC	France, Spain, N. Africa	24	50
March/April 1933	G-ABOC	Jerusalem, Luxor, Tunis, Oran	23	77
April 1934	G-ABOC	Bathurst, Grand Canary	26	78
March/April 1935	G-ABOC	Across the Sahara, Khartoum, Cairo, Rome	33	119

Index

255